C000153432

DARE TO TAKE A PATH LESS TRAVELED

DARE TO TAKE A PATH LESS TRAVELED

A MEMOIR

FINDING YOUR WAY
TO SUCCESS IN
A NEW WORLD

HERVE ERUDITE GNIDEHOUE

Hardcover ISBN: 978-1-7332552-3-3
Paperback ISBN: 978-1-7332552-4-0

www.beyondbailiwick.com

Book designed by Jennifer Toomey

Printed in the United States of America

Disclaimer

This is a work of nonfiction. The events described in this book are based on true stories in my personal life and are recounted to the best of my recollection. Some names of persons and locations have been changed for privacy, while some have been maintained at my sole discretion. At times I have drawn on cultural, historical, and contemporary events to illuminate particular subjects and to express points of view that are mine and only mine. This work of literature is neither intentionally published to be used as a medium to air any grievance or grudge nor meant to offend anyone personally or any group of people or any place mentioned herein. However, I remain steadfast in my opinions and convictions with regard to certain topics broached throughout this book, while at the same time I remain a humble student of wisdom and always ready for philosophical arguments. This book does not claim to be a blueprint for achieving success in life or in any specific endeavor. The images in this book have been duly authorized for use.

To all those who have had the fortitude to take a journey to the unknown

Table of Contents

Prologue

The idea of writing a book, sharing stories about my life and my journey in and outside of my native land, was never something I thought I would do. Most of the time, when people decide to write their memoirs, they do it much later in life. But waiting will not necessarily polish my recollection of events in my life; after more than three decades of existing, I have had my share of trials, troubles, and joyful moments. I am not going to wait until I am much older before sharing them.

What if you are relatively young, still in your thirties, for example, and are known to only a few people, such as your family, friends, neighbors, coworkers, colleagues, and a few other acquaintances? Is it worth the effort to spend months writing a book about yourself and recounting particular events in your life? And will it be interesting enough not only to keep the reader in suspense but also to educate and entertain him or her at the same time?

We all have a story to tell. The accounts and stories in this book are drawn from my own life. It is the life of an immigrant in the United States. Like many before him, he left his native country for opportunities he saw lacking in his homeland and came to a destination reputed for the immense and limitless options that it offers, a promise of a prosperous life. The very first weeks he spent in his new country quickly dispelled some of the myths. He realized that the road to the American Dream is bumpy, but neither impossible nor impassable. There was an immense sacrifice needed to learn a new language, secure gainful employment, socialize with natives, educate himself, and above all learn how to navigate a country and a culture that is very different from the one into which he was born. How could he survive and succeed in this new country? Would he like living there? Should he assimilate or hold on to his roots: the customs and traditions of his native land?

When I was growing up in Benin, in West Africa, I had always thought about pursuing my university education abroad. I knew that one of my uncles had studied in Ukraine. It was not just going abroad and studying that I was interested in. No! Doing it in a language other than French, and being exposed to another culture and a different way of thinking, were the stimuli for me. But, of all the countries I entertained as places to attend college one day, the United States stood out. There were several reasons why.

First, when I was growing up in the 1980s, Michael Jackson was arguably the most prominent entertainer in the world, and his songs and videos were all the rage on the radio and television. As a child watching him on TV, I wondered where his country of origin could be. When I learned that he was from the United States, I started fantasizing about going there to meet him one day.

Second, Apollo 11 (the first human-crewed moon landing mission) and subsequent space exploration missions were also much talked about on national television and radio in my native land. It didn't take me long to realize that those engineering feats were achieved in the United States, by NASA (the National Aeronautics and Space Administration). I cherished the idea of working there someday. These thoughts and ambitions fueled my interest in that distant land—an ocean away—called America.

A third impetus to head to the United States was that in the 1990s, when I was in my preteen years, the national university in our small republic was having a strike almost annually, with students and faculty regularly appearing on TV threatening to boycott classes or invalidate the academic year. Unions often took the academic year hostage. Students started every school year under the looming specter of an invalid academic year, and they were usually the losers, because they would miss the opportunity to advance to a higher grade level. Back then, I did not know enough about politics to understand why the student body, the faculties, the organized unions, and the government were at loggerheads all the time. But I knew I did not want to be caught up in that once I finished high school and headed for college.

Another important consideration was that my own nation's university offered far fewer options when it came to courses of study than did those in the United States, which afforded a cornucopia of choices. These concerns, along with the self-imposed challenge of performing my studies in a language other than French, kept me hoping that one day nature would conspire to make my wish a reality.

My dream was not an uncommon one. The United States hosts one of the largest diasporas of Africans outside of the cradle of humanity, Africa. Many African Americans Stateside can trace their origins back to Benin and its neighboring countries. And so, for a myriad of reasons, from a young age, I hoped to join their numbers and follow my own path in the Land of Opportunity.

A note on the text that follows: Where necessary throughout this book, I have used fictitious names in order to maintain the privacy of some of the individuals involved. Those names are indicated by an asterisk (*) at their first occurrence. However, some of the names used are real names of the persons mentioned.

In early 2006, I left my parents and my native Benin for the United States. Still in my early twenties, I had just finished the mandatory internship that would validate my bachelor's degree. I had submitted and defended my internship report a few weeks earlier in front of some of my professors, family members, and friends. Now I was eager to leave and experience what would be in store for me on the other side of the Atlantic. However, even though my parents and sisters were supportive of my plans, there was a little bit of "less eagerness," given that they knew that at least for a while, they wouldn't see me for long periods. For the first time, I would be so far away in a place foreign to them. It is not an uncommon thing, of course, for someone to leave his family to go and live in another country with no expected return date, but in my family, I was the first to do it.

When I arrived in the United States, my host family—my cousin Alicia*
and her husband and children—welcomed me warmly. I stayed with them
for three months, and after that, I was on my own. I had to learn things my
own way, adapt, and navigate the new system into which I had brought myself. It was a new and entirely different culture than what I was accustomed
to: not only a different language, but a different attitude on life, a different
way of thinking. My number one priority was not just to survive or try to fit
in. No! It was the language. Early on, I knew that investing time in learning the language and speaking it well would be the key to success. Not just
speaking it simply to get by, but gaining mastery of it in a way that would
rival that of a native speaker.

When I started living on my own, I adapted quickly to the system. In a
matter of six months, I had gotten the full picture of the economic, social,
and political system of the United States. The St. Louis County Library
became my refuge when I was searching for employment, and also when I
was hungry for knowledge about a particular topic.

The idea of writing a book did not settle in my mind until May of 2016,
once I had embarked on my career as an electrical engineer. I had briefly
entertained the thought of writing a book a few years earlier, while I was
still in college, but I was not certain what topic to choose. At that time, I
quickly dismissed the idea without losing sleep over it. In fact, I was very
busy with schoolwork. Each semester, I was taking as many classes as I
could with the goal to graduate quickly. So it wasn't until the spring of 2016
that I started seriously considering writing a memoir.

In fact, 2016 marked the 10-year anniversary of my departure from
Benin for the first time to head to the United States. I remembered the
hugs and kisses from my parents and sisters at the Cadjehoun International
Airport. Over the years since then, many of the people I knew wanted to
have news of me. They wanted me to share my experience abroad. I had
written letters to my father, and of course, I have maintained close contact
with both parents and my sisters. As I was reminiscing about the beginning
of my journey, I had an epiphany as to the topic I could write about: myself.

---

*   Some names have been changed.

Yet even then, I did not have a strong motivation to do it. My profession as an electrical engineer was becoming a bit demanding, and weekends were pretty much the only free time I had. I did not want to burden myself with a self-imposed book-writing assignment.

In the summer of 2016, I went on vacation to Germany and stayed with a friend of mine, Alena Shaffer, who was beginning work on her PhD in botany. I knew that a doctorate requires a lot of writing, and once my friend's PhD was complete, her work would forever be available for posterity. It is much like leaving behind a legacy. That was what spurred my motivation and ardor to write this book.

Many Americans would probably never leave the United States to live in a foreign country. There are some who travel to other countries for vacation. A few relocate temporarily to do volunteer work for the Peace Corps or to study as exchange students. Some find themselves required to travel because they are members of the US armed forces, who serve in many other nations, such as Germany, Japan, and South Korea. That being said, the reasons why Americans might immigrate to other countries are certainly not the same as the one that typically draws a foreigner to the land of George Washington. Emigration from the United States is a move that is more popular among older Americans looking for an affordable country to retire in. Countries such as Mexico, Costa Rica, Panama, Colombia, Nicaragua, and Malaysia have become trendy destinations among US expats. The US dollar goes further in those countries. There are challenges that immigrants face when they move to another country—the United States in my case.

The US policy on granting citizenship to immigrants is multifaceted and diverse. In this book, I discuss only the avenue that I followed. Centuries ago, the quest for opportunity and a new life began driving people to America from very remote parts of Europe. They arrived in the Western Hemisphere, settled, started a new life, and accomplished things that could not have been possible in their native lands. That same spirit has spread throughout the world, and even today, it is as alive as it was back then. I have been touched by it, and this is my story.

CHAPTER 1

The Genesis of the Journey

When, on a Saturday morning in July 2004, I decided to accompany my father on one of his biweekly business trips to Nigeria, it was just another trip for me. I did not always tag along with my father on his travels, because most of the time he went between Mondays and Fridays and occasionally on Saturdays. On that particular day, when I decided to ride along when he drove to Lagos, Nigeria, he was glad that I wanted to come with him.

Two hours after we left home, we were at the international border between Benin and Nigeria. For Beninese citizens entering Nigeria, there is less formality because both countries belong to the Economic Community of West African States (ECOWAS). No visa is required. But entering Nigeria by car is not that simple. After crossing the border into Nigerian territory, you pass through a series of checkpoints that stretches several miles. Before hitting the checkpoints, my father stopped at a kiosk on the Benin side of the border to exchange Beninese currency (CFA francs) for Nigerian currency (nairas). Although I don't recall the exchange rate, I remember that the CFA traded higher than the naira. Goods in Nigeria were relatively affordable to Beninese citizens by virtue of the strength of the CFA with respect to the naira.

There wasn't much distance between the checkpoints. Officers at the checkpoints routinely stop vehicles, subject drivers and passengers to questions, and often demand to be given "something" (a bribe). They show absolutely no shame about it. Some officers are more direct than others. From the tone in which the officers ask questions and conduct their belligerent inquiries, a driver can sense when to give the officer that "something" in order to quickly extricate himself from their harassment, move on to the next checkpoint, and repeat the same thing: the giving of "something" to the officers. Otherwise, one can expect to be unashamedly groped, verbally and physically abused, and manhandled with utter impunity.

I had noticed that my father usually kept wads of banknotes in his front pocket and under the dashboard. When he was stopped at a checkpoint and badgered by annoying questions from the officers, he knew that it was time to pay that officer and move on. He would gently slide one or two banknotes to the officers, and they would let him go, sometimes with no questions asked. It is how the game is played. For an unaware driver, the consequences of trying to play tough, or trying to come across as a man of rectitude or probity in those types of situations, can turn very sour very quickly. The officers are well armed and are more than willing to savagely rough up anyone who dares to challenge their egos. The money given to those officers will never, of course, see the coffers of the Nigerian government. Pay to pass. That's the game.

My father was very familiar with the routine and had made friends with some of those officers, who knew him very well. They knew that he was a good payer of "something"—his dues—to the point that those who recognized him just let him go. He gave them that "something" only when he felt like doing so.

It is a system that I hate and deplore because it is one of the reasons many African nations are still economically behind compared with, say, other countries in Europe and North America, for example. Although I do not endorse bribery or any kind of corruption, I am well aware of the realities that many of those officers and other government workers have to deal with, such as low and stagnant salary, and also their government which routinely fails to pay them on time. Arrears of monthly compensation are quite common in many countries across the continent. It is a fact that drives workers to put money in their pockets by any means.

With a myriad of checkpoints behind us by now, my father was set back a few Nigerian nairas. But I don't think he was concerned about the money. He is a businessman, and he eventually passes that cost on to his customers.

One hour later, we were in the small city of Badagry. Going through that city alone took us more than two hours. The traffic jam was infernal. In Benin and other neighboring countries, Nigeria, the most populous country in Africa, is also known as "Go Slow." As a matter of fact, a traffic jam is called a *go slow* in Nigeria. The term *traffic jam* is more formal and left to textbooks or newspapers.

Traffic jams in Nigeria are nerve-racking, depressing, infuriating, and interminably long. There are traffic jams everywhere. One of the reasons is that the streets are not only mostly narrow but also riddled with potholes. Another is that a lot of traffic lights are no longer working and have not been fixed, leaving drivers relying on one another's courtesy. Occasionally there will be police officers at major intersections, directing traffic. Sitting for long hours in a traffic jam was something that I became used to very quickly. It came with the territory.

Peddling at traffic lights has grown and flourished, thanks to the traffic jams. With cars not being able to proceed at their desired speed, peddlers can approach drivers and their passengers to offer their products: fast foods, cookies, magazines, cigarettes, stationery, newspapers. The congestion also gives beggars an opportunity to solicit help. My father usually gave those people some money. I did it too. Giving to those people makes one feel good. They shower their benefactors with blessings, and no one can have too many of those!

It had been an hour since we'd stopped still in that traffic jam, and we had barely moved a quarter of a mile. A peddler with a newspaper approached my father's window and asked if we would like to buy the periodical. My father bought one from him and handed it to me in the passenger seat. The official language in Nigeria is English, but several other languages are also spoken, such as Yoruba, Hausa, and others. This newspaper was in English. My knowledge of the English language was not very strong at the time. I knew some English, having taken a few lessons in school, but not enough to read and fully comprehend the formal vocabulary and issues discussed in those articles. That day, the image on the cover of that newspaper caught my attention. It was not an image related to any current affairs in Nigeria. The image plastered on the front page was about the annual visa program, the Diversity Visa lottery (or DV), to the United States.

What is the Diversity Visa? By way of a brief history, the DV program came to life in the mid-1990s. In fact, it started in 1995, although it was conceived in 1990 and signed by President George H. W. Bush. During that year, Senator Chuck Schumer of New York and some members of the House of Representatives introduced the Diversity Visa bill as part of the new immigration law package. The purpose of the program was to grant visas to citizens from countries around the globe that have low or very low immigrant populations in the United States. About 50,000 visas of this type are issued each year.

For a candidate to be eligible, he or she needs various pieces of documentation, as well as a sponsor. An application will not be processed if the name and address of the verified person known to the applicant and living in the United States are not provided. A lot of aspirants give up because of that requirement alone. Some, who may not know anyone living in the United States, talk to friends, family, and acquaintances in the hope of finding someone Stateside who would be willing to allow their name to be put on the application that's sent back to the US immigration services for processing. The address of the sponsor is put on file, and that is both where the applicant is expected to land once he or she arrives in the United States, and where his or her Green Card will be sent. The Diversity Visa is valid for six months from the date of issuance. Therefore, the applicant has to enter the United States before it expires.

I had heard about the DV before in Benin but had never paid too much attention to it. Why? I had heard that there was a lot of paperwork to marshal before and during the process, and there is no guarantee of an interview. Even some interviews result in rejections, with no money refunded.

From the newspaper article, I learned that the period to participate in the DV had just begun. I had never seen anything like that in Benin, where the DV program was not publicized to that extent. For me, in Benin, I had never taken the DV program seriously, because I had always thought of it as a legitimate program hijacked by some unscrupulous scammers. There was indeed a valid reason to be distrustful of the program, given that I had heard stories about people manipulating the lottery and making money out of it through the promise of marriage. Because the spouse of a DV winner is also legally eligible for all the benefits that a Green Card confers, the credential is highly sought after. The Green Card gives a person the right to work in the United States and to apply to become a US citizen after five years of permanent residence.

From what I knew, the United States and Canada were the two nations that had such programs. Both countries were born thanks to immigration. So, for generations, they have found ways, crafted policies, and enacted legislation allowing them to bring in folks willing to be part of their society, or at least experience it. In many developing countries like Benin, there is a prestige associated with someone who has traveled and lived and studied in North America, especially Canada and the United States. I grew up with that thinking, too, hoping that one day I would make it to either one of these countries under the right circumstances. A few years earlier, I had tried the Canadian equivalent of the US DV program and had never gotten a return answer. I assumed that the selection process might be rigorous—as it should—and I probably wouldn't make the cut. That was another reason why I was not too hopeful that I might get lucky with the American visa lottery.

With my head buried in the newspaper, I summoned all the imagination I had to try to comprehend the English I was reading. I could clearly understand that the program would start in just a few weeks. At that moment, it dawned on me that the DV lottery of the United States was legit. Why would a respectable newspaper put its reputation and credibility on the line by backing something that wasn't true? I knew right then that I would give the DV lottery a try after my father and I returned to Benin.

Once we were home, I followed through with my application for the DV program. If I had not accompanied my father on his business trip that day, not only would my curiosity not have sparked, but I wouldn't have taken any action, and I certainly wouldn't have left my native land.

I had always felt that I would be a better fit anywhere else in the world. But as I was growing older and becoming aware of geopolitics and cultures in different parts of the world, I had narrowed down my preferences to only a select few countries. The United States spearheaded that list, followed by Canada, Japan, Germany, Russia, and Australia. The mental preparation I'd had over the years had prepared me, and I was convinced that one day, under the right conditions, I could indeed go live in the United States. My father had encouraged all of us, his four children, to complement whatever field of study we would choose in life with the study of languages. In Benin, several dozen languages are spoken throughout the country, but French is the official language or the lingua franca. Businesses, official affairs, and education are conducted in French. Of the other dozens of tongues that are spoken, some have been conferred some official status by virtue of a large population of the country that speaks them, but these dialects are not put on the same pedestal as French.

My father fluently speaks nine languages: French, Fon (or Fongbé), Goun (or Goungbé), Hausa, Mina, Nigerian Pidgin, Toli, Xla, and Yoruba. My parents are from two different parts of the country, and they grew up speaking different languages with the exception of French that they had learned in school. I can fluently speak the two most dominant dialects of the South: Goun and Fon. My command of Yoruba and Mina is fair, not great, but I can understand when people are conversing in those dialects. Because French is the official language, everyone who has been to school in Benin has a good command of it, depending upon how far they have gone in their education.

I had always enjoyed those trips to Nigeria with my father because they gave me the opportunity to learn from him doing business there. He haggled over prices like no man I've ever seen. Haggling is very common in the region. Even items in shops with prices clearly and visibly marked can be bargained for. It's quite an interesting practice and culture. The same cannot be said of North American countries like the United States and Canada, or most European countries, where the merchandise sticker price is the amount to be paid at the register, plus tax. Women in the West African region and across the continent learn at an early age how to dicker over prices by watching their mothers haggle at the markets. It is a skill that helps make one's money go far. Below is a typical interaction between vendor and buyer.

Buyer: "How much is this?"

Vendor: "It costs $50."

Buyer: "Really? $50? Leave it to me for $20."

Vendor: "$20? No. I'll give it to you for $45."

Buyer: "Why is it that expensive? $45? That's too much. I will take it for $25."

Vendor: "You are buying a good product. Give me $40, and it's all yours."

Buyer: "I think $30 is my last offer."

Vendor: "Okay. You are my friend. Give me $35, and I will give it to you."

Buyer: "No, $30 is my last offer. Deal or no deal."

At $30, the vendor can decide whether to sell or not. It all depends. He can accept the shopper's $30 offer, or the buyer can meet him halfway. My father was a master at this game and impressed even my mother on various occasions.

My father is in the retail business. His trips to Nigeria consisted of buying television sets, radio sets, electronic parts, and electrical components such as diodes, capacitors, integrated circuits, amplifiers, and computer accessories. He purchased these items in bulk in Nigeria and resold them to customers in Benin. Before I turned 10, I probably knew about most of the different components that can go in an electrical circuit long before I took my first Introduction to Electricity class in junior high school.

My father's business is undoubtedly what got me interested in electronics. The business of selling these spare parts is viable in Benin, given that people do not discard their TVs or radios; when their electronic devices start malfunctioning, people always seek the services of repair shops.

My father is very well known among the electronics repairmen in Cotonou. The economic capital, as it is unofficially called, Cotonou is the largest and most populous city of Benin. It is where I was born. Cotonou is a vibrant city with an abundance of businesses and shops. It has seen an increase in migration, given that people come from all over the country to seek training, jobs, and business opportunities there. From the early 1980s until the late '90s, my father almost ruled the electronic-parts business in Cotonou. His shop was where almost all the radio and TV technicians went to buy parts. For more than two decades, not only was he the main parts supplier, but he would also take requests to place orders for technicians when the items they were looking for could not be found in his store. He would resell the items for close to the buying price; in other words, he made minimal profit reselling them.

I have found my dad's way of doing business very interesting in the sense that he has managed to stay in business making minimal profit from his sales. I asked him one day why he doesn't charge his customers enough to make the maximum profit per item sold. He answered that the practice of overcharging customers is cruel and that one should think about being in business to help and provide services at the minimal cost instead of ripping people off. What I have learned from his philosophy of business is that one can efficiently operate a business and stay in business for much longer making essential profit than by trying to rake in unreasonably high profit per sale. He's a man of a generation that grew up under a different economic system. I, on the other hand, have been fond of capitalism and maximum-profit-seeking ways when it comes to businesses.

When he goes on business trip to purchase these items, he has to declare them to customs upon his return to Benin and pay customs fees on the merchandise. People know the wringer one has to go through in going to Nigeria and back to Benin. Most people in Cotonou do not even dare. The checkpoints on the other side of the border are too much to deal with for most people. At times, the Nigerian officers can be very intimidating and aggressive when one doesn't know how to deal with them. They mostly speak Yoruba, Hausa, and Pidgin or Broken (a mixture of informal English with local dialects that is very challenging for non-Nigerians to understand). Sometimes hearing formal spoken English among the officers is an oddity. Broken is the preferred form of communication. For a foreigner who knows nothing about the languages spoken in Nigeria, dealing with the officers can be terrifying, and some officers pounce on that and demand a "something" before they let go of the travelers.

But my father has never taken advantage of the fact that he is the one who knows the ropes of traveling to Nigeria and buying goods for resale in Benin. In his store, the items are reasonably priced and affordable for his customers. He also once told me that when you charge customers more than is necessary, it will be expedient for a period, but they will think twice before stepping into your store again. They will constantly be looking for another alternative. He said to me that he didn't want a customer to think twice before entering his store. He wanted to be the only one they would think of, even though there might be other alternatives available. In fact, there were a few other stores that competed with my father's, but customers found his items more affordable.

My father has earned the respect of many of his customers, who believe that he is easy to get along with and is also an honest man. At times, I witnessed customers coming in to buy items with less money than the going rate of some of the merchandise, and in spite of that, they were able to walk out with those items in hand. They would later pay my father back what they owed him. Sometimes they didn't, though, but I do not have any recollection of him badgering them for that. The trust between him and his regular customers is so strong that there is usually no dispute over a debt or anything of that nature. His store was often flooded with customers, all of them in search of a bargain. I've seen customers haggling with him over a price for almost an hour. My father would tell those customers the cost at which he would sell an item, but some would haggle to the point of beseeching him. It could be quite a scene at my father's store. Sometimes he stood his ground; sometimes he yielded. At times, customers would buy items for less but come back a few days later with the difference to pay what they'd bought a few days earlier. My dad used no accounting software.

However, he managed to keep track and stay on top of everything going on in his business. It's remarkable.

In the 1980s, when my father's business was nascent and he had just started traveling to buy his merchandise, he was taken advantage of, by paying the "tourist price." In other words, as a foreigner, he was unfairly charged more for his purchases. Upon returning to Benin from his trip to Nigeria, he would realize that some of the merchandise was not affordable to his customers. He had to resell some things at a loss just to get them off his shelves, but that period of underselling was short-lived. Once he mastered the art of bargaining, the world was his. He became shrewd and canny—a superior negotiator. It is undoubtedly one of the skills that I have learned from my father. At an early age, I understood the art of bargaining. There were times when I had to put those skills on display when I was alone face-to-face with a seller.

Bargaining skills come with practice. Bargaining is more than just offering a lower price than the seller is asking. It is a game that is an art in itself. The buyer and seller engage in body movement, using eye contact, tone of voice, and a posture that suggests that both of them are serious about the potential transaction.

The mastery of haggling is something that is handed down from generation to generation, especially from mother to daughter. I learned it from my father, but I have honed my skills by learning from my mother. At a young age, as early as girls are old enough to go to school, their mothers take them to the market to shop. In this context, the market is a vast, reserved open space, comparable to the traditional farmers' market found in North America, but perhaps 10 to 20 times bigger, where merchants set up their booths and display their products for sale. Inside the market, it is not uncommon to see enclosed shops where customers can go in and out. The stores and improvised booths together make up the market where thousands of people congregate for shopping. Usually, the markets are dominated by women, both as shoppers and as sellers. Young women follow along with their mothers. It is during these interactions with vendors that one can see the young women who have accompanied their mothers observing and learning the art of price haggling, an initiation process that takes years.

From an early age, girls need to know how to do this, because one day they will be the ones in charge of shopping for their families.

Occasionally, my father would go to the market to do the grocery shopping, to help my mother. Anytime he went shopping and came back home with the purchases, my mother knew with certainty that he had not paid the "man price." The "man price" is an expression mostly used to refer to an overcharged purchase made by a man. Given that men, compared with women, often are not naturally good at bargaining, vendors frequently take advantage of them. That is why in most cases, men prefer to leave the shopping duties to women, because they know that a female vendor will probably be a little intimidated when dealing with a woman as the buyer.

When I was in elementary school, my mother took me along on several of her trips to the market, and I saw firsthand her bargaining skills. My mother's approach was different from my father's. Upon a vendor's initial price suggestion, my mother would usually counteroffer by asking the vendor if he or she was really serious about the stated price. In effect, but in different words, she was saying to the vendor, *"Are you kidding me?"* She would ask the vendor to come clean about the correct price, otherwise, she would leave and go back to another vendor of the same product who had offered her a better price for it. This is a master-class bargaining technique, and definitely intimidating. I saw my mother play that game over and over again. I usually accompanied her once every two or three months to Cotonou's largest market site, called Dantokpa, which straddles Lake Nokoué. Dantokpa's name is not by happenstance. *Dan* in the Fon language means "snake," and *tokpa* means "lakeside," "riverside," or "by the water."

According to a very popular legend, the Dantokpa lakeshore was a ritual place for sacrificial offerings to a majestic snake considered to be a spirit that used to dwell in the lake. Usually consisting of live goats and chickens and such, the sacrifices to the snake were for different purposes: health, success, fertility, and so on. Even though the snake itself was rarely seen, it was believed that it usually came out at witching hour and took with it to the lake the objects of sacrifice that were left there.

The legend also had it that the snake did not accept all sacrificial offerings. Those supplicants who returned later to find that their offerings had vanished saw this as a sign that the snake had come out of the lake to take their gifts. For those people, this was a sign of a prayer accepted, or soon to be fulfilled. But those whose offerings were never taken from the shore viewed this as a sign of prayers rejected.

To this day, there are conflicting reports as to whether the snake of the lake accepted human sacrifices, but those who are descendants of the previous inhabitants of the lake's surrounding areas claim that the snake has never taken a human sacrifice.

Lake Nokoué is one of the largest and longest in Benin, stretching from the western third of Cotonou, the economic capital, all the way to Porto-Novo, the political capital. During the day, fishermen, some in canoes and some in motorboats, can be seen casting their nets. According to the legend, some fishermen spent days on the lake without catching anything meaningful that they could sell on the market or even use for their own consumption. As you may have guessed, the reason was that the snake god of the lake demanded sacrifices. The elders, or those who were initiated to communicate with spirits, could communicate with the snake god to understand what it wanted. Only after the sacrifices were made and accepted would the snake god, propitiated, bless the fishermen with a decent catch.

In the early 1900s, a construction project was begun to build a bridge across Lake Nokoué, connecting two sides of what's now the Dantokpa area. Accounts from those who knew suggested that the project was sporadically struck by delays, and it was reported that there was a loss of life at the construction site at one point. The work stalled, and that was how the authorities grew convinced that something out of the ordinary needed to be done. It was thought that these strange and unexplained events had occurred because an appropriate "permission" or "request" had not been addressed to the snake god of the lake. So the elders who could communicate with spirits were hired to communicate with the mystical snake. They submitted their request on behalf of the entity or company in charge of delivering the bridge, and then asked the snake's blessing.

Most people in Benin are well aware of the existence of the spirit world, which can be both a blessing and a curse to those who seek to summon it. The latter may consist of an actual curse or witchcraft, the dark side of the spirit world. In this instance, after months of work and sacrifices, the bridge was finally completed.

〜

I have learned a lot from both of my parents. My father lost both of his parents when he was still young, and he did not grow up with a lot of money available to him. Therefore, when he started making money, he understood how hard it was and got into the habit of tracking all his expenses and saving as much as he could. These habits that he inculcated in himself later made him successful at running his own business.

At work, my father was always presentable, and that was one of the things his customers often pointed out to him. My mother once confessed to me that his being presentable and well dressed, yet not at all pretentious or cocky, was one of the things that attracted her to him. At the time when he met my mother, in the late 1970s, he had not started his electronic spare-parts business, and the motorbike he drove left a lot to be desired. My father had just left the military and was taking business law classes at the University of Benin while helping his older brother with his vinyl-records business. Though my father didn't have a whole lot going for him, he had plans to own his own business someday. My father courted my mother with the help of her mother (my grandmother). As a matter of fact, my father was a regular customer of my mother's mother. My grandmother at the time was a porridge vendor with a lot of customers; porridge was the most popular choice for breakfast in Benin at the time. She got most of her patrons between 5:00 and 10:00 a.m.

Back in the 1970s, cooking machines of the sort that we have today as fixtures in our houses were not available to households in Benin. People cooked using dry wood, which could be bought at the market or collected away from home. Collecting wood outside is very common, especially for families who are trying to save money or can't afford the bundles of three-foot-long wood pieces readily available at the market or from specialized merchants. Even though the cooking happens in an open environment, inhaling the smoke is unavoidable. My mother and grandmother used to sit or stand next to the fire with a handmade fan called an *afafa* in the Fon, or Fongbé, language. The *afafa* is a semicircular or quarter-circle-shaped, hand-agitated fan. This was cooks' way of warding off the smoke that comes belching out of the piles of dry woods. Even though for generations this way of cooking has remained the same, with all the smoke that is produced as a result, one would imagine that the women would develop lung and respiratory problems later in their lives, but surprisingly that has not been the case.

My father at the time was in his early thirties. He used to stop at my grandmother's stall for breakfast around 8:00 a.m., but by that time, my mother had already left for school. One day, he had errands to run early in the morning before work, so he had to eat breakfast earlier than usual. Therefore, around 6:00 a.m., he went for his porridge. And there he met my mother for the first time, as she had just finished chores with her mother and was ready to go back home for a second shower before heading off to school.

I believe that my father was beauty-struck, as he couldn't stop thinking about my mother. It didn't take much effort for him to realize that she was the daughter of the person whose business he had been patronizing for months. That first day, he didn't approach my mother but made a veiled attempt to inquire whether she was indeed my grandmother's daughter. When my grandmother confirmed it, my father left for his errands, but the image of my mother's face had taken a deep seat in his mind. He knew he had to see the girl again. For that to happen, he had to adjust his schedule and start having breakfast at 6:00 a.m. daily instead of his usual 8:00.

According to the customs of the land, a man in his thirties was expected to have started a family. Men usually started a family in their mid- to late twenties. Among his brothers and sisters, my father was the only one in his midthirties who did not have a wife and children, and that was something the family was not too happy about. His older sister, with the help of acquaintances at the paternal village, found a woman for my father to marry, but he rejected her—a move that caused some rancor between my father's family and that of the village girl. But eventually the two families were able to get past the "misunderstanding," and the girl's family wished my father well in his quest for the type of woman he was looking for. My father's family around that time had tried to set him up with dates or downright force women upon him, but he shunned them all. This prompted the family to question his male potency, in what is often a shame tactic used by family members and the society to call men to "action." In some traditions in Benin, there were rituals to prove men's virility. There is one in particular that I know of. Here is how it goes.

The man whose potency is questioned is made to stand in a barrel, naked and surrounded by other men. Some rituals call for seven men, others nine. Then, the dried scrotum with testes of a goat, attached to the same goat's dried intestines, is tied around the man's hips. Once these are in place, the barrel is filled to the man's waist level with water that contains certain other closely guarded ingredients. With no sexual stimulation at all, one expects the man's private part to rise and stay afloat in the water. Supposedly, this shows that the man is indeed virile and potent and capable of performing sexual acts when necessary to honor his woman. If, on the other hand, the man's private part does not rise to stay afloat, that man needs treatment. Treating this kind of male condition is easily solved by elders, and other people know all too well the "secrets of the plants" to cure it.

Fortunately, my father never had to go through this kind of family-orchestrated humiliation. Like my father before me, I started getting the same pressure to marry and start a family when I turned 30. Even though my parents were thousands of miles away, my mother once in a while would call and ask me when I would make her a grandmother. From time to time, during our phone calls, she asked me very personal questions—both seriously and jokingly—as to whether my reproductive organ was as healthy as it should be. I always answered in the affirmative. Yes, ma'am! It is a pressure tactic that is well known. Mothers candidly speak with their grown-up sons about sex and women. Men start receiving that pressure around 30 years of age, while women face it at around 25. In Western societies, when a man is in his thirties and is not married with children, his parents may simply view that as a matter of personal choice. In contrast, in my native land, for example, such a man's virility is brought into question.

As I've said, my father started going for breakfast at around 6:00 a.m.

so that he could see my mother. At first, she did not pay too much attention to him, because there were a lot of new customers patronizing my grandmother's business. For my mother, my father was just another regular customer. But Father's sudden change in breakfast times did not escape my grandmother's notice. One day she innocently asked him why he had started showing up a lot earlier for his porridge.

I have seen pictures of my mother when she was young. She was a little bit on the curvy side, with ethnic markings on her face: two half-inch marks on each cheek. She was from Ouidah, a historic city of Benin renowned for the variety of pythons that can be seen there. Ouidah is also known as the emblematic capital of voodoo and has become over the years a hotspot for tourism. Every year on January 10, Ouidah hosts the annual voodoo festival. The city and its surrounding areas become the cynosure of breathtaking demonstrations of the occult and awe-inspiring ritualistic dances performed by priestresses called *hounssi, hounyo, héviossossi* and other divinities such as *gélédé* "homage to motherhood", *kouvito* or *égun* "the revenant" and *zangbéto* "guardian of the night". Some people also refer to Ouidah as the kingdom of the pythons, and it is called that way in some history books. After getting the blessing of her father, my own father began dating my mother.

In the house where my father lived at the time, which later became my childhood home, lived some of my father's nephews—his older brother's children. For years they had wondered if my father would ever get married. His nephews knew that the family had tried to set him up with a woman to marry, to no avail. When my parents began their courtship, nobody except my mother's people was aware of it. Nobody in my father's family knew. A few weeks after their courtship started, a woman arrived looking for Alfred, my father. He was not at home at the time, but my cousins welcomed the woman in. She agreed to take a seat and wait for him.

It had been years since any woman had ever come to ask for Alfred. She was seated and served some water. After a while, one of my father's nephews was curious enough to ask her who she was. She dropped a statement nobody was expecting: "I am dating Alfred," she said. To their astonishment, she told them that she and my father had been dating for several months now. It was breaking news in the house.

As that woman, my mother, later reported to me, the question they were most interested in was how she had managed to captivate Alfred's attention. Why? Because Alfred was a mystery to a lot of women, and also to his own family because nobody knew what he was looking for in a woman. Agnes, my mother, gave them a brief history of how the courtship had started.

After winnowing the list of her suitors down to a single man, my mother moved in with my father in the early 1980s. My father started working harder than before in order to grow his electronic parts retailing business. There was a woman in his life now, and he was planning to start a family. For years, he had remained steadfast, because he knew the kind of woman he was seeking. There was also a trend that the family wanted him to follow: to marry a woman of the same ethnic background as him, and preferably of the same village. My father is of ethnic Goun, a people found in the province of Ouémé. This is the region that encompasses Benin's capital, Porto-Novo. My uncles, all of them, took wives that were Ouémé natives and spoke the vernacular. It appeared that my father was not much into the idea of having to marry a woman of his own ethnic background. He lived and had his business in Cotonou and thus was exposed to people from every corner and every ethnicity of Benin. Meeting my mother, who was of ethnic Fon and also a city girl, was for my father definitely a breath of fresh air.

CHAPTER 2

Welcoming Me: Customs and Traditions

When I was born, President Ronald Reagan had just entered the second year of his presidency; NASA had just launched the STS-3 mission; *USA Today* had its first publication; *Rocky III*, starring Sylvester Stallone,was released; Italy had won the soccer World Cup; and later that year Michael Jackson would release his album *Thriller*. It was a joy to both my parents when I was born. My mother was still attending high school. She continued going to school while she was pregnant, but later she had to cease attending school to prepare for my birth. Schools do not allow women to attend classes while being conspicuously pregnant, so she had to put her schooling on hold. However, she had the option of returning after giving birth.

My parents are Catholics. I was baptized a few weeks after I was born. One of the names that I was given was Yemanlin, which has the same meaning in both in the Goun and Fon languages. A name with a deep meaning, it is the combination of three words: *ye-man-lin*. Ye means "they," *man* means "don't" or "didn't," and *lin* means "think/imagine/anticipate/guess/foresee." On the one hand, when all that is put together, the name means "someone who has exceeded expectations" or "someone who has achieved or attained a success that no one could have foreseen." On the other hand, it also means "They never thought about it" or "That was

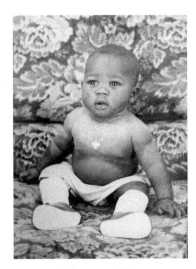 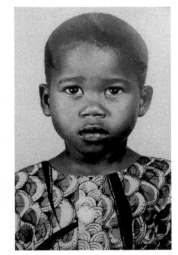

Me as a toddler   *Me at three years old*

an unexpected surprise." According to my father, one reason he chose the name was because as he was already in his midthirties, and no one in his family had thought that he would ever get married, let alone have a child. For him, my birth was proof that they were wrong about him.

In my first years in school, I did very well academically, often finishing at the top of my class. That earned me several nicknames, but the one that would stick with me and that I have made almost a middle name is "Erudite." In fact, if it didn't sound more like a word than a name, it would have made it to my birth certificate, because it was on the list of possible names that my mother had thought about shortly before I was born. She was an honor student when she became pregnant with me. She was probably imagining passing on to me some academic-excellence genes. As I later learned more about the true story—in my teenage years—I was surprised that I was coincidentally nicknamed so. Therefore, I have adopted it ever since.

In Benin, as it is in most African countries, there are rituals that ensue after a baby is born. These are usually done in the ancestral village of the newborn. If that's far from where the baby was actually born, or if the infant and the parents cannot, for whatever reason, travel there, they can send the baby's chosen name to relatives or elders in that village, along with some money if necessary to buy ingredients and items that will be needed to perform the rituals. This is how the newborn is officially welcomed into the family. Although there is usually nothing strange or arcane about those rituals, there are exceptions. Their purpose is to ask the baby's ancestors to provide protection and guidance during the little one's journey on Earth and be with the child during his or her entire life. In some families, the rituals are just a matter of a few minutes to a few hours, but some spread over days or weeks. And in some families, the rites cannot be performed without the newborn actually present. There are at least a couple of reasons why.

One reason is to confirm that the child is indeed the father's biological offspring. When a newborn bears a resemblance to his father, as I do, for example, this may reassure the father's family. But even if the resemblance is evident, the rituals welcoming the child into the family must go on. Although I'm not entirely privy to what occurs behind the scenes during the ritual, from what I have learned and heard from those who have witnessed it, it is done mostly by the women (aunts, grandmother, and so on) of the father's family. They toss the baby in the air and catch it a certain number of times while uttering incantations. From the way the infant screams while being tossed and how he or she lands back in the arms of the person doing the tossing, the family can tell whether the baby is the father's.

The other predominant reason for the baby's need to be present for the rituals is so that the family can apply minor scarifications to the newborn's face, chest, back, arm, or flank. These are meant to protect the infant from witchcraft, and from evil spirits that could seek to harm the baby's well-being or success later in life.

There are societal realities in Africa that to this day still perplex and bewilder those from outside the continent who do not know much about them. Some know the phenomenon as black magic, while others call it voodoo or other names. It's worth mentioning here that the word *voodoo* is etymologically derived from *vodoun*, which is its name in the language Fon, or Fongbé. More than a practice, voodoo is a religion that encompasses a body of rites and rituals, including libations, animal offerings to gods and other venerated deities, and a lot of incantations. The incantations can be carriers of good wishes or ill wishes.

Even though adherents who are initiated, called priests and priestesses, who know well the power of voodoo, advocate its use for commendable purposes such as healing of diseases, protection against misfortune and witchcraft, and so on, others privy to voodoo's secrets can still use it to do just the opposite of what the religion's high priests promote. A victim of a voodoo hex, for example, might catch a mysterious disease that can be extremely hard, if not impossible, to cure, even with modern medicine. Only someone who is initiated, an acknowledged healer, can help the victim/patient overcome the curse or strange disease; and even with help, it's not always guaranteed that the victim will fully recover or even survive.

For example, it is not unusual for a patient who goes to the hospital for treatment for an ailment to be discharged because the doctors have tried all they can but cannot cure the patient of the disease. Some doctors even advise the patient to seek help from an initiated healer who knows the secrets and the power of plants and other very guarded methods of healing mysterious diseases. Yes, there are doctors, trained in modern medicine with degrees from Western countries, who sometimes confess to their patients that they'd better seek traditional treatment, because the remedy for the disease they're suffering from might be beyond the ken of modern medicine.

On the one hand, it can be argued that these health-care specialists lack the skills to treat the patient adequately, and this surely may be true. But on the other hand, there is also an undeniable reality that witchcraft exists and is well practiced and used by some to harm others. The form of the harm that witchcraft can bring to its victim is wide-ranging. Illness is only one manifestation. In some cases, patients go abroad (mostly to western Europe) to seek treatment, to no avail. They might get better once undergoing treatment abroad, but they might succumb to the disease or curse when they come back home. All these things can sound strange, mysterious, or even laughable to some, but to those born into those cultures who know well the realities, for them, it is not a laughing matter. It is serious.

Another question most foreigners pose is "How can an educated person believe in such things?" Of course, these phenomena would make no sense to a person born and raised outside of sub-Saharan Africa. But those who were born and raised there, and who have seen with their own eyes the direct results and impacts of conjurations, cannot deny the reality. For generations, many in Africa have known the art of conjuring spirits to heal or harm other people. In Benin, the initiated practitioners are called Ázétó, *Bókótónón*, or Ámannón. In some other countries, they are referred to as *Marabous*. All this being said, how can I personally testify to this reality? After all, I was born into that culture, and I have seen and experienced a thing or two. Here is what I can share.

In the spring of 1998, when I was in ninth grade, I had a personal experience with a life-threatening malaise that rendered me incapacitated for several days. One afternoon shortly after 12:00 p.m. when I was attending a biology class, with all the students' gazes directed at the teacher, I inexplicably started feeling feverish. My body temperature began to rise, I started quivering, and my teeth chattered uncontrollably. My fingers trembled. Unable to regain focus to pay attention to what the teacher was saying, I felt my eyes becoming wet. My throat was dry and tight. Gasping for air, I felt as if something was trying to pull my tongue out of my mouth. Somehow I managed to sit through the lesson and went home when we were dismissed at around 12:20. We were supposed to reconvene at 3:00 p.m. after the recess, but I was not able to make it back to class that afternoon. My body's temperature had reached a crescendo by the time I got home. No sooner had I arrived home than I started vomiting massively. My eyes were turning green at that point, by my mother's assessment. Fortunately, she was at home, and I was immediately taken to the hospital. I was hospitalized for three days, then discharged when the doctors estimated that I could continue treatment at home.

In actuality, my discomfort started two days earlier, on a Saturday morning when I was returning home from shopping at the city center in a section called Ganhi. It was sunny, and I was riding my motorbike in traffic at around 6:00 p.m. The bridge linking Ganhi to Akpakpa, the district of Cotonou where I resided, was packed with cab drivers and motorcyclists, also known as *zémidjans* or *kèkènons*—taxi drivers offering rides or transport services using motorcycles rather than cars. As I was wending my way through the traffic to reach the other side of the bridge, I felt a sudden burning and sharp pain on my upper-right chest. In a matter of about three seconds, the full intensity of that pain spread throughout my pectoral muscles. Instinctively, I tried to relinquish the gas handlebar in an attempt to cup my chest with my hand and feel what could be the cause.

I panicked. It was as if I had just been struck by a bullet. With only one hand holding the gas handlebar, I almost lost control of the motorbike. I swerved left and right. Flanked by heavy traffic, with plumes of exhaust belching from the surrounding vehicles, there was no way to break through and speed home. As I continued riding, the pain grew more and more severe. I looked up at the sky, wondering whether I would make it off that bridge alive, or whether this was the last time on Earth that I would see the beauty of the immense blue sky over my head.

For about five minutes, the traffic was at a standstill. With the pain piercing deeper and deeper through my lung and then slowly diffusing through my back and shoulder, I started loosening my grip on the gas handlebar. With my left hand holding my chest and my right hand on the handlebar, I was tempted to cup my other pectoral with my right hand as well because of the intensity of the pain on both sides. But I knew that there was absolutely no way for me to ride that motorbike with no hands. I would fall and possibly, God forbid, be run over by the frenetic drivers who were visibly impatient, occasionally cursing at each other in their hurry to move. For a moment, I entertained the idea of just getting off the motorbike, leaving it in the middle of the traffic, and walking home. But I didn't follow through. If I had, not only would I have singlehandedly exacerbated the traffic jam, but the *zémidjans* would have gone nuclear on me with their invective. Some of them are notorious for their vituperations; they don't mince words when it comes to condemning other drivers or pedestrians.

I'd begun losing focus when the deafening blast of a horn from the car behind me jolted me out of my dizziness. As I looked up, I saw that the traffic ahead and surrounding me was moving again. Thank God! Regaining my strength and focus, I followed the traffic flow until I made it off the bridge, then found a safe place to pull over and catch my breath. I sat down on the ground, wondering whether I would faint right there or be lucky enough to recover and find my way home. If anything were to happen to me, I preferred that it would happen at home.

After about 15 minutes, the pain went away, but I continued gripping my chest, dreading that the stabbing sensation might suddenly return. I got back on my motorbike and headed straight home. I thought I might be having a heart attack, but somehow I knew that what had just happened to me on that bridge was not a symptom of a heart attack.

Though the doctors at the hospital never identified exactly what I was suffering from, they treated my case as though I had malaria. In fact, given that malaria is the most common disease in our part of the world, it's not unusual for doctors to treat cases like mine in that way, whether they are indeed malaria or not. Unfortunately, it doesn't always work well for patients.

Once I returned home from the hospital, my health did not seem to improve, despite taking the medication as recommended. It was then that, upon the advice of a close family member, my mother took me to a healer for an alternative, more traditional treatment. The healer lived about an hour away from my parents' home, in a remote area in the district of Godomey. The healer—for convenience I'll call her Mêhó (an appellation showing respect, and also meaning "elderly and wise")—was a woman probably in her midfifties. She knew in advance what had brought us to her house. In my own words, I answered her questions about what was going on with me and how it had all begun. She asked me some very specific questions. It was as though she herself was right there inside my body, feeling it all and seeing it all. For a moment, I got scared. How could she know all that? She proceeded to reassure me not to be afraid and added that I should feel better soon. I glanced at my mother. She sat quietly, listening to my conversation with Mêhó. I also felt at that moment that I would be fine.

After a few rituals, Mêhó invited me to an area immured with dry palm tree branches. Little did I know that Mêhó was about to bathe me in a way that I had never been—not even at the hands of my own mother. I undressed down to my underwear. Mêhó asked me to step inside a bucket of water sprinkled with leaves and herbs. The water was clear enough that I could see the bottom of the bucket as I stepped in. Once I was standing in the bucket, Mêhó bathed me with a sponge that I believe was made of tree roots and herbs. With the sponge tightly clenched, she thoroughly scrubbed my head, my arms, my back, my legs . . . while uttering invocations in the

Fon language. The words she was saying sounded as though she was re-citing proverbs one after another. Only she knew the power behind those words. Each scrub was deep and hard. It felt as if I was being bathed with a jagged stainless-steel kitchen scrub brush. As a result, I started feeling burning sensations all over my body, but I remained stoic. After about ten minutes or so, Mêhó was finished.

Upon her direction, I remained standing in the bucket for a while un-til she asked me to step out. Once I was out, she directed me to take a deep breath and then look in the bucket. At first, I checked my body to see whether I was bleeding anywhere, due to the abrasive scrubbing I'd just undergone. To my surprise, there was not the slightest sign of laceration on my skin, but the sensation of burning remained. I felt good.

Then, when I looked in the bucket, I saw shards of glass, carpentry nails, and thorny plants similar to prickly pears. Where had they come from? How had they ended up there in the bucket? They hadn't been there when I'd stepped in. Otherwise, I would have stepped on them, causing serious injury to my feet. I was baffled, but knowing where I was and why I'd been taken to the healer, I knew that my visit to Mêhó had not been in vain. She had just cured me of something that she would later reveal to me as *Tchákátoú*.

"Who would wish you harm enough to do something like that to you?" she asked. I shrugged my shoulders. To my knowledge, *Tchákátoú* has no translation in any of the United Nations' official languages—Arabic, Chi-nese, English, French, Russian, Spanish. However, you can find it in other dialects in Senegal, Mali, Nigeria, Ivory Coast, etc. For brevity and sim-plicity's sake, I'll just define it as a harmful spell intended to cause malaise, infirmity, and even death to its victim. It is well known in West Africa and supposedly exists in different forms and intensities. It is not unusual there to see people, from newborn to elderly, with amulets as jewelry around their waistlines, necks, or wrists to protect themselves from evil spirits. But mi-nor scarifications—also known as *átíndjidjá* in the local vernacular—on the chest, back, and other body parts are more discreet than amulets and have been part of the rituals of protection against evil spirits for generations. Scarifications of protection are not a once-and-done proposition. They can be done several times over the years, at any age.

Though I'd had baptismal scarification when I was an infant, I had it redone shortly after my health scare that had led my parents to take me to see Mêhó. My grandmother took charge of the scarification process soon after I returned home from Mêhó's place.

It was a Friday evening. The sun had just set. I was lying in bed recovering from the healing ritual I'd gone through the day before, when a knock on my door woke me up. It was my grandmother, accompanied by my mother. My grandmother was dressed in a traditional garment and was holding a small craft handbag. I would soon discover the contents of that bag: a razor blade and herb ashes. As she revealed the bag's contents to me, I knew that I was about to get fresh scarifications. It was not a happy feeling, because I knew that it was going to hurt a lot. Mentally, I began preparing myself for the pain.

On my grandmother's instructions, I turned my back and lay facedown on the mattress. No sooner had I taken a deep breath than I felt the razor blade penetrate my flesh. I felt the blood oozing out of that first cut and spilling onto my back. The second cut followed immediately, and the third one right after that. I felt a sharp echoing all over my body. The razor cuts on the skin were about a quarter of an inch long.

A few other parts of my body went through what my back had just endured. As my dear and beloved grandma finished, she took a handful of the ashes she had brought and spread it on her palm, squeezed the handful between her fingers, and then spread the ash over the lacerations. This burned like having ground red hot chili pepper spread over a wound. It hurts, but it does marvels for the body.

Afterward, my grandma reassured me that everything was fine and that I should worry no more. Her words reassured me that all would be well. I gave my grandma a hug and thanked her for coming. She left the room with my mother, who had watched it all.

I did not bathe for two more days, so that the cuts would close themselves, taking in as much of the residual ash as possible. Like modern-day disease-protection methods such as vaccinations, ritual scarifications might not offer protection against all "evil spirits" or hexes cast at someone, whether by another person or even by conspiring invisible forces of nature, but there is a common saying among the locals that goes "Better a little of something than nothing." It is an adage that carries more weight and has a deeper meaning than any other language can adequately convey.

My recovery was very swift after Mêhó treated me. I stopped taking all the medication prescribed to me at the hospital and solely focused on the infusion Mêhó had prepared exclusively for me to take home. For me personally, that was the moment when, for the first time, I was awakened to some of the realities of bewitchment that I had often heard of.

CHAPTER 3

Inside the Family

As first-time parents, my folks had to make a lot of compromises and adjustments. Having still been in school when she became pregnant with me, my mother had planned to return to school at some point to earn her high school diploma. But as time went by, that plan became dimmer and dimmer until, after a few years, it was dashed completely. She entertained the idea of going to nursing school, but my father did not seem to like that idea. Although his electronic-parts business was still fledgling, its future looked promising, based on the revenue it was generating. Therefore, he, like most men at the time, was not keen on his wife's having a job outside the home, because there wouldn't be anyone to take care of the children. The Republic of Benin, like many other African countries, is very patriarchal. The man is supposed to be the breadwinner, the provider, while the woman is the homemaker. Over the past few decades, that mind-set has shifted a little bit given that men can lose their job or do not bring home the necessary income to cover all the family needs.

At first, my parents made ends meet by sharing a home with other members of the family. I grew up in the same house with some of my cousins. In fact, during the first eight years after I was born, we lived in the house of my uncle—my father's older brother. My father raised all of us—his own children and his brother's seven children. So, there were many of us in the house. My uncle himself did not live in the same house with us. He lived in the family's ancestral home in the village of Tchaada.

Almost two years after I was born, my parents welcomed a new member of the family: my sister Edwige. Three years later they added another daughter, my second sister, Aurelle Christelle, and finally, four years after that, my youngest sister, Sonia.

Where I grew up, living with close and extended family members is very common. My mother cooked for all of us and maintained the house. But, despite her efforts, some of my cousins, who were a little older at the time, some in their late teens, some in their mid- to late twenties, made life a bit difficult for her. At times, some of them casually disrespected her by reminding her that she was living in a house that belonged neither to her nor to my father. To this day, I remember vividly a few of the direct provocations some of my cousins made toward my mother when I was young, perhaps four to five years old.

One day Marlene,* a daughter of my uncle, got into an argument with my mother, who at the time was pregnant with my sister Aurelle Christelle. Marlene threatened my mother with a stick and said that she was going to use it to remove the child from my mother's womb. I witnessed the quarrel and heard most of the invective. My mother sacrificed her time to make sure that food was always ready and that the house was well cared for, but at times, my cousins did not appreciate her work. These contretemps usually happened behind my father's back, when he was at work. I believe my mother reported to my father when the incidents occurred. But my father, being a quiet man, did not generally rebuke or confront them, to my recollection. However, some of my cousins did respect my mother, and all of them feared my father.

In early 1990, I was about eight years old. For financial reasons, my uncle put the house up for sale, so my father rented an apartment in the neighborhood of Sènadé, where he moved us, my mother and my siblings. My mother was very happy and relieved after we moved; rightfully so. For eight years, it had been like a roller-coaster ride for her in the house with my

---

*   Some names have been changed.

cousins. A few incidents here and there have stayed with me. Even though I was young at the time, I remember those things. Because I witnessed those disputes and still recall vividly to this day some of the insults hurled at my mother, over the years I have calibrated my relationships with some of those relatives accordingly. But, after all, whether I like it or not, it's still my family, and no family is perfect. The instinct to protect took root in me when I was witnessing those sporadic microaggressions toward my mother.

Remembering almost perfectly these incidents that I witnessed when I was a child has caused me to try not to do anything that might be offensive or disrespectful to another person in front of a child. I know that children have good retention of memories. Traumatizing events might stay with them, and, as has been the case for me, that child will likely carry them, in the form of grudges or resentments, into adulthood.

But despite the strife of those years, my mother stayed strong. She knew that it was just a matter of time before my father, too, bought or built his own house. Eventually, her prayers were answered when we left my uncle's house. After staying in a rental apartment for about a year, we moved to my dad's newly built house.

Finally, after years of praying and waiting, my mother could now live and raise her children in her husband's home. There is some pride and dignity that comes with that. It was all my mother had prayed for, all those years. Nobody in my dad's family would ever again dare tell her that she was living and raising his children in a house that didn't belong to her husband.

In a twist of fate, after we moved to our house in the district of Avotrou, some of those same relatives had the audacity to plead with my parents to let them come and live with us in our new home. My mother did not have the best days of her marital life living in the same house with her husband's nieces, nephews, and other relatives. Clearly, she was not going to accept that and relive the same experience.

CHAPTER 4

A Brief History of the Native Land

At the time of my birth, Mathieu Kérékou was the president of Benin. A little over a decade before my parents welcomed me into this world, army captain Kérékou and a few other key members of the national army led a brilliant coup d'état that put an end to a rotation system in which three political figures had been alternately assuming the office of the presidency. The agreement was that the three men, Hubert Maga, Justin Ahomadégbé, and Sourou-Migan Apithy, would each serve two years. At the end of the two-year term, the incumbent president would hand over power to the next person among the three, and so on.

The reason for a political system in which the presidency was rotated among three men was to bring diversity to the post. Benin is ethnically diverse. Each member of the trifecta represented either the North, the Center, or the South. It was an attempt by those leaders to ease the fear, resentment, or concern among the population that just one person of a particular ethnic group was holding on to power. Though the intention behind this presidential system was understandable, it was not efficient. Eventually, the army started to plot a stratagem to do away with it and bring order to the office of the president, so that Benin could have one clear president just like any other nation in the world.

Later known as La Révolution du 26 Octobre 1972, the coup was not bloody. The three members of the dissolved presidential trifecta, fortunately, were not assassinated, but they were placed under house arrest for several years. Benin in 1972 was still a very young country that had just gotten its independence 12 years earlier, on August 1, 1960. It had been a French colony. Between 1960, the year of the proclamation of independence, and 1972, several men had assumed the presidency. Coups d'état were routine. The country was still looking to find its way. Politicians tossed around several different political ideologies. The country was clearly doing some soul-searching as to the most adequate ideology and political and economic system that would best serve everyone. The shortest presidential tenure on record in Benin was 24 hours—yes, just one day. Power struggles were something the new nation had to grapple with.

Once independence was gained, the French left Benin. The country was now on its own and had to carve its own destiny. The presidency being unstable at the time, Benin was becoming a laughingstock in the region, even though other West African countries were facing similar challenges—but nothing like Benin's 24-hour presidency. It was high time someone brought order to the chaos. This was why Kérékou and a group of loyalists carried out their military coup, seizing power on October 26, 1972.

With the military in control, things started to change drastically, as one would expect. Respect, strict discipline, and intimidation became the new reality for nearly two decades. The country under Kérékou between 1972 and 1991 was ruled like a dictatorship. It was a military regime. Freedom of expression was a foreign concept to Beninese during that time. There were political prisoners, and there was not much that journalists could say against the Kérékou-ruled government or anyone in his entourage, for that matter. This was particularly true during the 1970s, when anyone who had just made a radio or TV appearance in which he or she criticized the president would be accosted on the street or picked up at home and ushered into a military van by heavily armed soldiers. Critics of the government were reportedly taken to the nearest military base, where some were made an example of with corporal punishment. It was an era of intimidation by the Kérékou regime. The near absence of an opposition party was viewed as the key to "stability" within the country.

In the late 1980s, with the fall of the Soviet Union, several African countries had to rethink their political systems. Benin under President Kérékou was run under the model of the Eastern European bloc. The people of Benin audaciously and without fear for their lives demanded a change, Kérékou yielded under pressure, and in 1990 a general conference was called. Benin decided to embrace democracy. The sons and daughters of Benin who had fled the country during the "reign" of Kérékou were called upon to return from exile and help usher the country into a new era. The scholars both living in the country and abroad called for a national conference to be held. During that conference, the Constitution of Benin was drafted. The international community and other African countries in particular watched in bewilderment as the conference concluded without a single shot being fired, without a drop of blood, and without turmoil. It was surreal to many observers who had bet that Kérékou would never agree to what would transpire. Many observers, local and international, had predicted that the country would descend into chaos.

The Catholic Archbishop of Cotonou, Isidore De Souza, chaired the conference, during which prayers were organized all over the country each day. Archbishop De Souza is often remembered for warning before the conference that he would not condone any type of violence anywhere in the country. As much as people were praying, the nation was also ready for an outcome that might bring upheaval and turmoil, because Kérékou still had a lot of supporters and loyalists at the time, especially in the military. Surprisingly, he accepted the new Constitution and agreed to relinquish power so that a fair presidential election could be organized. It was remarkable, and not many people outside of Benin, or even within the country, had thought it possible. The economic system of Marxism-Leninism that he had spearheaded, championed, and promoted since seizing power was coming to an end before his very eyes. Prior to Kérékou's stepping down, there was no African leader in the region who, solely under the pressure of his own countrymen, ceded power to make way for a democratic election.

African presidents were very skeptical of democracy. My history and geography teacher in junior high school once compared African presidents to a typical newborn being breastfed. Newborns usually do not want to let go of their mothers' breasts during suckling. For generations, this has been true of Africa's leaders, but things have changed a bit—for the better—in some countries, where presidents leave power after their two terms.

As one can see, I was born under a dictatorship, a country ruled by the military, where discipline in all aspects of life was the law of the land. Excellence in school and at work, and respect for authority, were instilled in me at an early age. In a country where criticizing the president or any member of his cabinet or administration can land you in trouble, or even in jail in some instances, I have come to appreciate countries with longstanding democracies, like the United States, where the freedom of expression is inked in the Constitution, and the military can probably never be used against the citizenry upon the order of the President of the United States. In many other countries, the military is often casually used against the people.

A few years after Benin was ushered into democracy, the other country on the African continent that democratically organized a peaceful presidential election was arguably South Africa. But the difference between Benin and South Africa was that the latter yielded to international pressure to abandon Apartheid. I vividly remember growing up in the late 1980s—the campaigns and songs playing on national television condemning the political system in the Zulu nation, and the visceral condemnation of Apartheid spewed on the airwaves. During the Apartheid years, South Africa was banned from participating in the most prestigious soccer tournament on the continent: the African Cup of Nations. A few years after the end of Apartheid, South Africa won the privilege of hosting the tournament, and the South African men's national soccer team played with brilliance and won the competition that same year. It was an opportunity for the world and especially the entire African continent to witness the talent of those men repressed to be expressed on the international stage because of the infamous political system under which they were living.

CHAPTER 5

Off to School

In the late 1980s, I started kindergarten. My mother, who'd had to drop out of school when she was pregnant with me, had prepared me for my very first day at school. That day I saw a lot of other children around my age. If my memory serves me well, I was a little surprised, because I thought I would have the entire classroom to myself. My mother had trained me in reciting the alphabet and in counting. Before I went to school for the first time, my idea of school was that it was a place where I would continue learning, but also where I would receive undivided attention from someone other than my mother. My father was almost never home because of his work, and therefore my mother was the one who had guided me and helped lay the elementary educational foundation upon which I needed to build.

As I progressed through elementary school, I was usually ranked as the best student in my class. Once, in third grade, for the first time, I briefly lost the top position and slid to second. When my mother saw my report card for that trimester, her disenchantment and anger were evident. She was not at all happy with my slide to number two. That day, my mother put me on notice. Her message was clear: "If you ever slide down to number two again, don't even bother to come home." My mother was very strict.

But by the time I was in fourth grade, my mother had loosened up a little bit. My youngest sister, Sonia, had just been born and demanded more attention and care. By then, however, I didn't really need much supervision or tutoring. I was ten years old, and I had learned the drill. I knew what my parents, especially my mother, wanted from me academically. From there, I was on my own. I did not disappoint them. I was bringing home excellent grades, and they were proud.

In first grade, I could name and pinpoint on the map all the different countries on the African continent. My knowledge of the world expanded dramatically by second grade. I remember that during the soccer World Cup of 1990, when countries were opposing each other during the tournament, I made sure to locate each one on the map. I had also realized that there were more languages in the world than I had previously thought. I wanted to learn as many of them as I could. I was just in second grade, and my fluency in French was still in its infancy, but I already had the curiosity, the willingness, and the drive to learn other languages. I had to wait, though, until junior high school to get my first English language introduction class. There was not much stress put on learning and acquiring fluency in any language other than French. In elementary school, teachers drilled the French language into pupils by any means necessary. Corporal punishment is allowed, and instances of young kids being severely beaten with whips and sticks made particularly for that purpose are ubiquitous. It is the culture, and it is not illegal, though the practice is clearly illegal in other countries around the world.

In my case, I have a whip mark on my left arm: a reminder of a punishment I got in third grade for failing to find the correct answer to a division problem that my teacher asked me to solve in front of the class.

Because I had done very well in class, the teacher called my name to go up front and perform the operation. He thought I would be able to do it, but my confidence was not where I would have wanted it to be. To confess, I was not entirely ready, because the material that we had just covered in class had not sunk in yet. Once my name was called, I had absolutely no choice but to stand up, weave my way among the seats and tables in the classroom, and go to the blackboard to solve the problem. All my classmates gazed at me, almost all of them knowing that I should be able to do it.

When I got in front of the classroom, my teacher handed me a piece of chalk. I started the operation well, but midway through it, I had to resort to counting on my fingers, because I wanted to be certain that I got right that part of the multiplication table that I needed to work out the answer. The teacher saw me counting on my fingers and shouted my name. At that moment, I lost all focus and became paralyzed by his voice. My feet started trembling; my voice replied unsteadily. I began stuttering. I knew at that moment that I was in trouble. Without further ado, he grabbed his whip and hit me a few times. In an attempt to use my arms to ward off some of the barrage of lashes, I was left with a few protuberant marks, one of which was very pronounced. I bear the scar on my left arm to this day.

For fear of corporal punishment, I have developed the habit of staying focused and paying attention whenever I am in an audience. The small details that you don't pay attention to are the ones that are usually critical. That kind of stern education has made me a very disciplined and scrupulous person.

In junior high school, my focus was medicine, because that was the career choice that my mother wanted for me. It was also a passion that was fueled by a TV program called *Savoir Plus Santé*, which showed actual surgeons performing real surgical procedures and operations. But that passion for medicine didn't last long when in my third year in junior high I took my first introduction to physics. A year before that, which would be eighth grade, we received a brief introduction to electricity in school, but it was a smattering. It didn't command my interest, because I was more absorbed in the thought of becoming a medical doctor, just as my mother wanted. I didn't want to be an electrician, as I would say to myself. I was more into mathematics and natural sciences.

But as the months went by and we went through one chapter after another, I developed a liking for physics. My childhood ambition of going to the United States one day and working as a NASA engineer started catching up with me. My interest in medicine dwindled, and the discipline of physics began to come easily to me. I was doing very well in both physics and mathematics. By the 11th grade, I was sold on everything physics, especially the lessons pertaining to electricity.

Even though I liked physics a lot when I was in junior high school, I had not decided on the exact profession I would pursue later in life. Although becoming a NASA scientist was often on my mind, I knew that the agency was on the other side of the globe, and I might never get to work there after all. However, electrical engineering, civil engineering, and business were on my top-three list. In those three fields, there was only so far that one could go in Benin, as far as higher education was concerned.

The electrical engineering program offered at the university level was mostly geared toward prospective electric power engineers—power engineers to serve on the national market. The other branches of the field, such as control engineering, microelectronics, signal processing, computer engineering, and telecommunications, did not have a noticeable presence, and any desire for specialization in one of those fields would require the student to study abroad. Canada, Europe, and the United States have gained popularity among students seeking knowledge and an advanced degree in those focus disciplines.

The United States and Canada were always my target destinations, with Germany a distant third. Even though I was fluent in French, France was never on my list. I wanted to pursue my university studies in another language, preferably English. The United States was always the top choice, but I was not sure whether I would ever make it to the US because of the difficulty of obtaining a visa, at least from what I'd been told at the time. I knew Canada would be relatively easy, but just like the US, it imposed some visa requirements pertaining to financial support that I knew would be hard to let my parents know about, especially my father, given that he was the one who paid for our—his children's—schooling. I couldn't summon the courage to tell him about the proof of financial support that he would have to pledge in order for me to get a visa.

I had always believed that if I couldn't immigrate to the United States or Canada, I would probably make it to Germany. Why Germany? I studied the German language in ninth grade and did well. Moreover, the opportunity to study in Germany was available, and earning a scholarship was relatively easier than receiving one to the United States.

A minimum test score of 15 out of 20 on the high school exit exam at the national level would make a fair case for me to apply for a scholarship in order to study abroad. It is one of those grades that are not easily attained. At the national high school exit (college entrance) exam, an aggregate grade of 17 out of 20 is in itself a feat that can draw media attention to the student. I was a hair shy of the minimum of 15. It was not my chef d'oeuvre, but I had to move on.

I had been confident I would score at least the required minimum, but when I fell a bit short, I knew that it would be a little challenging to win the scholarship I had so coveted. With my exam grade, I was still eligible to apply for some scholarships that could cover me to study in other countries in North Africa, but I was not interested in them. In high school, I had made it clear to my friends that I would seek a way to make my visa application robust enough so that I could get a visa to go to North America and pursue the degree that I actually wanted. While still in high school, I wrote to a few universities in the United States. They sent me packages containing their brochures and information about their different programs. The projected annual tuition fees, along with the costs of health insurance, books, and dormitory lodging, were very high compared with what my parents could afford, so I never bothered to apply to those schools.

But all hope was not lost. I wrote letters to the US Embassy inquiring about scholarships for which I might be eligible. I knew little about the system at the time, but it was my way of seeking and exploring all the avenues I could to make my dream a reality.

CHAPTER 6

The Visa Interview

Two months after the proclamation of the high school exam results came an event that would change the United States' geopolitics and visa issuance: the terrorist attack of September 11, 2001. The news coverage of that event sent shock waves through the long list of those who had applied for a visa and were preparing for a visa interview. Those who were entertaining the idea of applying for one in the near future were no longer certain about their chances and were wondering if it was even worth the effort. The word was out that more visa applications would be denied. And the *Denied* or *Rejected* stamp is something that a lot of people dread to see on their passports.

It dawned on me that I needed to come to grips with reality, put the idea of trying to pursue my educational goals in one of my top three preferred countries behind me, and just stay home. I definitely wanted to go to a university and get a higher-level education, but as I looked around, I really didn't like the programs offered by the institutions of higher learning in my country, including the University of Benin. I had known that all along when I was still in high school, and that was why I was looking for a "way out" to go where I would have a wide range of options.

I asked myself whether I should take a sabbatical year, enroll in a local university, or help my father with his business. I decided to enroll in the mathematics and physics program at what was then the National University of Benin. I don't remember exactly how many times I attended class that year, but I am sure it couldn't have been more than 90 days combined throughout the year. My attendance was sporadic. I logged perfect attendance for the first two months, but after that, I was hard to find on campus.

The following year, I enrolled in a private university, L'Institut Universitaire du Bénin, to study computer engineering and information systems. It was a new school, and the program it offered was a bit closer to what I was expecting. Not quite what I wanted, but that's what was available to me. For the next three years at that school, I studied a wide range of topics, such as computer programming languages, website development, electronics, telecommunication, and networking.

In my senior year, while I was doing my internship with an Internet service provider company, I got news from the US Embassy that my immigrant visa application had been accepted and that I was scheduled for an interview. The year before, in 2004, I had applied for the Diversity Visa upon returning home from the business trip with my father. Before applying, I spent countless hours translating from English to French the entire newspaper article that my father had bought for me. Upon hearing that I was scheduled for an interview at the US Embassy, I could feel my heart skip a beat. For the first time in my life, I started picturing seriously what life might be like where I would probably be headed soon: the United States of America. Even though I was graduating that year, there was no promising employment opportunity in my field that I was expecting. Taking over my father's business was all I was planning for.

That phone call from the embassy changed the equation for me. For years, I had waited for that moment. I started reflecting on that day when my father had bought that newspaper for me when I'd accompanied him on his business trip. I remembered that once we returned home from that trip, hardly had the engine of my father's car cooled down before I grabbed my English-to-French dictionary and retreated to my room to pore over the newspaper. Articles written in newspapers tend to be in formal English with a more advanced vocabulary, for all the obvious reasons. I knew that even though English was not foreign to me anymore, I would be dealing with a lot of words I didn't know.

It was a huge and heavy paper, as they usually were, but I was only interested in one article: the one on the front page, dealing with the Diversity Visa open application. I wouldn't let a word go untranslated from English to French in that article. I was determined. After about three hours of going back and forth between the languages, I became tired and fell asleep on my bed. I still had not finished translating the article in its entirety. I had remained patient and determined to translate every word, to the last.

A few days later, I did it.

Now, with the real prospect of a visa interview, I had to prepare myself and gather all the necessary documents. On the day of the appointment, I would be offered the choice to be interviewed either in French or in English. I had prepared myself to elect English if presented with the choice. I knew it wouldn't be perfect, but at least that would be my way of showing that I had some familiarity with the language spoken in the country in which I was applying for the visa. I wanted to impress!

In the days leading up to the interview, I prayed a lot. I really wanted it. My mindset: now or never. On the day of the interview, I put on my suit, borrowed my father's car, and headed to the embassy. A security guard greeted me at the entrance. Once inside, I explained the purpose of my visit and signed in.

The confidence that I had that day was palpable, at least to me. I was not nervous at all. I was ready. The waiting room was set at a good temperature, and barely could one hear a noise from the outside. It was the perfect setting for an interview. I was in the middle of mentally rehearsing my responses to some of the anticipated questions when my name was called. At that moment, I have to admit, once more my heart skipped a beat. It was my moment of truth. It was my win-or-go-home moment.

The interview room was compartmentalized in such a way that there was a wall with an aperture separating the interviewer and the interviewee. My interviewer was already there, standing and waiting for me. He was wearing a white dress shirt and gave me a warm smile as I approached. He had my application in front of him. He asked me to confirm my name and date of birth, which I did, without stuttering, of course. From there, the next question he asked me was whether I would like the interview to be conducted in French or English. I bravely chose English, despite not being fluent at that time.

While answering some of the questions, I intermittently paused, not because I was providing the incorrect answer, but because I was substantially vocabulary-challenged at that moment, and some of the English words I needed were not coming as easily out of my mouth as I would want them to. However, I pressed on anyway and got my points across. All my years of practicing, the business trips to Nigeria with my father, listening to BBC Africa, I poured all out that day. In the jargon of sports commentators in the United States, it's called *being in the zone*. Yes, I was *in the zone*.

The interviewer at times even helped me with some words, but I did well enough to remember lines from some of my rehearsals. The interviewer was quite impressed and asked me at one point where I had learned English. I believe he just appreciated the effort I was making. At times, he would smile; on occasion, he would keep a straight face. For a moment, doubt started creeping inside me. Knowing that there was also a probability that I might get a "Rejected" stamp on my passport, I started imagining the reaction of my family when I told them that I wouldn't be going to the United States. At least there would be my father's business that I would be taking charge of. For a moment, that was the thought that consoled me, but deep down, I knew I wanted what I had come to the interview for. I got a jolt of hope and greater confidence in obtaining the visa when the interviewer started complimenting me on my aspirations and what I planned to do once I arrived in the United States.

It was time to wrap up the interview. We had to finish it off in French, because of some important US national security messages that needed to be read to me so that I would understand them properly. He asked me to raise my right hand and take an oath. That's when I knew I was approved. A chill went up my spine. I was very excited, but I didn't express my enthusiasm. I kept it within me. After the recitation of the oath, the interviewer gave me a congratulatory handshake and wished me immense success in my endeavors in the United States.

⤸

The day of my departure had arrived. My luggage was ready. My mother was visibly nervous. For the first time in two decades, I was leaving her bosom; I was going alone to another country to live. How would I fend for myself? Would I be safe? Would I be treated right? These were some of the concerns that my mother had and discussed with me before I left.

I reassured her as much as I could. I saw tears in her eyes. She was happy I was going, but also worried about my safety. She told me that she knew I was going to a great country that was constantly in the news making good headlines—and also making less-good headlines. I understood what she was feeling at that moment. But I also knew that it was just a matter of time before she would get over it. I enfolded my parents in a strong embrace and whispered "thank you" to them. I waved them good-bye as I headed through the security checkpoint to board my flight. Two days later, I was at my final destination: St. Louis, Missouri, USA.

CHAPTER 7

Welcome to America

May 11, 2006. My plane had just touched down at JFK International Airport. About 30 minutes before the plane had landed, the pilot had made an announcement about the weather on the ground and flight connection formalities. I did not understand everything he said through the speaker, but I cocked my head and strained my ears enough to get an idea of what he was talking about. I was not familiar with that accent—the English language as spoken in the United States.

When the plane landed, it did not head toward an assigned gate so that we could deplane through a jet bridge. Instead, it remained on the tarmac with officers on the ground to guide us toward immigration and customs. It was the second leg of my flight, after a stop in Paris at Charles De Gaulle Airport. As soon as I got off the plane and set feet on the ground, I knelt down on one knee in reverence and thanksgiving, touched the ground with my right hand, and made the sign of the cross. I had watched on television on a few occasions the chief of the Roman Catholic Church, the Pope, do the same thing when he traveled to foreign countries. As I stood and looked up at the sky, it was just as blue as I had seen back in my ancestral land. Was I expecting it to be different? Well . . . no, not exactly. I was still on Earth, after all. And yet I gazed up at the sky for a few moments.

At the customs and immigration office in the airport, I handed the officer my passport, along with a document that I'd been instructed by the US Embassy in Benin to give to the person who would register my entry into the United States. From that moment, I was guessing what might follow. Afterward, I was taken to a room for fingerprinting. I was expecting the officers to give me the third degree, but that didn't happen.

The airport was like nothing I'd seen before: It was truly enormous, and I was intimidated but impressed. I was afraid I wouldn't be able to find the gate for my flight to St. Louis, but I followed the signs and was able to get there easily. A few minutes later, I boarded the plane for a two-hour flight to the "Show-Me" state, Missouri. At Lambert International Airport in St. Louis, my cousin, Alicia;* her husband, Scott; * and their children, Logan* and Emily,* were waiting for me. They waved at me as soon as they saw me, the children rushing to hug me. They welcomed me and asked whether my trip had gone well. I reassured them that all had gone smoothly.

Before my arrival, my cousin and her family had debated where to take me for dinner. My flight from New York to St. Louis arrived around 8:00 at night. They decided to take me to one of the country's flagship eateries: McDonald's. From the airport, we headed to a McDonald's restaurant, and I tasted a burger for the first time. In Benin, I had always wanted to try a juicy hamburger. I studied the menu, placed my order—with Scott's help as my translator—and in just a few minutes, my food was handed to me. The meat, the dripping grease, the cheese, all sandwiched inside a fluffy bun, tasted exceptionally good. I savored every bite of it. As I looked out the window of the McDonald's, it dawned on me that I was indeed in a different country—in a different part of the world!

A few feet away from our table, other customers were placing orders. I strained my ears to understand what they were saying, but I couldn't. They were speaking English, but not the English I was accustomed to— the British English from BBC World Services that I listened to on the radio in Africa.

By the time we finished eating and headed to Alicia's house, it was almost midnight. When we got there, I called my parents to reassure them

---

*   Some names have been changed.

that I had arrived safe and sound. Alicia showed me to my room. My bed was made, and the room smelled nice. Once alone in the room, I got on my knees and said my prayers before heading to bed—my first night in America.

The following day, I got to see my new city of St. Louis. As we all gathered for breakfast, they wanted to know how my night had gone. Scott gave me a quick history of St. Louis and a description of some of the attractions around the city. Alicia worked as an esthetician, so she was busy most of the time, but Scott was a self-employed car dealer, and his time was more flexible. He drove me around town and showed me some of the sights, such as the Gateway Arch, Union Station, and Busch Stadium, where the St. Louis Cardinals play their home games. When we returned home from our tour of the city, I spent most of my time in front of the television, to help me better understand the language.

Alicia did her best to accommodate me in her house. I bonded quickly with Logan, their son, as he reminded me of myself when I was about his age, nine years old.

One night, we were all watching the *Late Show with David Letterman*. Letterman was telling joke after joke, and Alicia and Scott were laughing so hard. I wanted to as well, but I couldn't, because I didn't understand what Letterman was saying. At one point, Scott asked me if I understood, and I admitted that I was only getting bits and pieces of it. It was then that Scott turned on the closed captioning. It was a game changer for me. Once I could match what I was hearing on TV with the words being displayed at the bottom of the screen, my understanding of spoken American English took off from there. At Alicia's recommendation, I also enrolled in a free English as a Second Language (ESL) class held in a church nearby: the Fee Fee Baptist Church.

Fee Fee Baptist Church has many community outreach programs. One of those amazing services was the free English lessons that I attended. The class was taught by very experienced teachers who knew the pedagogy pertaining to teaching English to non-native speakers. Funded by the city, the free class was open to anyone who wanted to learn, such as recent immigrants and others for whom English was not their first language. During the class, I met people who'd received very little formal education in their countries of origin. The ESL class was a golden opportunity for many to learn the language.

On my first day of class, I met the instructor, Mrs. Leslie Sullivan.* After our introduction, she let me attend the first half of her lesson. During a break in the class, she took me to a room and handed me a placement test to assess my knowledge of English. I was a little nervous at first, although I was already familiar with some of the grammatical rules. For the next two hours, I took the test, answering a litany of questions on grammar, vocabulary, reading comprehension, and listening comprehension. I finished the test by the time Leslie finished teaching her class, and she graded it while I waited. She was pleased with how well I had done on the test. We spent the next 30 to 40 minutes chatting. She wanted to know everything about me. She was very personable, approachable, and eager to get to know her students.

When I shared my aspiration to complete a master's degree and later a PhD, she said that although her class would help with my English, it would not prepare me for the more rigorous placement tests that non-native English speakers must pass in order to enroll in English-speaking universities. The ESL class was not that challenging to me, but it was still a good opportunity to learn more about the United States—my new home. Leslie explained that I would need to prepare for the TOEFL (Test of English as a Foreign Language) and likely for the GRE or GMAT, too, depending upon the graduate-level program and the university I chose.

I attended the class for a few months, and it was one of the best decisions I made when I first came to the United States. In Leslie's class, we learned not only the language but also American history, civics, government, and laws. It was more than just an English class; it was an immersion into the American culture and society, the dos and don'ts, and the holidays and their history. I was very assiduous and diligent during her class, as I was eager to learn as much as I could, and as fast as I could. As the weeks and months ticked by, between Leslie's class and the closed-captioning function on the TV, the language became much less intimidating to me.

---

*   Some names have been changed.

I had polished my vocabulary enough to start speaking with other people.

After a few months, my ears and brain had become accustomed to the American English accent, and my memory of the English accent from BBC World Services faded. Scott would often buy me the local newspaper, the *St. Louis Post-Dispatch*, and I would randomly pick one or two articles and highlight the words I didn't know. I would then spend hours looking up those words in the dictionary. Sometimes I would write down their definitions and read all the ways in which those words could be used and the context in which they were used in the article I was reading. It was pretty much the same thing I did when I was given a newspaper on a business trip with my father.

The ESL classes take place in the same building as the Sunday church services at Fee Fee Baptist Church. This has given the church access to a pool of folks of international background. In fact, every Sunday morning between the 7:00 a.m. and 11:00 a.m. services, the Fee Fee Baptist Church held a class called International Bible Study. From time to time during the week, the instructors of that class visited students attending the ESL class to talk to them about it. The International Bible Study class itself was geared toward non-native English speakers, but it was also open to whoever might want to attend. Over time, as I became a regular attendee, I saw people who were Americans by birth coming to our class to learn the Gospel with us. It was during one of my English classes with Leslie that I met Mrs. Caroline Rodgers,* one of the International Bible Study instructors. She and her husband, Dr. David Rodgers,* were members of the church.

Even though I was a student of English at the time, I hadn't had the opportunity to really read or learn the Bible in English. My knowledge of the Bible in English was confined to snippets that I saw displayed on screens and monitors during church services. The idea of Bible study was very intriguing to me. I saw it as another opportunity to accelerate my learning of the language, to see it used in a different context, and of course to learn more about religious terminology along the way.

---

*   Some names have been changed.

Me with Fee Fee Baptist Church instructors during a
Sunday morning International Bible Study class

I attended my first International Bible Study class the following weekend. Mrs. Rodgers was thrilled to see me. She introduced me to the other
instructors, Mrs. Lucille Wilson,* Matthew Ryan,* and later Mrs. Danica
Peters.* The peculiarity of the Bible class was that it did not just involve
reading the Old and New Testament. We began the class with an opening
prayer and then dove into a 10- to 15-minute vocabulary-building drill.
The new words that we learned on the spot were selected from the Gospel
that we were about to read. After vocabulary study, we proceeded to read
the portion of the Bible scheduled for the class that day. A discussion of
the passage's message, instruction, or Commandment followed, and finally, we concluded with a closing prayer. It was a true language-immersion
environment.

---

    *   Some names have been changed.

Through the church, I had made my first friends. One of the unexpected surprises came when one of the instructors, Mrs. Wilson, organized a birthday party for me at her house. At a time when I felt quite alone, I found that there were people thinking of me and wanting to bring me joy on the days that are special to me. It was a gesture I really appreciated, and I knew I owed the Wilsons a debt of gratitude. The couple later left St. Louis and moved to Springfield, Missouri, after Mr. Wilson's health began deteriorating. I kept in touch with them through e-mails. Given what they had done for me, the least I could do was to pay them a visit. I chose to make it during the Christmas season. They confessed to me that my visit meant a lot to them. I was very honored in the way and manner in which they welcomed me into their home for three days.

In July of 2015, I received the news that Bob Wilson had peacefully passed away. I was devastated. It was like losing a very close relative. Bob was a man it was a pleasure and a privilege to know.

With Lucille and Bob

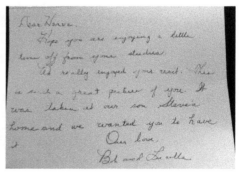

Letter received after visiting Lucille and Bob

After just three months in the United States, with the countless hours spent learning the language, I felt a confidence boost. Even though I was not understanding everything that was said, either on the street or on television, I really liked the level I'd reached. When I started understanding jokes, I knew right there that I was getting the hang of the language. I had learned how to write a résumé—different from the way they're written in Benin—and how to apply for a job. I did submit a few job applications here and there. At first, I tried for jobs in my field (I graduated with a bachelor's degree in computer engineering and information systems in Benin), but I did not find one. I was not that surprised, because some of the positions called for other qualifications, certifications, and technology exposure or proficiency that I did not truly have. I knew that for the same degree program, there was a gap between the curriculum in Benin and that of most universities in the United States. I concluded that I had a lot to earn if I wanted to gain employment in my field.

As weeks were going by, I needed some income. When I had left my birth country, my father had given me about $800 (US) to keep on me just in case. One of my maternal uncles, Abel, had given me $100. Another neighbor who was a tenant in the house next to my parents' gave me some money, too, in the local currency, which would be about $30 US if converted.

Despite all the meals being available to me every day at my cousin Alicia's, there were things outside that I saw and wanted to have: clothes, foods, and more. I dipped into the money my father had given me, and little by little, that money was running low. I decided then to open a bank account so that I could put the remainder away. Alicia also advised me to do so.

A few days later, I walked into a bank about a 15-minute drive from where I lived, and opened an account. I went there unaccompanied. At that point, after two months of intensive English lessons, I had built enough confidence to go out by myself and engage in conversation with other people. I didn't want to be "chaperoned" anymore by either Alicia or Scott, who had helped me navigate some of the key services I was unfamiliar with but that were unavoidable for my integration, such as the DMV (Department of Motor Vehicles), the Social Security office, and the Immigration Services office in Downtown St. Louis.

As soon as I had the necessary legal paperwork, I started applying for some jobs online, but to no avail. Monster.com was very popular at the time, and that was the website I used the most for job applications. I would have been a good fit for some of the jobs, but for the most part, they required certifications, several years of experience, and the exposure to certain industry technologies and software. I needed to gain new skills.

I started weighing enrolling in classes to complete some of the certifications and training I would need to compete for some positions. Most of the courses would require months if not years of dedication, and that comes with a price tag. I did apply to enroll in some of the programs that I targeted based on the demand that I saw in the job postings, but I did not start any of those programs, given the financial resources required. I did not have the funds at the time. Some schools would suggest that I apply for financial aid, but I have always tried to avoid taking on debt as much as I can, so I was reluctant to take a loan. How did the system work? I was still trying to figure everything out. After just under two months in the country, I needed to educate myself about its system rather than do anything that I might regret later.

A friend of mine, Peter, pointed me to a job placement agency near Downtown St. Louis. Previously, he had also given me a crash course on how the Metro and bus system worked. It had become my adopted transportation mode, given that I had no vehicle of my own at that point.

Equipped with several copies of my résumé, I went to the job placement agency to make inquiries. Upon entering the agency, I signed up. Then I had to wait for my turn. The agency was packed that day. There were a lot of computers around, reminiscent of a Cyber Café back in Benin. People were very focused, staring at their computer monitors, visibly applying for jobs. As I looked around the room, I did not see anyone smiling or having a good time at all. I would imagine that when one is looking for a job, perhaps having been out of work for months, there is not much in life to smile about. The seriousness and the stern countenances of the people I saw that day struck me very much.

After a few minutes, it was my turn to go talk to a "helper" who would handle my case. She was a woman probably in her midfifties, and she smiled at me as I approached her cubicle. Her face was radiating in my direction a glimmer of hope. *You are in good hands.* That was what I could read in her face. Once we'd introduced ourselves and she'd directed me to have a seat, she entered my personal information in her computer and then asked me how the agency could be of help to me. I handed her my résumé. At that point, of course, it did not list any local education institutions, and I thought that would hurt me in my job search. She gave me a booklet about how to prepare for and succeed in a job interview. Then she gave me a list of websites with job postings that I could apply for online.

I left the agency not with a job prospect, but with resources that I could utilize in my job search. The information I got by reading the booklets she'd given me was timely and necessary. I had to learn how the job market worked and acquire the skills I needed to succeed. I had to remember that I was living in a new country, and that I had to learn the way of success in this new country. Over the next few weeks, I revisited the booklets to refresh my memory regarding how to prepare for an interview and how to conduct oneself during a job meeting.

Following tips from one of the booklets, I rewrote my résumé, then resumed applying for jobs online with some confidence. But my lack of job experience with a US company had planted in me some doubt about my chance of landing employment in the field of my education—computer engineering and information systems. After weeks and months of trying, nothing really came my way.

Meanwhile, I was visiting the websites of universities across the country in an effort to identify one with a solid master's degree program that might be a good fit for me. I went on an online-college-application spree that of course resulted in my e-mail and mailbox being flooded with brochures from the colleges I'd applied to. Those universities, naturally, required tests like the GRE. Moreover, I had to send my transcripts to the schools, and also to an accredited institution that would evaluate the equivalency of my grades and the classes I'd taken back home to those in the United States. I contacted an accredited agency in Wisconsin and sent it all of my under-graduate transcripts, plus the fee required. At one point, I felt overwhelmed by all the things I needed to do. But at the same time, I was pleased to do all those things and learn the process.

A few weeks later, I received news from the agency in Wisconsin: my degree-equivalency tableau did not look very promising. As a matter of fact, it showed that I was fine on the grade side, but the challenge of course and credit transfer became real. The schools wouldn't accept the transfer of my previous course work. Evidently, the school requesting the equivalency of my transcript would not admit me into its master's program right away. I would have to start a lot of things all over again and retake a bunch of classes.

I had just spent four years in college back in my native land. Was I ready to begin as an undergraduate again in the United States? I was not too pleased with the prospect. In fact, I dreaded it. I was already in my midtwenties.

Facing this dilemma, I started asking around what I could do. I was surprised to learn that difficulties with degree transfers from other countries to North America were quite common, and it has always been that way. Around that time, I also looked into tuition: how much it would cost me to study. The tuition was high. If I decided to enroll in any school at the time, I would have to take out a loan. The mere idea of taking out a huge loan to go to school was very scary to me. I was born and raised in a country where the concept of borrowing to study does not exist. Either you can afford it, or you cannot.

Facing all these challenges and questions, and with no job offer in my desired field on the horizon, I was then ready to do anything. Anything.

The *St. Louis Post-Dispatch* became my go-to job announcement source. I started applying for all types of jobs, mostly those that did not necessitate a lot of skills. I got a break a few weeks later, when I received a call from an airline that operated at St. Louis Lambert Airport. The company was looking for ramp agents—people who work on the airport tarmac, load and unload aircraft, push them out of their gates for takeoff, and direct them to their assigned gates when they land.

With the job interview day looming ahead, it was for me the perfect opportunity to put into practice everything I had learned in the booklet I'd been given at the job placement agency. I was mentally ready to go to that job interview. At that point, I was no longer living at Alicia's. I had moved in with my friend Peter. He practiced with me how to answer key questions and manage my demeanor (eye contact, assurance, positive attitude). He himself had gone through this before and was well equipped to mentor me.

On the interview day, I woke up early in the morning to get ready. I was appropriately dressed. Deep down inside myself, I was confident. The only trepidation I had at the time was my delivery. The heavy influence of my French on my English could still be felt, and I was still developing my vocabulary. I did not know exactly how that would play out during the interview. Would the interviewer like it? How would I come across to him? Even though these questions were humming inside my head, I was still confident.

Upon entering the building, I arrived at the location where my interview was to take place. It was a sunny morning, and a little bit cold outside. With the help of the office secretary, I found the interview room, where my interviewer, Frank, had been waiting for me with a copy of my résumé in his hands. I entered the room and gave him a firm handshake. In fact, it was a firm handshake on steroids; I firmly pressed his hand and shook it about three times—just enough not to hurt his wrist and shoulder. I measured it accordingly. I could tell that he was not used to getting that kind of handshake. I did not do that per happenstance. I did it on purpose.

In my defense, I did it because the job I was applying for would be physical in nature, as was stated clearly in the job description. My handshake with Frank was my statement to him, before the interview had even begun, that I had enough strength in me to do what the job entailed.

Once we were seated, he again picked up my résumé and asked me a few questions, but most of the interview was not what I was prepared for. He went through the ramp agent job description and just wanted to make sure that I could fulfill the duties. I responded in the affirmative each time. He asked me when I would be ready to start. I proposed that I could start the following week. I was excited when he asked me that question, because I knew that I had just gotten the job. At the end of the interview, Frank shook my hand, congratulated me, and told me that he would be expecting me on the first day of my job orientation.

After the interview, I took the bus home. When Peter returned from work later in the evening, I announced to him that I had gotten the job, and I detailed for him how the interview had gone. We shared a celebratory round of beer. The following day, I went shopping for the clothing I would need for my work. I reported for orientation a few days later.

CHAPTER 8

Cultural Differences Firsthand

My first job in the United States was a rite of passage. The job of an airline ramp agent was very physical in nature. But first, I had to be trained. The company paired me up with a mentor, Harry Moore,[*] who would train me for two weeks. After that, I would be on my own. Harry had more than a decade of experience. He knew the ins and outs of the job, and I was glad the company had selected him to train me.

Even though I was happy to be hired, it was not how I'd envisioned things would be when I got to America. I had to start earning money at some point, and I didn't care where it would be coming from as long as I was doing it legally. Unfortunately, at that moment, it was the only option I had. It was both discouraging and depressing to me. At least the job at the airport would allow me to get some work experience while I was thinking about what to do next with my future. As weeks went by, I embraced that experience fully. I became more appreciative.

Harry took me to the luggage room, which was filled with a web of conveyor belts. This is where airline travelers' luggage is kept and dispatched to their next destination, and it's where we spent most of our time. The avalanche of bags rolling down the belts was overwhelming at times. I had

---

[*]   Some names have been changed.

almost no rest, and I sweat a lot. We loaded the bags onto a small tug truck and then into the aircraft.

At work, I became a curiosity. I was a new hire, and my coworkers wanted to know more about my background and origin. It was something I had expected, given my speech: English tinged with a French accent. I had practiced sounding like a native, but it was not easy for me to pull that off. My vocal cords had been shaped by more than two decades of French, Fongbé, and Goungbé. But I was always happy to share my story and background with my coworkers. When I was talking with them, they would have me repeat some words two or three times, because I was not pronouncing them as perfectly as intended. I got some of them pronounced right and others not, usually stressing the wrong syllable. My coworkers would guess what I meant and would correct me, which helped me refine my pronunciation.

One of the baffling questions I was asked was from a coworker who wanted to know by what transportation method I had come to the United States. In fact, that coworker, who had just learned that I came from an unknown country in Africa, wanted to know where I had parked the horse or the elephant that I had ridden to come to the United States. The seriousness in his facial expression told me that he was not joking. At first, I thought he was asking me if people rode horses and elephants in the country from which I came. I answered that, yes indeed, horseback riding is still very popular in the northern part of Benin, but not so much in the country in general, or even in the rest of Africa, for that matter. But hardly had I finished giving him that answer than another coworker rephrased the question for him, saying that, in fact, he wanted to know if I'd traveled from Benin to the United States on horseback or by riding an elephant. To their utter astonishment, I informed them that I had flown in. Then ensued an avalanche of other bizarre questions. They started asking me the airlines that operated in the country I came from. Their questions included: *What airlines operate there? Are they American-operated airlines? Are there cars in Benin? What types of clothes do people wear there? What type of work do people in Benin do to be able to afford a plane ticket? You guys there, in Africa—Benin—probably don't need to go to the zoo to see wild animals, do you? What pet lion do you have, a small one or a big one?*

I was dumbfounded by the questions.

As I explained to them exactly the flight connections that I had made from my boarding in Benin all the way to the United States, some of them looked bewildered. In their minds, the whole of Africa was one gigantic jungle with men in Tarzan-like garments leaping from tree to tree, riding on elephants and cohabitating with lions, panthers, zebras, and giraffes. This was the year 2006. The nature of the questions I fielded during that exchange made it clear to me that some people were still living in absolute darkness when it came to knowledge of the world beyond the confines of where they were born. I believe that the television images of people on safari in Kenya, Zimbabwe, and remote areas in South Africa have a lot to do with that broad misconception. I was taken aback by the questions, but I genuinely, politely answered them in such a way as not to insult my coworkers or make them feel like ignoramuses.

The African continent has almost never gotten good press in the American media. Africa is usually portrayed as that desolate place, that war-torn place where violence is pretty much the way of life and where famine and political instability reign. For most, Africa is kind of viewed as a single country, with its countries perceived as cities within it. As a matter of fact, it is a continent with about 54 nations, each with its own government, traditions, and culture. Some countries on the continent, such as Angola, Sierra Leone, Liberia, and Congo, have endured decades of war, while the rest of the continent has enjoyed a relative peace that rivals that of any other industrialized country in the world, though under despotism, authoritarianism, and military regimes. But the news stemming from the war-torn countries is what makes it into the news cycle in the western media. However, in recent years I have seen TV programs and documentaries produced by American media portraying the continent in a better light.

Political instability and wars are not confined to just one place or continent in the world. That kind of bad press has brainwashed some Americans, and even people living in other countries outside of Africa, to believe that the entire continent is all blood, fire, and famine. The images of starving Somali and Ethiopian children plastered on billboards or appearing in the news also tend to suggest to many people in the West that the entire African continent's children are poor, malnourished, and desperately in need of assistance from the rest of the world. News reports on violence perpetrated in the West are usually perceived as one-offs, while the same media outlets portray violence as endemic elsewhere.

As someone who lived on the African continent for more than two straight decades and who knows it fairly well, I'm aware that political instability has been an issue in some of its countries. In fact, the political upheaval in those countries has more to do with despotism than with actual internal conflict causing disruption or chaos.

The early 1960s brought a wave of independence in Africa, marking the end of colonial rule. As a result, power fell into the hands of individuals who clung to it and refused to relinquish it. The ideas of democracy and presidential term limits were at the time European concepts. The continent was an amalgamation of tribes and kingdoms before the Europeans arrived. And once they left to let the Africans rule their own countries, I guess the new postcolonial generation decided to pick up where their ancestors left off: restoring kingdoms. Many African presidents have been in power for generations. It used to be the continent of no-term-limit presidents.

When some countries started to experience the universal suffrage that comes with democracy, the elections were almost always contested, with losers refusing to concede defeat. This usually results in conflict that pitches the winner's and loser's camps against each other, and also, most often, the military gets involved. It is a scenario that is dreaded before and after elections in some countries in Africa, arguably even to this day. Thus, the reputation for political instability the African continent has had. Some nations have made progress to the point where the transition of power after an election happens so smoothly that it barely makes the headlines in the news outside of that country.

At work one day, during break, one of my coworkers, Curtis,* who was African American, was curious about my origins. After I answered his questions, I asked Curtis if he would consider one day taking a trip to visit the motherland, Africa. The reaction I saw on his face was everything but

---

*   Some names have been changed.

excitement. He winced and retracted his head back before giving a not-so-pleasing look. "I watched the movie *Hotel Rwanda*," he told me. "Africa—people over there are always in war and fighting and killing each other." I still remember his words to this day. He did not mince words expressing to me his personal beliefs about Africa. He made it clear that he would rather stay in America than venture to any of those countries in Africa where a violent death might be awaiting him. I was stunned by his reaction. He proceeded to tell me that he would rather meet a peaceful demise than a violent one. Little did he know that the likelihood of his dying a violent death is higher in the United States than it is in Africa. I was not pleased by his point of view, but I also understood that the gentleman certainly didn't know much about life beyond his city limits.

As our conversation went on, Curtis asked me whether I had ever taken part in a war as a child. That was another question that left me speechless. After a moment's pause, I tersely answered no. He was a little surprised by my response. I understood how his views of the African continent had been shaped. The images of war-torn countries seen on TV, with shabbily dressed teenage boys and men sporting AK-47 rifles, have made him believe that the same must be true across the continent. I explained to him and a group of other coworkers participating in the discussion that while the phenomenon of child soldiers is a sad reality in some of those countries, it is not the same across the continent. There are a lot of nations in Africa that no one has ever heard of, and that is probably because they are enjoying a relatively peaceful political stability.

As my coworkers were citing to me the violence they saw coming from the continent in the news outlets, I pointed out to them that the United States, for example, is a big country with 50 states, and that the daily reports of murders and gang violence that have plagued cities like St. Louis, Detroit, Chicago, Baltimore, Philadelphia, Oakland, Memphis, and New Orleans don't make it fair to paint the entire continent with a broad brush as violent. The genocide in Rwanda that Curtis had alluded to earlier happened in a span of three months. For years now, Rwanda has been one of the safest African countries to visit. But there are cities and especially neighborhoods in the US that routinely log several hundred murders per year.

Does this make the United States a perilous place in the eyes of foreigners viewing the country as a nation where people just kill each other? No! The 762 murders that occurred in Chicago in 2016, for example, aren't likely to deter many people from living there or visiting that city; nor will the 300-or-so homicide cases racked up in Baltimore and in Detroit during that same time frame. People do not define the US solely through the lens of violent crime or murders in those cities. And one of the sad aspects of all this is that communities of color have paid a particularly heavy price.

Black Americans make up 13 percent of the US population, but they account for more than half of the murder victims, according to the FBI's Uniform Crime Reporting (UCR). It is a staggering figure that has been consistent for years and that I find very depressing. Most murders are committed in-group. This kind of statistic clearly confers no bragging rights. The reasoning by fallacy practiced by people who think like Curtis is an intellectual dishonesty and a benighted thinking for which I have neither admiration nor respect.

The other flip side of the coin is the spate of mass shootings that have become routine in the United States where individuals armed with firearms, storm places of public gathering such as shopping centers, schools, churches, synagogues and they mercilessly mow down as many people as possible. Those gun-toting individuals leave nothing behind but a trail of dead bodies, grief, and victims' families that are scarred for the rest of their life. The United States is a vast country with a lot of people. Thus, there is a very low probability of becoming a casualty. Nevertheless, the simple thought that one may fall victim to such a tragedy is in itself terrifying. It's a state of affairs that seems likely to remain, with no end in sight.

Nonetheless, at work at the airport, I was pleased to be in the company of a diverse group of people. Most of them were African Americans with whom I had good working relationships. A few friendships came out of that, but not many. I got some pushback early on, but as weeks went by, I understood why, and I had to handpick accordingly with whom to socialize. For me, it seemed that some people tend to observe you from a distance for a while before they warm up to you. I was a coworker and a curiosity at the same time. I accepted it that way. Nevertheless, some of them always, at first sight, hugged me in a brotherly embrace and finished with a special type of handshake as a way to tell me, "We are brothers and family." I appreciated that.

As someone who was new in the country, I am indebted to some of my coworkers who gave me tips and advice about how to stay safe in St. Louis, the good and bad areas around town, and also the crowds with whom I should and shouldn't hang out. A group of three coworkers once gave me a lifesaving bit of advice as far as the color of the T-shirt and shoes that I should avoid. An orange T-shirt and matching shoes were something they advised me not to wear. The reason was that around 2006 and 2007, orange was the color of choice of a particular gang whose members were being targeted for payback by another, rival gang. If I mistakenly wore an orange T-shirt or shoes, I could be mistaken for belonging to that gang, and I could be shot dead. Gang-related shootings and killings are frequent occurrences in St. Louis. It was a serious matter at the time. So I thanked them wholeheartedly for tips like that to keep me out of harm's way.

Curtis's belief about Rwanda being a microcosm of Africa was something that stunned me and had me searching for arguments and examples to dissuade him of his misconception. Allow me to digress for a moment and give you some relevant history.

Hotel Rwanda is a movie starring Don Cheadle and depicting the genocide in Rwanda between April and July of 1994. The film gives viewers an insight into the massacre that happened in Rwanda that year. It was a merciless civil war between the Hutu and Tutsi peoples that claimed an estimated one million lives, mostly of the Tutsi ethnic group. What exactly happened in Rwanda in 1994? Several books have been written about the Rwandan genocide, or the genocide against the Tutsi, as some literature dubs it.

Rwanda, a small nation in central Africa with neighboring countries such as Burundi, Democratic Republic of Congo, Uganda, and Tanzania, is populated by two major ethnic groups: the Tutsis, constituting about 14 percent of the population, and the Hutus, who make up about 85 percent of the population. A third ethnic group, the Twas, comprises about 1 percent of the population. The Hutus and the Tutsis lived relatively in peace for generations. Armed conflicts between forces representing both ethnic groups over political power-sharing issues arose in the early 1900s and continued after the country gained independence in 1962. History has it that in the early 1930s, when the Belgians took over the modernization of Rwanda, they introduced the identification card: each person was identified by their ethnic group. Like the German occupiers before them, the Belgians at the time showed a preference for the Tutsis, a minority they viewed as more human and superior to the other ethnic groups, including the Hutus, who were mostly farmers. Therefore, key administrative roles were entrusted to the Tutsis. That situation did not make a lot of Hutus happy. After all, they were the majority in the country. For this reason, the Hutus harbored a grudge against the Tutsis.

After Rwanda gained its independence in 1962, the power shifted, and the Hutu majority claimed most of the country's leadership positions. The subsequent years saw a power-sharing struggle between the Hutus and Tutsis, as the Tutsis felt excluded from leadership positions. The international community through the United Nations mediated the conflict between the two groups so that a sustainable government of national unity could be formed, but there had never been a true success in forming that idealistic unity government. The reason was simple: The Hutus did not trust the Tutsis. For too long, the Tutsis had held power. That was how the colonial authority—Belgium—wanted it, and that had created resentment. In addition, the Hutus dreaded that if they shared power with the Tutsis, the latter would try to bring back the monarchy and rule Rwanda again for generations to come. As a matter of fact, when Rwanda was a monarchy, Tutsis were assuming the crown. But from its independence in 1962 until the mid-1990s, the Rwandan government was a majority Hutu administration.

On April 6, 1994, what would later be known as the catalyst to the genocide took place in the sky. The plane carrying the Rwandan president, Juvénal Habyarimana, was shot down. Aboard his plane was also the president of Burundi, Cyprien Ntaryamira. Both men were ethnic Hutu. The incident occurred when the plane was about to land in Kigali, the capital of Rwanda. Both presidents were pronounced dead at the scene. It all happened during power-sharing talks between the majority Hutu-led government and the Tutsi minority.

As the news of the death of Rwanda's president started to spread, some key leaders in the national army, including Colonel Théoneste Bagosora, formed an ad hoc committee to address the power vacuum that had just been created. The prime minister at the time, Agathe Uwilingiyimana, legitimately the next in line to the presidency, was poised to be sworn in as the new president of Rwanda, but the army leaders, especially Colonel Bagosora, would not allow her to accede to power as prescribed in the Rwandan Constitution. She was denied the presidency. Colonel Bagosora became the de facto self-appointed leader, and it was not long before he issued orders to kill all Tutsis. The narrative at the time was that the Tutsis were the ones who had plotted to kill President Habyarimana, and therefore they should be "removed."

The edict urged Hutus wherever they were in the country to spare no Tutsi's life. Hutus throughout the country were instructed to kill their Tutsi neighbors with any weapon they had. Some radio stations were instrumental in spreading Bagosora's orders. Several checkpoints manned by Hutu and other militias began to be erected across the country, and every person going through the checkpoints was identified. Given that people's ethnicity was clearly printed on their ID cards, those identifying as Tutsi were immediately executed.

The militias, sympathizers to the Hutus, received help from Hutu civilians armed with machetes or whatever sharp object they could find. They would maim, behead, and mutilate any Tutsi they came across. The children were the most targeted, as they were viewed as the future generation. But pregnant Tutsi women died the most atrocious deaths, as they were first raped at machete point, and then their fetuses were cut from their wombs alive, yanked out, and hurled to the ground or a nearby wall while the mothers were left to bleed to death. Friends turned against their neighbors, hacking them to death. It was savagery and barbarism on full display as it had not been seen in recent memory.

One of the most powerful tactics the Hutus used was the systematic looting and burning down of Tutsi houses. When the genocide was escalating, a lot of Tutsis, fearing for their lives, sequestered themselves in their homes. The Hutus realized this and began torching the Tutsis' houses, forcing them to come out. Then the Hutus hacked them to death. In most cases, they killed the adults first, leaving the children defenseless. The kids watched their parents being slaughtered in front of them.

The other weapon that the Hutus used was the rape of Tutsi women. This led to the spread of HIV, and numerous children were later born to infected mothers. Several churches throughout the country offered refuge, especially to women and children, but the blood-thirsty Hutu killers desecrated those holy grounds and massacred the children anyway. After the genocide was over, those churches and other places were turned into mass graves. Their blood-stained walls indicated that most of the children died from trauma to their heads as they were thrown against the walls and their skulls split. For three months, similar scenes played out throughout the country. The smell of death was everywhere.

The genocide ended in July of 1994 when the Rwandan Patriotic Front (RPF), a minority Tutsi-led force, heavily armed and meticulously organized, took over the country. That force was, in fact, a fringe battalion that had long been known to the central Rwandan government but had been marginalized because it was viewed as hostile. The RPF was led by Paul Kagame, who would later become president of Rwanda.

The Rwandan genocide was one of the darkest chapters in the history of humankind.

∽

I did not give Curtis a one-on-one history lesson about the Rwandan conflict nor did I try to convince him to rethink his views about Mother Africa. However, I did learn a few things in the process. The interchanges with my coworkers at the airline gave me the opportunity to learn a great deal about the cultural differences between my ancestral land and that of the United States. Later, I had to take those differences into account in my interactions with the natives, as well as in my judgment overall when it came to certain circumstances and courses of action.

CHAPTER 9

The Pursuit of Happiness Continues

After four months as an employee of the airline, I decided to part ways with the company and start a new phase in my life. The job was not something I wanted to keep doing. I took it upon myself to find a different one. At the same time, I enlisted the help of some of my friends to inform me of any job opening they might be aware of somewhere. Who knows? Even though I became unemployed when I left the company, I was never worried about the future. I did have some money saved, although nothing near what would tide me over for months. However, I was not in a panic mode. I was just confident that I would find something before I drained my savings. That confidence kept me going during my job search. At the time, there was not a single day that I was not at the library using the computer to apply for jobs and send résumés. The local library became my refuge.

It had been two weeks since I had left gainful employment. Although I had started looking for a new position, I wasn't doing so with the same enthusiasm I'd had when looking for my first job. I began to wish I had stayed longer at the airline, but once in a while, there had been rounds of furloughs, layoffs, disciplinary actions, and terminations that often resulted in sudden cutbacks or changes in personnel among the ramp agents. Observing all those things happening around me, I realized the precariousness of the job I was doing. The position could be taken away from me at any moment for any reason. That was very concerning to me. I needed to find a job that would give me at least some safety. Even though a college degree would not completely cloak an employee from the precariousness of a job, the positions one can obtain with a degree under his belt are much better than those that require no technical skills, where employees are easily expendable.

Being without a guaranteed source of income, even for the shortest amount of time, is a scary thing. The rent and utility bills have to be paid on time. Those are expenses that don't care whether you have a job or not. I have developed the habit of saving money in case of an emergency.

My persistence in seeking a new job paid off when I found one at a home improvement store. Even though I was glad to have landed another employment opportunity, I was nowhere near starting what I had initially planned to do when I'd arrived in the United States. The reality was different from what I had thought. I had to start making some money as soon as possible.

This new job at the home improvement store put my body through something I had never experienced before. One thing that was different about it was that I worked the night shift. I would report to work at 7:00 p.m. and finish at about 4:00 the next morning. The job was very physical in nature. At night, there are not many people in the store. The job consisted of replenishing the shelves. First, a truckload of store-ordered merchandise would come. We would unload the truck and stack some of the goods in the stockroom. Certain items were relatively easily carried; others required a pallet jack to be moved. After everything was unloaded, we would head to the store floor, where heaps of items on pallets would be waiting to be unpacked and put on the shelves.

A home improvement store has a lot of stuff. We were each assigned certain aisles. I found unpacking and stocking bathroom supplies, tiles, and ready-made doors very challenging because they were heavy materials. Some of the items are stored at the floor level, but some go up on the shelves. So, I had to use a ladder while carrying them up. Sometimes there were entire boxes of ceramic tiles, tools, or paints that needed to be put up on the shelves. Two of my coworkers wore back braces. At first, I thought they didn't really need them, but after a few weeks on the job, I saw the necessity of buying and wearing one myself.

My body took a long time to adjust to the night shift. I found myself fighting off sleep numerous times. I could not afford to be found snoozing on the job. That surely would have gotten me fired. As a matter of fact, I heard through the grapevine that an employee had been released a few days earlier because he was caught sleeping on the job. I had gone through a lot to find that job, and there was no way I was going to contribute in that fashion to my own termination. So, throughout my shift, I tried to avoid remaining still. I had to stay up and awake and keep restocking those shelves. But there was no shortage of stuff to keep me moving. Sometimes it took an hour or more, depending on the merchandise, to unpack a pallet and shelve everything on it.

The supervisors micromanaged a lot, and I didn't like that a bit. But in spite of that, it was a good atmosphere at the store, especially after midnight. Music was our companion. Either a radio station would be turned on, or some sort of CD would be playing.

After a few months on the job, I started rethinking the future. I began seriously asking myself how long I would be able to do that type of job. There was no question that it was paying the bills, but I needed to work out an exit plan without straining my finances. At that time, I hadn't saved much money. It would have been premature to leave that position.

I was searching for a better job opportunity, but the idea of enrolling in a school, learning some skills, and especially resuming my studies toward a degree was constantly in my mind. The year before, I had looked into that, but the cost of school and the time commitment had held me back. I was not really ready to sacrifice four more years, or start as a freshman in my midtwenties, sitting in the same classroom with recent high school graduates. The thought of that alone just depressed me.

Even while I was mulling over all that, I was still committed to my job. Due to the physical exertion it required, I lost a lot of weight at that time. Almost every Sunday afternoon, I met with some of my friends to play soccer. My weight loss caught their attention. Some asked me if I was starving myself. I answered no, of course not. However, their question definitely made an impression on me. I felt bad for myself. I paused for a few moments, reflecting on my employment situation. I had to fight back tears. I did not express my emotions in a conspicuous way, but I knew then that I could not go on with that job much longer.

The physical nature of my work was definitely taking a toll on me. This was not how I wanted to be seen. That was when one of my soccer crowd, Nathaniel,* suggested I think about finding a wife. Nathaniel said that if I had a wife, she wouldn't be happy seeing me losing that much weight, and she would take charge of making sure my meals were ready so that I didn't skip meals. I found his suggestion very intriguing, but I assumed he was joking. He might have been serious, though, because he was a married man with a wife who by all indications catered to all his needs.

Nathaniel was originally from the Republic of Togo. His wife had a part-time job as a hairdresser but only worked very few days and very few hours a day. He was able to maintain a semblance of a traditional West African family. Once in a while, he invited us to his house for parties. Those parties were like family reunions of the West African community in St. Louis. His wife cooked all the food. Once we arrived at his parties, it didn't take too long for us to notice the sometimes ostentatious assortment of West African dishes: sauce *gombo*, *fufu* and peanut sauce, *atièkè*, *kédjénou*, *goussi*, *gbómán*, *télibo*. It was a way of reminding us where we came from. Only at those gatherings did I get to taste West African foods. Nathaniel's wife was very good at putting those dishes together.

My mother, too, cooked very well, and there was no shortage of restaurants serving traditional dishes back in Benin. There was no question in my mind that Nathaniel consumed his wife's homemade dishes daily. He was indeed a happy man, with a wife who catered to all his needs, at least his gustatory delights. A very well-built man, Nathaniel wanted me to look as fit as he was.

But for me, getting married was not on my mind. I didn't have solid employment at the time, and there was no way I would get married with an hourly job making barely $12 or $13 an hour. And yet it was around

---

* Some names have been changed.

that time that I started seriously entertaining the idea of finding at least a girlfriend to start with. Hanging out with the soccer crowd was good, but wouldn't it be better if I were spending much of my free time with a woman friend as well? I decided I should put myself out there.

My first two attempts at pursuing a romantic interest were not successful. In spite of the effort I put forth, there was not a mutual interest. So I had to let go. Those two forays happened in broad daylight in the gentlemanlike, cold-approach style that I grew up seeing. I was exceedingly polite during those two tries at striking up an acquaintance with a woman, in the manner in which men in my native country are brought up to initiate those types of interactions. They show complete reverence for their intended conquests, usually in very formal French. I replicated that same approach in English, and it quickly dawned on me that in this new country, that was probably not the best way to do it. To paraphrase Albert Einstein, doing the same thing over and over again and expecting a different result is tantamount to insanity.

In a country as diverse as the United States, courtship might not be initiated the same way across all races and ethnicities. I had made new friends, all of them American males, yet they hadn't given me the tips I might need to break through in my quest. But at that point, in the spring of 2007, having been in America for about eight months, I had seen a few things that pointed me in the "right" direction in that regard. As the saying goes, "When in Rome . . ."

My third attempt at courtship that spring worked so well in a way that it even bothered me a little, because I had to do something out of character. As it turned out, imitating the "Romans" didn't come naturally to me.

When I was working as an airport ramp agent the year before, one or two things I observed some of my coworkers doing as first steps in pursuing a love interest had me scratching my head. For starters, the fact that some of them did it on the job seemed brazen to me. Granted, our work environment was not like one with office spaces where people are more formal and professional in every way. Even so, these coworkers were quite bold and unequivocal about their intentions. It was something I came to admire and respect. On numerous occasions, I saw guys talking to females in an endearing and very flirtatious way. The guys' tone was not condescending but definitely commanded attention. I had seen some women wait and listen, and I had also seen guys whose introductory flirts were summarily dismissed by the women they were trying to impress. It was quite a culture shock for me, witnessing all that.

In my spare time at that point, I sometimes hung out at Union Station Mall in Downtown St. Louis, where a friend of mine had a store. At the mall, I saw men calling out come-ons to which some women—mostly very young women—acquiesced, and some obviously did not pay attention other than by turning their heads to see who was addressing them. Little by little, I formed an idea about how to endear myself to whoever I might be interested in next time. But there was one thing I could not do very well: speak Ebonics.

Another thing that I observed being used together with Ebonics was what some people refer to colloquially as *swagger*. Could Ebonics and swagger get me what I was looking for? At least for a few minutes, I would have to reinvent myself or play some character, so to speak. I practiced Ebonics for fun. As for the swagger, I knew it would come naturally when I was in the situation. I wanted to put my Ebonics and swagger to the test, but I did not want to do it in broad daylight, for fear of being humiliated or being rejected coldly. I thought that it would be "safe" at nighttime.

One evening, my friends and I decided to visit a nightclub in East St. Louis: the Oz nightclub, one of the most popular in the city. That night, the club was crowded. It is patronized by a lot of rap and hip-hop artists in the area. I was casually dressed. After my friends and I showed our identification to the security guards, we were patted down. As I was contemplating the nightclub from the outside, I could feel the adrenaline rushing through me. I was very excited to get in.

Once inside, we waded our way through the boisterous crowd and started dancing to the music. Hip-hop and R&B songs reigned supreme inside the club. As I was dancing, I spotted a woman with a friend of hers. I made eye contact with her first and stared for a few seconds. There was no smile on my face. I summoned my courage and walked up to her. In Ebonics, I opened the conversation with a line like this: *How y'all doin'?* From there, I went on to compliment her on her hair. She was wearing a wig, and I wouldn't dispute that she'd been at the hairdresser's not long ago. I'll call her Nicole.* She was born in North Carolina. I did not pay attention to her friend at all. It was a way of showing Nicole my undivided attention. It worked like a charm, as she agreed to dance with me. We danced until the song played itself out.

As we came back to sit, the first thing she said to me was "You sound kind of cute. Are you from here? Where are you from?" Though she could tell that I had an accent, that did not deter me from speaking the best Ebonics that I possibly could. I did not hide my intention to get to know her better, and she agreed. We exchanged phone numbers and started dating afterward. I had to "code-switch" when we were together or spoke over the phone, but it became harder and harder for me to keep on doing so.

What is *code-switching*? It refers to a change in one's style of speaking to please, conform to, or appeal to a particular group. In my case, I thought at the time that speaking Ebonics was my only chance to blend in, integrate, and feel welcome in the African American community, especially when it came to having a relationship with the opposite sex.

I have gone as far as downloading rap music lyrics from the Internet in order to improve my proficiency in Ebonics. It was only years after the experience with Nicole that I realized that code-switching is an integral part of the life of minorities in general in the United States, and African Americans in particular. On the job or at a more formal occasion, a perfect English is spoken, but a less grammatically correct English comes out among one's peers. Code-switching can undoubtedly be easy for a native of a language, but in my case, it was a difficult exercise. Words' pronunciations and the manner in which they are said are the keys to Ebonics. I had to learn how certain words are pronounced in Ebonics and how the same words are said in formal English. It was a lot of pressure that I put on myself.

After just a month of trying to speak Ebonics and putting on a swagger while I was with Nicole, I simply couldn't keep doing it. To be frank, I didn't have it. It was not innate. It was too much effort. And in the same

---

* Some names have been changed.

vein, during the first three weeks of dating, Nicole and I clashed over what I would wear. She wanted me to wear more urban clothes. One afternoon, we were going out together to a bus stop on our way to Downtown St. Louis when she called me out again on my choice of attire.

"Who are you going out with dressing like a white boy?" she said. I was wearing a tennis hat, a golf shirt, PGA Tour–style short pants, and tennis shoes. I started laughing, but it was not a laughing matter to her, as I quickly realized. She suggested I put on another outfit, but I did not comply. We went our separate ways shortly after.

My short-lived relationship with Nicole was something I chalked up to experience. As time went on, I realized that the Ebonics-and-swagger method isn't how courtship happens for most people in the United States. It did give me for a short period the companionship that I sought, but the whole Ebonics-and-swagger "theatrics" drew me to someone with whom I couldn't have a meaningful, respectful and serious relationship. The ways of meeting a mate in this country are almost as numerous as the people involved. But only some methods—generally the less successful ones in the long run—require a person to pretend to be something he's not. Nevertheless, it was a testament to my personality that I could adapt to any situation anywhere, and that I was very capable of putting in the work and effort to reach my goals.

∾

Just under three months after I started working at the home improvement store, a wave of layoffs swept through the store. It was around the summer of 2007. As one of the most recent hires at the time, I was laid off, along with other employees. I was not too pleased with the news. The precariousness of the jobs I had done thus far became clear to me. I started then researching the types of jobs that would provide me with relative security.

Given that I could not use my foreign degree at the time, I was definitely looking for a job in high demand, with no formal academic degree required, and that would be less prone to its employees being fired or laid off. I couldn't find many such options, but the one that I saw constantly coming up was in the trucking industry: an over-the-road (OTR) truck driver. When I realized this, it gave me a sense of relief. Job searching had become something that I hated. Looking for a new job was like a full-time job in itself, in which I spent countless hours on the Internet and sending résumés to potential employers.

CHAPTER 10

A Job with Some Peace of Mind

Back on the job market after being laid off from the home improvement store, I remembered vividly what I'd gone through the first two times I'd been on the job hunt. The prospect of having to do it a third time in a span of seven months started to weigh on me. It was mentally fatiguing. I didn't know for sure how long it would take me to find employment again. For a while, I thought about whether there was some type of small business that I could start, but I didn't have the capital. I was like a pacing lion in captivity, hungry and looking for prey. That layoff disoriented me for a while, and I spent a few days contemplating what my next step should be. It had become clear to me that I was not made for those types of jobs, or, I should say, that those types of jobs were not meant for me.

My soul-searching led me to a goal that I decided to pursue by any means necessary: returning to school to earn a university degree. The engineering career that I had always longed for would require a degree anyway. As I've said, I am someone who is reluctant to take on debt. Therefore, the only way around taking out loans to return to school was to save as much money as I could. I needed to set aside, at minimum, two years' worth of tuition plus a two-year apartment rental budget before I could quit my job. According to my projection, I would need to work for three more years to save the $55,000 that I planned. From there on, I gave myself a deadline for how long I would keep on working in jobs outside my chosen field, with the aim of returning to school to pursue a degree.

I tried going through a job placement agency, but the jobs available to me through the agency were not to my liking. At this point, I resolved to take matters into my own hands and once again find another job by myself.

During my two-week training at the job placement agency, I applied for positions mostly with trucking companies. After deep thought, yes, I was ready to get a commercial driver's license (CDL) and become an over-the-road truck driver. In order to attain my savings objective for school expenses, I needed to find a job that was steady and reliable and offered a good income as well. Becoming a truck driver answered all those needs. There are several reasons why truck drivers do not get terminated or laid off as often as those in other lines of work.

First, driving a semitruck (an 18-wheeler, as it is colloquially called) in itself is dangerous, and it is a risk that not many people want to take. As a matter of fact, truck driving is among the top 10 most dangerous jobs in the United States. It is even more hazardous than being a police officer.

Second, there is loneliness associated with it that may not appeal to many, and truck driving, OTR in particular, takes you away from your family. Drivers go out by themselves for weeks at a time without seeing their loved ones. It is one of the reasons that the divorce rate among truck drivers is very high. Most truckers are male, and if they have children, the family will not have the father-figure presence at home that their counterparts with regular nine-to-five jobs can provide.

And third, even though OTR truck driving pays relatively well with years of experience, the paychecks might not be steady, because drivers are not salaried employees, nor are they paid by the hour. As with any other job out there, truck drivers do get fired or laid off, but the drivers who are let go usually don't have much trouble finding another company willing to hire them. This was a very important point for me, because I didn't want to relive the experience of having to hunt for a job for weeks, or even months. A driving record riddled with accidents or traffic citations is usually what keeps a person with a CDL from finding employment as a truck driver. It is a good industry to be in if one is ready for the risk and life over the road.

But it is definitely not an appealing lifestyle for most people.

I applied with several trucking companies across the United States: Schneider National, Prime Inc., Stevens, Swift Transportation. Some companies called me the very same day that I applied.

With the influx of offers from trucking companies, I felt a boost of ego. I felt wanted. The feeling that rushed through me was indescribable. I knew it was just a matter of personal availability before I would be hired again. For the first time, I had the dilemma of choosing the company for which to work. I had had direct phone calls with recruiters from all over the country. I felt like a high school football or basketball prodigy who had just been discovered by talent scouts for universities and courted by their athletic programs. It was up to me then to decide. I nailed my choice down to three companies: Werner, C.R. England, and Swift Transportation. But I ultimately decided to go with Swift.

The truth is that when trucking companies hire and train, the new drivers receive no compensation during the training, regardless of its length. Once I had decided to formally accept Swift's invitation to enroll in its truck-driving school to acquire my CDL, I was at peace with my choice. I felt ready to do the job. But when I shared that decision with some of my friends, most of them were skeptical. Some jokingly admired my courage in even thinking about doing that kind of job. One of them clearly told me that I might not be able to pass the CDL test, let alone be hired. There were several reasons for my friends' skepticism.

To begin with, I did not fit the profile of a truck driver. I am about 5 feet 8 inches tall, and at that point, I weighed about 160 pounds. Though I was in my midtwenties, my appearance suggested otherwise; I looked as if I was in my late teenage years, and most of the time I sported golf or tennis T-shirts and tennis shoes. The perception of truck drivers generally is that they are older white men and that they are unkempt, scruffy, sometimes overweight, and taller. In April of 2018, the *Financial Times* magazine published an article about the shortage of truck drivers in the United States, referring to them as middle-aged and not highly educated. Even though some trucking companies asked that applicants have at least a high school diploma or equivalent, it wasn't a requirement that they enforced. Having a high school diploma is not a prerequisite for a CDL. That commercial driver's license is all that trucking companies want.

Another doubt my friends expressed was that a few years prior, one of them, who was older than me, probably in his early forties at the time, found the driving test too challenging, and therefore had to abandon his dream of becoming a truck driver. He believed the same thing would probably befall me.

I understood their concerns, but I was undeterred. Besides the search for a more stable and "secure" employment opportunity that spurred me to acquire a CDL, I wanted so badly to get an education as soon as possible so that I could land a job in the technology field. When I opted to go for a commercial driver's license and become an OTR driver, I did not intend to make truck driving my career. Life's circumstances were putting that type of work in my path at that moment. Enrolling in a university and earning an engineering degree was the goal.

Actually, I was still a trifle bitter over the fact that I could not really validate my foreign engineering degree, but that anger had subsided. I had decided to turn that page and focus on the future. I had met several immigrants like myself, who were content with jobs like those. They worked and stayed in those jobs for years and years, enduring all the grind of grueling labor. I, on the other hand, wanted a way out. With a laser focus on saving as much money as I could in the next two and a half to three years in order to return to school, I was determined to go all the way in.

I could have started a small business or trained in a trade, but I had different aspirations. I had come a long way. When I was a teenager back in my native country, the reason I had wanted to immigrate especially to the United States, was that I believed it was where I would have better options in terms of fields of study. I knew there was nothing I would want to specialize in that US schools couldn't provide. It did not take me long to realize how important an education is in the United States, how much it is valued and encouraged, and in general, how much better the quality of life is for those with a college degree than for those without one. In my case, the issue was not about the degree; I had one, but I had a hard time finding employment with it. It was clear to me that re-educating myself was the only option.

All I had in mind was to do the truck-driving job for a few years, save some money, and use those savings to start college. I did not care anymore about being a freshman at 25 years old. In my native country, that would be laughable. But I was no longer living there. I could start school without any pressure. It was the game plan I had set.

I contacted the Swift Transportation recruiter who had reached out to me a few days earlier. I informed her that I was willing to enroll in Swift's driving school to get my CDL and then work for the company. She was very pleased. She asked me when I was ready to start, worked out the details with me, and mailed me more information about the Swift Driving Academy and its class schedule. The driving school is located in Millington, Tennessee, which is a suburb of Memphis, but the company itself is head-quartered in Phoenix, Arizona. I agreed with the recruiter about when I would be ready to start the CDL training classes. I would be required to go to Memphis for the three-week-long training at the company's expense.

Swift sent me a Greyhound bus ticket to Memphis. I was excited about the journey I was set to embark on. For me, success was a must. Under no circumstances would I return to St. Louis without any tangible form of success and accomplishment in my hands.

When I arrived in Memphis, the company assigned me a room. In it were four beds, and there were already about seven people in the room when I got there. Four of guys were just there to chat with their friends. Three of the beds were visibly taken, so I knew that the one that was un-done was mine. As I laid my luggage on the mattress, nobody seemed to say anything. So I knew I had just claimed my spot. I quickly introduced myself to my roommates. They asked which state I came from, and I informed them that I was coming from St. Louis, Missouri. Then they took turns introducing themselves by their first names and telling me the states from which they came: Minnesota, Texas, Mississippi, Maryland, and Florida.

The following day, we got down to business. According to the schedule that day, we were to have a Department of Transportation (DOT) physical test and a drug test. The physical exam was to make sure that the prospec-tive driver was indeed physically fit to do the job. Even though it was a driving job, there would come times when the driver would be required to unload his or her trailer. The physical exam is a federal requirement that must be passed before an individual can acquire a CDL. I underwent a host of required medical tests, such as vision and hearing, and also a drug test to check for illegal substances.

With regard to illegal substances, I had not smoked or taken any of those products my entire life, so I was not too worried. However, I was a little bit nervous, because back in St. Louis, I lived in an apartment complex where some people smoked marijuana. The smell permeated the air so much that it could be felt everywhere. Its odor is unmistakable. Even though I never smoked it myself, I knew its smell. I did not know for sure if my inhalation of the smoke would cause any trace of that substance to be detected in my urine. I was just hoping for the best. Fortunately, I passed all the physical tests, and my urine specimen did not reveal any trace of an illegal substance.

As the training got under way at the driving academy, the course material covered a litany of indispensable subjects, such as the DOT safety rules and regulations, preventive maintenance of the commercial vehicle, skill range, vehicle inspection, and highway driving.

The first time I stepped inside a tractor-trailer truck to do a driving exercise, it took my breath away. The steering wheel itself was wide and massive. The dashboard was full of gauges and control instruments. It was like the cockpit of an airliner. The gear stick looked almost three times bigger than what I had seen in cars. I felt my heart pounding inside of my chest, and a spurt of trepidation rushed down my spine. But when I sat in the driver's seat and was able to see the pavement through the windshield, the intimidation ebbed. I adjusted the seat to my comfort, along with the cabin and side-view mirrors.

I started the truck, following the instructions I'd been given. As I put the rig in first gear, it started moving slowly. I eased up on the clutch and gently maneuvered the steering wheel to keep the vehicle going straight. I was able to successfully steer the truck in a straight line from the get-go. At times I could feel that the truck wanted to bear to one side, but I made the necessary adjustments to keep it heading forward. The instructor's words to me before I'd hopped on the truck had been "Don't fight with the steering wheel! Be gentle with it!" I followed his instructions to the letter. I was inside the truck. It was a good feeling. Just as the previous student drivers had done before me, I drove around in a circle and brought the semi back to where I'd picked it up.

Over the next few days, we learned several other skills. The most important and the most dreaded of them all was the backing test. It was challenging for everyone, including me. What makes this particular maneuver difficult is that it is done in a manner opposite to how we do it with a car. For example, in a car, if a person wants to move backward to the right, he or she will turn the steering wheel to the right. To move backward to the left, the steering wheel is turned to the left. But in the case of a semitruck, the driver wanting to back up to the right has to turn the steering wheel to the left, and vice versa. It takes a while for the brain to get used to this. Even when one gets it, one also has to learn that just rotating the steering wheel a few degrees creates a large swing of the trailer. However, there are very specific maneuvers and very few situations that require the steering wheel to turn all the way in either direction. Those situations have to be known by heart. This was an area that upset many students. Several failed the test, and as a result, the school terminated their training right away and sent them back home. It was not a surprise to us, because each of us had been warned beforehand.

To be honest, I did not see myself getting a failing grade or being forced to drop out of the program and be sent home for lack of skills. If I did fail the backing skill assessment and the instructors deemed that I could not drive a semitruck on a public highway, what would I do when I returned to St. Louis? I had left everything behind. It had taken me about three months to find my previous job at the home improvement store. How long would it take for me to find another one if I returned home without the commercial license? I didn't have enough savings left. I was on a tight budget. I had bet on the opportunity to get a CDL, drive for a few years, save money, and use that money to start college. Obtaining a CDL was my plan A, B, C, and D. To be honest, I did not have a backup plan.

During the entire time, we were at the Swift driving school, we were not getting paid, because we were not yet officially employees of the company, even though a job was (almost) guaranteed to us when we finished the four-week program. In other words, I did not have a source of income while I was in Memphis for the training. So I knew that I had to put in all the work and effort to get my CDL when the training finished—by any means necessary. Failing any test was not an option. I told myself that if everyone else were to fail, I would be the only one to pass. I was ready, focused, and determined. Most of my friends back in St. Louis had bet that I wouldn't pass the CDL test. I imagined my humiliation if I failed. I would become their laughingstock.

The backing exercise was indeed tough. It was quite a spectacle to see some student drivers maneuvering the truck into awkward positions, making it harder or even impossible for them to complete the intended exercise. We were given the opportunity to retry several times when we didn't get it right the first time around.

When it was my turn to do the backing trial, I was a little bit nervous, but at the same time, I was confident. I had paid careful attention during the lessons, and also, I watched attentively to see where those who went before me failed. I knew what to do so as not to repeat the mistakes they made. The key to success was the two side rearview mirrors. I also knew that I had to avoid turning the steering wheel too much except at certain specific moments. When I climbed inside the cabin only to get off a few minutes later after I impeccably put the vehicle within the bounds of the orange cones, I pumped my fist in exhilaration. I reminded myself of Tiger Woods winning his first Masters tournament in 1997 ten years earlier. As Mr Woods did it, I was not overly emotional but fully aware of the importance of that moment. I did it!.

At that moment, I knew that I had just successfully completed one of the most dreaded tests. I let out a sigh of relief. I'd dodged a bullet. I stepped out of the cabin with a triumphant air. Passing that test had kept my dream alive. The pride and enthusiasm I felt after passing that test created in me a momentum that carried me through other essential milestones, such as the brake and highway driving tests. With all the tests behind me, I was anxiously expecting the final result.

But meanwhile, I had realized that my projected yearly income wouldn't be enough to allow the amount of savings I had planned. The fact of the matter was that a few students dropped out of the driving academy because of the compensation package the company offered to new hires: $0.29 per mile driven. It is known nationwide that new truck drivers, especially the ones with no prior experience, do not make much money. But the longer they stay and acquire more experience in the industry while maintaining a good driving record, the more their mileage pay can increase. The average annual income of new truck drivers back in 2007 was between $30,000 and $35,000. Unfortunately, trucking companies promise and entice new drivers with a yearly income of $50,000, but the reality is that it is hardly true. It took me a few arithmetic operations to determine that it would require a tour de force on my part to barely make $28,000 the first year and maybe $30,000 the second. These were not the numbers upon which I had based my plan to save $55,000 for my university tuition. Ultimately I realized that I could still earn higher than the median in order to reach my savings goals, but it would require a sacrifice. I was determined to do whatever it took.

At the end of the program, after I passed all the tests, the state of Tennessee sent me my commercial driver's license. As I was looking at the license in my hands, I was very pleased and proud of myself. It had not been easy to get there. But I did it. Yes, I did. Now that I had a CDL, the company could officially put me on its payroll, and indeed Swift offered me a job as soon as I had my CDL in hand. As I was looking at my picture on the license, it brought a big smile to my face. Over the past few weeks of training, several students either had dropped out of their own volition or had been kicked out because they'd failed crucial tests. Once again, I was triumphant.

At the conclusion of the training in Memphis, I returned to St. Louis. My friends were happy to see me again. It had been almost a month since I'd seen them. They were eager to learn how things had gone in Memphis, and I shared my most memorable experiences with them.

Before Swift Transportation could entrust me with a semitruck, I had to go through its five-week mentorship program. The company needs to make sure that its new drivers are indeed ready to be out there by themselves hauling an 80,000-pound rig on public highways. In this part of the training process, the recruit is paired up with an experienced driver who shows him what it's actually like to be a truck driver on the road.

While I waited in St. Louis, the company tried to find a driver mentor from among its ranks. I only had to be patient for a few days, but when three days had passed and I hadn't heard anything yet, my patience was being tested. I was bored being at home. However, I seized the opportunity to reflect again on my life at that moment. It would take years before I attained the objectives I'd set, yet I was convinced that I was on the right track. I was optimistic.

It was in October of 2007, while I was at home in St. Louis, that the presidential campaign for the 2008 general election was heating up. While I was still in Memphis a few weeks earlier, I had witnessed other student drivers debating about the upcoming election and particularly about one of the Democratic presidential hopefuls, Illinois senator Barack Obama. News of the ailing economy was being leaked as we, the student drivers, were discussing how the economy might potentially affect our employment down the road.

There were several candidates in the presidential race at the time, but why was the discussion mostly about Obama? Because he was an African American seeking to be elected to the presidency of the United States.

In an ideal world, ethnicity or racial identification shouldn't matter, but in the United States, it mattered. Historically and culturally, racial politics and attitude against those who identified as blacks have been ugly, to say the least. The perception, the prejudice, and stereotypes associated with persons identifying as black or African American, do not in general play in their favor. Thus, when someone of that racial group seeks to garner the support of a majority-white country, you wonder how that is going to happen. Yes, 2007 or 2008 was not the 1900s or the 1960s, when the idea of a black person running for president of the United States would have been deemed ludicrous. The assessment of his winning chances became an unavoidable debate across the country.

A few decades ago, as recently as the 1960s, even though African Americans with deep roots in the United States legitimately considered themselves citizens, they were not treated or even viewed as such in the eyes of many white Americans. For African Americans, America is their home, but they knew they were pretty much considered *personae non gratae*. The race-based laws that were in place said it all. The American society they lived in had made sure that they didn't get close to the ballot box, because people of African descent were deemed inferior and therefore couldn't be trusted with power, let alone power over the white man. It wouldn't be too far-fetched to assert that black Americans never truly became citizens of the United States until the early 1970s, after the passage of the Civil Rights Act in 1964.

As I was watching the presidential campaign unfold, I was inspired by the audacity of Senator Obama in what he was trying to achieve, despite the end result not being certain.

I remembered when he'd announced his candidacy for president earlier that year, in February of 2007. I had not really paid much attention. With respect to the other candidates in the race, such as Hillary Clinton, Joe Biden, John Edwards, John McCain, Mike Huckabee, and Fred Thompson, I thought there were obstacles that Obama would face that the other candidates would not, and therefore at some point he would just drop out. To win the presidency, he would have to convince the majority-white electorate to look beyond skin color or racial background and vote for him.

I knew it was just not going to be that easy for him. Truth be told, I wouldn't have bet on him, either. Even since the "I Have a Dream" speech of 1963 by Rev. Martin Luther King Jr., it could not be said that King's dream had been fully achieved in America. However, undeniable progress has been made. More minorities have been elected to positions in government than ever before.

To my knowledge, before Senator Barack Obama, there had been two serious black candidates to seek the office of the president of the United States: Shirley Chisholm in 1972 and Rev. Jesse Jackson in both 1984 and 1988. It did not work out very well for Chisholm, but Jackson did score some points. I started looking at the Obama candidacy with some modicum of hope, but as to his winning it all, I definitely would not have bet on it. Ironically, most of the states where Jackson won primaries were in the South, including Mississippi. For him, winning anything in Mississippi must have been in itself an accomplishment, because for African Americans, it was one of the states considered to be the ground zero of oppression back in the day. As King put it in his 1963 speech: "I have a dream that one day even the state of Mississippi, a state sweltering with the heat of injustice, sweltering with the heat of oppression, will be transformed into an oasis of freedom and justice." If Jackson could pull off those victories, it seemed probable that Senator Obama could do likewise. It was an indication that a black candidate could get some acceptance. However, could that acceptance spread nationwide to the point of entrusting him with the highest office in the land? The White House? As it turned out later, the answer was yes. It came on the heels of Obama's defying all the stereotypes associated with a black man. My joy in that victory was not for him, but for the United States of America as a nation.

CHAPTER 11

The Mentorship in Moberly

S wift Transportation contacted me about two weeks after I returned to
St. Louis to inform me that it had found a mentor for me. His name
was Jacob.*

Jacob had been a professional truck driver for several years. He used to
be an OTR driver, but he had scaled back a bit and now did only regional deliveries. He lived in Moberly, Missouri, and delivered freight mostly
in Missouri, Iowa, Illinois, Minnesota, and Nebraska. In fact, Swift has a
small terminal in Moberly, but it is not a terminal in the true sense. It is
more like a distribution center for Walmart, but the drivers are Swift drivers
who deliver goods to Walmart stores across the Midwest. Two days after I
learned that Jacob would be my mentor, he gave me an introductory courtesy phone call, and we agreed to meet at a bus station in the Moberly area.
From there, he took me along to his delivery assignment.

Moberly is located about two and a half hours west of St. Louis. When
I arrived there in November of 2007, I was very much impressed with its
cleanliness. The quiet, the tranquility, and the calm surrounding it were
undeniable. It could be a good place to retire or raise a family. For the past
year and a half, the only cities I had known were St. Louis and Memphis.

---

*   Some names have been changed.

So, for me, comparing Moberly with those big cities, especially St. Louis, was unavoidable. For the next five weeks, Moberly was where I would be residing and training for my new job.

Jacob and I returned to the Swift terminal late that night after he made his delivery, and he took me to the dispatch center, where he introduced me to all the dispatchers on duty that night. I was well received. They reassured me that Jacob would be a good mentor to me. They vouched for him and assured me that the company had put me in good hands. The next few weeks that I would spend under Jacob's tutelage were crucial in the sense that he would be sending weekly performance reports to my company-assigned driver manager. If a new driver received a bad review while being trained, the company could decide to part ways with the new hire. Once again, I had found myself in a situation where the stakes were very high.

I couldn't have had a better mentor. From the dispatch center, Jacob took me to the driver lounge and introduced me to a few drivers who were there watching TV and having dinner. Then Jacob left for home. He would leave his truck at the distribution center and drive home in his car.

The distribution center did not have rooms to accommodate guests, although there were bathrooms where drivers could take a shower. Therefore, I did not have a room where I could sleep. For the next five weeks, Jacob's truck would be my room. Most modern commercial vehicles have a sleeper berth inside the cabin. Jacob's had a two-level sleeper berth, like most trucks these days. The inside of his rig was very clean and well maintained. He was someone who took a lot of pride in correctly maintaining his vehicle. For me, it would be the first time I'd slept inside a truck. As it turned out, I found the sleeper berth more comfortable than I'd expected.

At about 5:00 a.m., I woke to a beeping sound from inside the truck. I guessed what that might be: probably one of the onboard communication devices I had learned about in driving school. As I stood up to look for the source of the beep, I saw that I was right. It was a Qualcomm-made onboard computer used for communication between drivers and the dispatch. The beeping sound that woke me was a signal to Jacob that he was assigned to go make a delivery. I read the message, but I did not reply to it. It was his job to do that. At that time, he was at home, not at the distribution center to respond to the dispatch order, but it turned out that he had set things up with the dispatch to also receive delivery assignments via his mobile phone.

Later in the morning, Jacob sent me a message to inform me that he had already accepted the order and would come late in the afternoon for pickup. According to the assignment, we were scheduled for two delivery stops up north, in the state of Iowa. We would make one stop in Ottumwa and another in Waterloo. Around 5:00 p.m., Jacob showed up. We went to the trailer staging area where the trailer that we were supposed to pick up was parked. We'd already received the trailer number and its spot location via the onboard computer. Jacob did a quick inspection of the tractor and connected it.

Connecting the tractor to the trailer is in itself an important skill to have. As soon as the tractor was hitched to the trailer, I could feel it. Once the connection was established, Jacob and I got off the truck, and he performed a thorough pre-trip inspection of the ensemble: tractor and trailer. After that, he logged it in his book, as required by law. I sat in the passenger seat while he explained everything to me. As his student, I was to sit in the passenger seat and watch him drive. I was excited to go on my first delivery trip with him.

Before we set out for Ottumwa, Jacob showed me our itinerary and pointed out the different roads we needed to take to get there. Not all routes are suitable for semitrucks, so it's important to choose one's itinerary accordingly. Failure to do this can sometimes result in the driver finding himself in a very uncomfortable situation, such as getting a citation or, even worse, ending up on a small, winding country road that is not designed for tractor-trailer traffic. Thus far, my learning experience was going very well. An experienced driver had once told me that a truck driver rarely goes for a month without any incident or something worth recounting. I knew that I would be out with Jacob for five weeks. So, it was likely that something would happen on the road. But what would that be? I wanted the entire duration of my training to be incident- and accident-free.

As we headed to Ottumwa, I enjoyed the scenery along the stretch of highway that we took. It was my first time traveling to Iowa. I was really excited about that.

We took highway US-63 and headed north. In less than two hours, we had crossed the Missouri-Iowa state line. We were then in the Hawkeye State. Along the stretch of highway, there was not much to see in terms of scenery, but as we were inching deeper into Iowa, I couldn't help but notice the vast succession of seemingly interminable agricultural lands. I did not know exactly what the economy of Iowa was based on, but I could tell that farming must play a vital role in it. There were cornfields left and right. To me, those lands did not show any sign of dereliction. From the truck's cabin, higher up than someone riding in a car, I could appreciate it more. The landscape was gorgeous. A few minutes later, when it was already dark outside, we arrived in Ottumwa. Our customer there was a Walmart Supercenter.

We were on time—even a little bit ahead—but we knew that the customer was expecting us to arrive at any moment. As we pulled in, Jacob drove around the building to find the docking area and positioned the truck so as to back in. He called receiving to let them know we were there. I was watching everything he was doing, the way he was turning the wheel, the way he was moving his eyes to scan the side rearview mirrors, how he applied the brakes. A few minutes later, he successfully docked the truck.

While we were still seated in the truck, I suddenly heard a screeching, rolling sound coming from behind us. It was the docking door being rolled up from inside the store's receiving area. We got off the truck, and the receiving manager opened a door for us to go inside. Jacob asked him to verify the plastic trailer seal number on the bill of lading against that on the trailer door. This was one of the receiving steps to show the customer that the seal on the trailer door had not been tampered with, or removed and replaced on our way there. A customer's rejection of a load for any reason is bad for business. After the manager confirmed that the numbers matched, he gave us the go-ahead to break the seal. Jacob broke the seal and handed it to him. There were already three or four employees there with pallet jacks. As soon as Jacob opened the trailer door, the employees started going inside the trailer to remove the merchandise.

Once the trailer had been emptied of all the Ottumwa store items, Jacob closed the trailer and asked the manager to witness his putting on another seal. That was the seal that would be shown to the receiving man-ager of the Waterloo store, our other stop on this trip. Jacob collected the appropriate acknowledgment of signature receipt. With that formality tak-en care of, we were off to Waterloo.

Waterloo is a few hours north of Ottumwa along the same stretch of US-63. We got there in pretty much the same amount of time it had taken us to travel from Moberly to Ottumwa. From Ottumwa to Waterloo, the scenery was almost the same. Cornfield, cornfield, and more cornfield.

Tractor-trailer dock-backing was undoubtedly something on which I should focus. However, another area where I needed more practice was pre-trip inspection. I would hate to have an issue with my truck because I hadn't paid enough attention to something before setting out. From our conversa-tion, Jacob knew the areas in which he needed to coach me some more.

We arrived in Waterloo later that night. Once at the receiving dock, Jacob repeated the exact delivery protocols he had followed in Ottumwa. After he'd obtained the delivery confirmation signature, he and I went back to the truck. He alerted the dispatch center in Moberly, and we left the store. Before heading back to Moberly, we stayed in the area a bit for some much-needed rest. In my first delivery trip while on the job, I'd seen ev-erything from pickup to final delivery. It gave me a sense of what it was actually like to be on the job as a professional driver.

After a few hours of rest, we set off toward Moberly. Over the next couple of days, we made more deliveries in the region: Davenport, Mount Pleasant, Ankeny.

On the third day, Jacob estimated that I had observed him enough and that it was my turn to get in the driver's seat. Was I mentally and physically ready? Absolutely yes! Jacob later got a dispatch order that would take us through Des Moines, the capital of Iowa, and later Council Bluffs. Jacob wanted me to take charge. He too was ready to see me get behind the wheel and drive. We agreed that I would do everything, and Jacob would just be there to observe. I followed and executed the exact same steps that Jacob did each time we prepared to leave the distribution center with a delivery: pre-trip inspection, air-brake test, weight check. The compliments he gave me were very gratifying. I learned a lot from him.

Doing a pre-trip inspection

I got behind the wheel. With Jacob in the passenger seat and me doing the driving, we headed to Des Moines. I was very excited to be the one to take us there. Occasionally, Jacob would correct a mistake I made or bring my attention to something. One thing he stressed a lot was how often I should be checking my left-wing and right-wing mirrors. As I was just going straight on the highway, my belief was that I needed to focus on the road ahead of me. He taught me that I needed to check my mirrors at least every five seconds. Now, with Jacob right there by my side and instructing me to do so, I had no choice. It was a good habit to adopt. Moreover, I knew I was doing a dangerous job. I could get killed doing that job or even accidentally kill someone else while doing it. I wanted neither. Therefore, it behooved me to listen to him. It didn't take too long for me to start really doing as he said. I was very disciplined.

We arrived in Des Moines a few hours later. There was a lot of snow on the ground. It was late 2007, and snow had already started blanketing much of the Midwest. Although some areas in the immediate vicinity of the store's loading dock looked messy due to the snow, the overall milieu was quite pleasing to the eyes. The colors of the rooftops of the houses around were in such harmony. Caps of snow well seated on the treetops had me thinking that the area would definitely be in for a white Christmas.

As I had seen Jacob do several times before, I informed the customer that I was there to make a delivery. Even though I had watched Jacob at work several times, it felt quite different when I was doing it myself. It felt easy when he was doing it. I did not get the same feeling when it was my turn.

In backing the semi up to the dock, there were two x factors I had to take into account. The first was the snow itself, and the second was that the dock door was positioned a bit lower than the surrounding area. The docking area was all snow-covered, and there were no tire tracks of any previous trucks. It looked as if there was about a foot of snow on the ground.

Given that the dock area was in a descent, the truck could slide downward, and I could lose control if black ice was lurking under the snow. I wouldn't know the situation until I really started. As I was maneuvering the truck, backing it to the dock door, I was incessantly glancing at both side mirrors. I felt that I had positioned the trailer in a way that would have made it a little difficult for me to properly align it with the loading dock. At one point, I felt lost and confused during all the maneuvering of the steering wheel. Jacob noticed this and brought my attention to a few details, and how to get out of certain situations like the one I was visibly in. That was when he reminded me of something I'd been taught in driving school. It was a maxim that is written and plastered on almost all walls at Swift Transportation facilities and terminals across the United States. It is called GOAL: *Get out and look.*

It has been shown that about 25 percent of truck-related accidents occur during reverse or backing. That figure shrinks to 15 percent when the driver *gets out and looks* around the trailer at least once.

Per Jacob's advice, I stepped out to see from a different perspective how the tractor was positioned, and in particular how skewed it was with respect to the dock door. That observation alone would give me a lot of information about what I needed to do. This was my first real test and challenge. Knowing that Jacob would be grading me, I knew that I had to take that test very seriously. When I alighted from the cabin, my foot went straight through the accumulation of snow around the truck. I picked up my foot, and as I took another step, I realized that the snowfall was even all around. About two feet deep. The temperature outside was about 5 to 10 degrees Fahrenheit as I walked around the truck. I climbed back inside. Once behind the wheel, I knew exactly how I needed to maneuver it. From there on, my execution of all the maneuvering was flawless. The receiving crew unloaded the trailer, and after that, Jacob and I headed to Council Bluffs. The personal pride that I felt that day in succeeding at the docking procedure on the first try was indescribable.

Over the next few weeks, Jacob and I became true team drivers. But one day, the unexpected happened—an event that put me on notice with regard to the dangerous nature of the job.

⤻

On December 4, 2007, Jacob and I had just made a delivery in a small town in Iowa called Marshalltown, and we were on our way back to the distribution center in Moberly. That day, I was sleeping in the sleeper berth, and he was driving. There had been freezing rain in some parts of Iowa the night before, and also in parts of Missouri. We had made deliveries in numerous inclement weather conditions previously. It is part of the job. Whether it snows or rains, the truck has to roll. I had driven to make a delivery the night before, and it was Jacob's turn to drive us back.

I was profoundly sleeping inside the truck. All of a sudden, I started hearing Jacob speaking loudly to himself as if he were in distress. The sound of his voice was so loud that it woke me from my deep sleep. I knew there was something unusual going on. As I woke up, I tossed aside the curtain.

Jacob suddenly shouted, "Herve, don't move, please don't move! Stay where you're at!" I instantly froze. My eyes were still begging for some sleep. I had just realized that Jacob was dealing with an uncomfortable if not dangerous situation. From the sleeper berth, I could see that the truck was literally gliding on the ice-covered road. It had completely lost traction, and my trainer was trying to control it or bring it to a stop. I looked around through the window and saw that we were on a two-way street with a ravine on each side.

From the cabin, I could feel the trailer wiggling at will. I too was being shaken left and right. The sleep left me instantly. Jacob was fighting with the steering wheel, trying to steer the truck clear of the right-hand ravine. I looked ahead to see if there was oncoming traffic. Luckily, there was none.

My heart started pounding heavily inside my chest. At that moment, we were at the mercy of the truck. As I glanced at the mirrors and the windshield, I could see that there was ice everywhere. The side mirrors were wholly covered with plaques of ice, impeding visibility. The truck, in its motion, was taking the entire pavement. A head-on collision would have been unavoidable if there had been another vehicle coming from the opposite direction. At one point, I saw the truck heading straight down to the left-hand ravine. I was staring helplessly at the slope, but as I realized we were going down there, I turned my head quickly in Jacob's direction to see what he was going to do.

Then, Jacob let out a series of *"Oh my God! Oh my God! Oh my God!"* I looked around, lowered my head, and closed my eyes for a second before opening them quickly and widely. I was staring at death itself. I knew at that moment that there was nothing I could do. In that instant, I saw a flash of my life. I thought about my family 6,000 miles away. I looked at Jacob as he was still trying to regain control of the truck. I neither tried to utter a word nor even entertained the idea of making any sudden movement. It could distract him. I was fully aware of the situation. Again for about a couple of seconds, I closed my eyes, because I was seeing the inevitable coming our way at that moment: death. Instead of keeping my eyes closed, I decided to open them and look death in the face. The tractor and trailer were slithering on the road like a snake being chased.

When I reopened my eyes, I could see that the trailer was utterly straddling both lanes of the highway. With the trailer making a sharp angle with respect to the tractor, it seemed to push the ensemble downward on the road and toward the ditch. I took another quick glance at the right-hand ravine. I could tell that there was no way either Jacob or I could survive if the truck fell. No way! We would be crushed by the impact and under the weight of the truck.

In these types of situations where the driver is at the mercy of the truck, stepping on the brakes is instinctive. However, it's hazardous to do so. Jacob did at first try to bring the truck to a stop by stepping on the brake. But when he realized that he'd completely lost traction because of the black ice on the road, he removed his foot from the brake pedal. He started then to maneuver gently. The truck must have been going about 50 miles per hour when it lost traction. Can you imagine what a near-80,000-pound rig going 50 miles an hour on black ice looks like? It is like a cruise missile barreling toward its target. There is no stopping it.

The danger of a vehicle that heavy moving that fast under those circumstances resides in Newton's laws of motion.

- Newton's first law of motion: A body acted on by no net force moves with constant velocity and zero acceleration.
- Newton's second law of motion: If a net external force acts on a body, the body accelerates. The direction of acceleration is the same as the direction of the net force.

$$\Sigma \vec{F} = m\vec{a}$$

In physics classes, there is also the concept of momentum, used to quantify the idea of "oomph" (vitality, energy) that an object with a certain mass, going at a certain velocity, carries:

$$p = mv$$

The laws of physics suggested to me that there was no way out for us. Still, miraculously, the truck started coming to a stop, but it was veering to the right side of the road, toward the ravine. At that particular instant, the trailer was almost completely off the pavement. The tractor's rear tires were also off the pavement. The trailer and the tractor's tires were sitting on the edge of the ravine, just a few inches from it. The front tire of the tractor itself was barely resting on the pavement. The tractor-trailer ensemble was tilted. A strong gust of wind was all that would be needed to sweep the truck off the roadway and down into the ravine. Yes, the truck stopped just on the edge of the ravine.

As the vehicle came to a complete stop, I couldn't believe it. The logical explanation would be that Jacob had successfully maneuvered the truck like a pro. Yet what I witnessed that day was much more than pure skill. It was beyond that. As soon as the truck stopped, I saw a car coming from the opposite direction. If we had met that car a mere 10 seconds earlier, a head-on collision would have been inevitable.

Did the truck stop thanks to Jacob's skill, or did it come to a complete stop by the grace of Providence? Before the truck came to rest—just a few inches from the ravine—Jacob too had both of his hands almost cupping his head. Just like me, he saw the inevitable. I felt that we were going to die that day. There seemed to be no way that the truck could have stopped. But it did. It was a miracle. A guardian angel probably saved us that day.

As my trainer was getting off the truck, he asked me to do likewise. I couldn't dismount from the passenger side, because the vehicle was leaning to that side. If I'd dared to do that, it would have precipitated the truck into the ravine, dragging me along with it. In addition, there was barely any ground there to step on if I'd tried to get out on that side. The ditch was right there staring me in the face with arms wide open. It took me about two minutes to descend from the cabin. I was being very careful not to make any sudden or jerky movement that could ripple through the truck, causing it to tilt further and slide into the ravine.

I was extremely cautious about everything I touched and how I was taking each step inside the cabin. I finally managed to exit the truck. Hardly had I taken my second step on the pavement when I slid. I fell to the ground, prostrate. I'd hurt my knees, but I had to ignore the pain and get up as soon as I could. The problem was, I didn't know how to get up. When I first tried to stand, my shoes couldn't get any traction. There was absolutely no traction to be found. Black ice was everywhere. The only way I could safely move off the pavement without risking another sudden tumble was to crawl on all fours like a baby.

The tread on the shoes I was wearing was no match for the slippery pavement. Jacob was already on the other side of the road waiting for me to reach the shoulder, having taken a tumble once himself before he'd successfully tiptoed his way there.

Somehow I managed to lever myself up onto my feet. I stayed standing for a few moments, wondering what I should do. I chose to slowly lower myself back to the ground and start crawling toward the shoulder. At one point, I realized that my hands were not making a good grip on the pavement, either. I stood up again, bent forward, and after a few more steps, I too was on the other side of the road. I joined Jacob.

The car coming toward us from the opposite direction was moving very slowly with its four-way flashers on. Its driver could see much of the spectacle from afar. That day was undoubtedly one of the scariest of my life. To see myself a few seconds from a clear and inevitable death had seared an indelible memory into my psyche.

On the shoulder, Jacob and I looked at each other in dismay. We both knew that we had just escaped the jaws of death. Jacob took out his phone and called for help. As he was calling for roadside assistance, I was staring at the truck. For some reason, despite the slippery state of the road, the truck did not seem to be moving. The parking brake and distress signals were on when we left the truck. A moment later, Jacob told me that help was on the way but that we might have to wait a little. The temperature outside was below freezing. As I touched my lips, ears, and nose, it didn't seem to me that they were there. It was dangerously cold. Not far from where we were, there was a hotel. We needed a place to rest.

Jacob decided we should go to the hotel to get some rest while we waited for the roadside assistance folks to arrive. The way the truck was positioned on the highway would require a lot of care and finesse to extricate it from the edge of the ravine. It wouldn't be just a hook-and-pull operation. Once at the hotel, Jacob booked us a room with two beds. For the first time in weeks, I had found the comfort of a bed. I was falling asleep, but also, I was fighting it off. We still had our truck out there, and the roadside assistance crew hadn't shown up yet. All of that was weighing on me.

The roadside assistance crew arrived a few hours later. I witnessed that day a truck rescue effort that took about 90 minutes to pull off. It was one of the most delicate operations I have ever seen. Rescuing an impala from the jaws of a lion would be a close comparison.

Due to the inclement weather, and obviously the dangerous road conditions, Jacob and I decided to remain at the hotel until the following day. Until my very last day of training with him, we didn't really discuss what had transpired that day. I never broached the subject with him. It was too scary for us even to mention.

One thing that was undeniable was that my trainer was an experienced driver. His experience helped save our lives that day. But I still believe that divine Providence had a hand in our survival. It was a miracle that the truck stopped on frictionless pavement, and right on the edge of a deep ravine. It was simply a miracle.

CHAPTER 12

Going Solo

Soon after the incident on the ice, my five-week mentor-assisted training period came to an end. I showed Jacob my appreciation for the time he had taken to train me, and for his patience, instruction, knowledge, and advice. In return, I rated him very well. He had been very good to me. He genuinely cared about my learning and my success.

With my training now over, it was up to the company to assign me my own truck. I had learned enough over the past two months. I was ready to be by myself. The company informed me that I would be contacted as soon as a truck became available. I was a little nervous upon hearing that, because I did not know just how long I would have to wait. I left Moberly and returned to St. Louis to bide my time.

A few days later, the company made good on its promise: A truck had been assigned to me. Upon hearing the news, I was thrilled. To pick up my truck, I would have to go to Memphis again, where it had all started. Before I left for Memphis, I knew that I wouldn't just be going there to pick up the truck and drive it back home to St. Louis. I took time to prepare luggage as if I were going on a monthlong vacation.

I left St. Louis for Memphis in a sunny afternoon. On the Greyhound bus, the only thing I was paying attention to was the truck drivers on the highway. Soon, I would be just like them, driving from city to city, state to state. As an OTR trucker, I would have the opportunity to see the entire continental United States. As someone who likes to visit landmarks and museums, I knew that this job would give me that chance.

The list of places I hoped to visit was long. Occupying the top slots were Grand Canyon National Park, Mount Rushmore, the Lincoln Memorial, the Statue of Liberty, and a much-lesser-known one: Lake View Cemetery in Seattle, Washington, where the founder of jeet kune do, the actor Bruce Lee, was buried. At that time, there were several other states, like California, Texas, and Florida, that I wanted to visit, but I did not know when I would ever get the opportunity to do so. Once I was an OTR truck driver, it would be highly likely that I would go to those states to make a delivery or pick up a load. I was admittedly looking forward to seeing these new places.

A few hours later, I arrived in Memphis. It was already nighttime. The streets seemed particularly empty that evening. The traffic was definitely less heavy than it had been when I was there the last time around, about two months prior. From the Greyhound station, I took a taxi to the Swift terminal, where I announced my arrival to the receptionist on duty. I was instructed to wait for a few more hours to get the keys to the truck that would be assigned to me. At 8:00 the next morning, I received the keys to my truck. It felt so good. At that moment, I was having flashbacks: the phone interview with the recruiter a few months earlier, my first trip to Memphis, the classes at the driving academy, the skill tests, the road test, getting my CDL, my weeks of training with Jacob.

Once I got outside, I went to the truck parking area to look for the truck that was assigned to me. I visually scanned the entire truck staging area in an attempt to get a glimpse of it. As soon as I spotted a truck whose number matched the tag on the key in my hand, I felt excited. As I was looking at the truck from a distance and walking toward it, I smiled. It felt like love at first sight. When I got up close, I touched it with my hands and caressed the frame. It was my way to form a bond with the truck. It was a white truck, with the company logo on it written in blue and gold. I walked around the truck to make sure that everything seemed in place. I didn't see anything out of the ordinary. I opened the door to the cab and got in. I put my belongings on the sleeper berth. The truck's interior was clean. Everything I expected to be inside was there. I verified the truck's registration and insurance, the decals.

Even though the truck looked clean, I decided to clean it once more. After all, it was inside that truck that I would be spending most of my time. I cleaned the truck, then opened the hood to perform a visual inspection and all the other inspections required by law. I was ready for my first solo trip, but I did not know where I would be going. I needed to wait until my driver manager assigned one to me.

The wait wasn't long. I received a message from the dispatch within a few minutes. I would be going to New York for my first solo assignment.

The load was ready to be picked up right there at the Memphis terminal. I was also sent a recommended itinerary from Memphis to the customer's address in New York. I had my own truck map book. It was a Rand McNally book featuring all the major highways, interstates, and county highways in the United States and Canada. I opened it to compare the suggested itinerary that dispatch had sent me with what was in the book. With the atlas open in front of me, I got a better idea of the states I would traverse from Memphis, Tennessee, all the way to New York.

I was working for a company that had programmed all its trucks' engines in such a way that the drivers could not go over 55 miles per hour. No matter how much a driver floored the gas pedal, the maximum speed the truck would reach was 55 miles per hour. Why was the speed capped at 55? Safety, safety, and safety. It can be frustrating for drivers at times, but for a lot of trucking companies, that is how they keep a check on their drivers' speeding habits. Given the time around which I was planning to leave Memphis to embark on my first solo trip, I figured out that it would take me a little over two days to complete the journey.

I did not have a GPS inside my truck at the time, so I had to write down my itinerary. I wrote my route on a yellow Post-it note and stuck it on the dashboard so that I could glance at it when needed while driving. On the Post-it, I put interstate numbers and important mile markers at which I might need to be looking for a connecting interstate. With my first solo trip to New York all planned, I was ready, eager, and excited to go. For the first time since I'd started driving school, I was by myself. I was my own man.

Jacob would not be there by my side.

Even though it felt strange to be sitting behind the wheel with no supervision for the first time, I was also glad that there wouldn't be anyone around breathing down my neck, micromanaging me. That's the freedom that being a trucker gives you. There is, of course, driver supervision, but not in the sense that most people are familiar with.

When I was planning my trip, I realized that I would go through Nashville, Tennessee. I was excited knowing that I would be passing through that city. I equated Nashville with country music. I wouldn't be making a stop there, but I thought I would drive slowly while going through the city to appreciate its beauty. Each day that went by would allow me to explore more of the United States. It was a great feeling. It was as if I would be getting paid to do some tourism.

My journey to New York began when I got onto Interstate 40 from Memphis. A few miles into my trip, boredom almost set in. I then decided to turn on the radio so that I could listen to the news and some music. It was an almost perfect blue sky that day. As I was seeing other truckers on the road, I felt proud that I belonged to their family. Occasionally a driver would pass me and give me a sign of greeting. I nodded back at them as I continued driving.

According to the weather forecast, there would be snow in New York when I arrived. On learning about the weather, I started getting flashbacks of the near-death experience Jacob and I had had. Remembering all that gave me a little bit of concern, but I also knew that I had driven in those same inclement weather conditions several times before. As I was approaching the New York state line, the rooftops of the houses that I could see from the highway were blanketed with heavy snow. When I arrived in New York, it was late at night. I didn't go straight to the customer's for the delivery because my appointment time had not come yet. I was ahead of schedule. Therefore, I decided to park my truck at a welcome center along the highway and wait until my scheduled delivery time the following morning.

As the delivery time neared, I headed to the customer's location. Much of the snow had been cleared from the highway. I felt very safe driving that day. It was my first time in New York, and it felt good. When I arrived at my destination, the receiving manager directed me to an assigned dock. I put into action everything I had learned during my training and followed all the processes. That delivery service concluded my first solo trip as a professional truck driver. Now, I could wait for my next assignment.

CHAPTER 13

The Incredible, Dangerous, and Fulfilling Life on the Road

I felt a sense of pride when I successfully and without incident completed my first solo trip. There would be many more trips in the future. I waited impatiently for my second pickup and delivery assignment.

I was inside my truck listening to some news when I got another notification from my dispatch. I checked the onboard computer to read the message. My next assignment was one that had me enthused in a way that I had not been in months. I was assigned to pick up cargo in Virginia and deliver it to the Sumner area in Washington State: a 3,000-mile trip. As soon as I saw the estimated mileage, I paused for a few seconds. I was not sure whether I was hallucinating or not. I wanted to make sure that it was not Washington, DC, but actually Washington State. Legally, I still had enough driving hours left. Once I assured myself that I was indeed going to deliver that load to the other side of the country, I was very pleased. I immediately replied ACCEPTED to the dispatch. As a new driver, I needed long trips like that so that I could make decent money. The trip in itself would take me almost a week to complete. Could I do it without incident? I hoped so.

As soon as I left the New York customer's premises, I embarked for Virginia to pick up my next load. But, needing a bit of rest, I stopped along the way at a rest stop to relax and stretch. I felt ready for another long trip, but it had been almost 24 hours since I'd eaten a decent meal. I had a lot of snacks in my truck. I knew that in order to remain healthy to make it in the new industry I had just joined, I needed to develop a good eating habit. It is not a secret that many truck drivers have the same problem: poor eating habits. It stems from the nature of the job itself.

In Virginia, I arrived at the customer's for pickup and was directed to the truck staging area. While I waited a few moments for my cargo to be prepared, I seized the opportunity to plan my trip to Washington State. As I plotted the route, I realized that it would take me at least five to six days to complete.

I felt very good about the trip I was about to embark on, because there were so many things I wanted to do along the way and upon arriving in Washington. Given that I would be traveling across several states, I planned to make occasional stops to do some sightseeing, going to popular landmarks and attractions in cities I would pass through, time permitting. Upon arriving in Washington—after my load delivery—I would visit the Space Needle, the Microsoft campus, and the Lake View Cemetery in Seattle to pay my respects to Bruce Lee.

According to my itinerary, my trip from Virginia to Washington State would take me through West Virginia, Kentucky, Illinois, Missouri, Kansas, Nebraska, South Dakota, Wyoming, Montana, and Idaho. I embarked late in the morning. There was still snow on the ground in Virginia. As I left the state and entered West Virginia, it did not take me long to notice the difference between the two states, even though they were adjacent to each other. West Virginia—at least, the part that I passed through—gave me the impression that there used to be factories everywhere. It seemed a little bit stuck in time compared with Virginia. I saw a lot of hills with houses built on them.

As I left West Virginia and entered Kentucky, it was growing late at night. So far, my trip had gone very well. I was driving and sightseeing at the same time. Admittedly, there is not much to see while driving on the highway, but even the scenery along the roads, the sunset and sunrise, and the pack of migratory birds I saw flying overhead were sights to behold. Coincidentally, St. Louis was on my itinerary. It was an opportunity for me to take a break in the comfort of my home instead of staying inside the truck. That's precisely what I did.

For me, it felt good to have a quick respite at home. Before I left St. Louis to continue on my journey to Sumner, Washington, I planned my next 550 miles or so. That was about how far I would travel between my pre-trip and post-trip inspections. Given the approximate number of miles remaining before I would reach my final destination, I was looking at about three more days on the road. The rest of my trip would take me through Nebraska and South Dakota. I noticed a change in scenery when I ventured west of the Mississippi River.

Nebraska was where I encountered some of the strongest wind gusts I'd experienced in the truck so far. I could feel the wind's impact on the tractor and trailer. I felt as if I'd entered a storm. When people drive in a car, gusts of wind might not feel like a big deal, but for someone higher up inside a semi, it is scary. As I was going through the windstorm, there were times when I felt as if the truck was about to flip over. I gripped the steering wheel with as much strength as I could. Wind gusts came crashing against the truck's cab several times. I slowed down and noticed that the impact of the wind diminished. But it was still there. During strong wind, it's not uncommon to see truckers pull over on the side of the road, or at an exit ramp on the highway, to wait until the gusts become less severe. Each second for me going through that windstorm was like being on a roller-coaster ride. It was terrifying.

I knew the truck was heavy enough to withstand the incessant wind onslaught and stay on the road. Nevertheless, I was afraid that the gusts might become stronger at some point and sweep me and the vehicle off the highway. At moments, it felt as if I had just left the turbulent zone behind. Everything would seem quiet around me, as if the windstorm had just stopped. Then, a few moments later, the wind would slam into the rig again, rocking it left and right. During those episodes, my heart raced inside my chest. I wondered if that second delivery trip would be my last. "What if I got swept off the road and ended up in the ditch?" I asked myself. Under those circumstances, driving became far less comfortable. It didn't take me long to notice that some drivers simply pulled over to wait until the windstorm withered.

During that windstorm in Nebraska, I kept my stamina. After a few hours on the road, finally, I had left the storm behind. For me, it was like passing a test, or should I say, dodging a bullet. Either way, I made it through the storm. I won another battle that day.

There were three more states to traverse between there and Washington: South Dakota, Montana, and Idaho. While driving through South Dakota, I was under the impression that I was on the set of a western movie from the 1960s or '70s. From the highway, I saw a lot of farmland, barns, horses, storage units, and bundles of hay. All of these signaled to me that I was now on the western side of the United States. I couldn't stop thinking about Clint Eastwood, Lee Van Cleef, Charles Bronson, Gary Cooper, Henry Fonda, Jack Elam, John Wayne. I did not know personally how many western movies, if any, were shot in South Dakota, but to me, its scenery bore a clear resemblance to what one would see in those movies.

From there, I entered Montana. Like South Dakota, Montana is not a densely populated state. What struck me in Montana was the immensity of available space and land, and the beauty of the mountains. In fact, the name *Montana* is from the Spanish word for "mountain," *montaña*. The state's scenery looked greener than that of South Dakota. I went through cities such as Billings, Bozeman, Butte, and Missoula. Interstate 90 runs through Montana and connects those cities. It is one of those highways where one feels lonely pretty easily. Given that there was less traffic on the road, I was driving very comfortably. It was one of the best-maintained highways I had ever seen. I later realized that most of the treacherous highways in the United States are west of the Mississippi River. In other words, the farther west one goes, the more dangerous the roads are, at least from a trucker's perspective.

There must have been tremendous efforts deployed building highways through and around those chains of mountains. It wouldn't have been possible to level all those mountains in Montana, Utah, Idaho, Oregon, New

Mexico, or Colorado just to build highways. The rapid altitude changes of those roads sometimes make things very uncomfortable for truck drivers. It is not just uncomfortable; it is dangerous. I just hoped that I would not fall victim to the treacherous nature of some of those highways.

Me and my ride at a rest stop in Wyoming

Another inconvenience of driving on those routes is that there are not many gas stations. There are even signs warning drivers to refuel as soon as they can because the next gas station could be, say, 200 miles away.

I took a break in Montana. With only Idaho and Washington ahead, I knew I would soon reach my destination. It had been more than three days since I'd started that trip. Before going through Idaho, I listened to the weather forecast and heard that the road conditions might not be great. It was mid-January. I can testify to what driving on a slippery road is like.

The mere mention of black ice in the weather forecast brought to me the memory of that day with Jacob. On a flat, straight road, I wouldn't mind too much. But I was not very prepared to deal with an ice-covered road or expressway in the mountains at a higher altitude, with treacherous sharp curves and hairpin turns where suggested speed limits were 20 or 25 miles per hour on a 70-mile-an-hour highway, with no guardrails, and wide-open drop-offs on all sides. With all these thoughts going through my mind, I started to realize how dangerous this job truly was. I had read a lot about those roads. I had heard about them. But I have never been the type of person to be easily scared. Despite all that was going through my mind, I was not deterred.

For a trucker, driving on the highways in the western US may be challenging, but one thing that I couldn't stop noticing was the breathtaking and gorgeous scenic views from the interstate. Everything I had seen thus far all the way from Virginia had convinced me that the United States is indeed not only a very big but also a beautiful and charming country. Each part of the country has its own distinction. What I had seen was awe-inspiring all around.

The scenery that I was contemplating gave me a better appreciation of the beauty of the job that I hadn't seen before. A quiet voice inside me urged me to stay longer on the job and make a career out of it. But I had other plans, and I had to stick to them. For now, I would focus on each trip and enjoy the beauty of each state that I traversed.

❦

Though the scenery in Montana was worth exploring further, I kept pressing on toward my destination. I still had to go through Idaho. Shortly after I crossed the Montana-Idaho state line heading west, I noticed heavy truck traffic. At that point, it was snowing, and it was very cold outside. Mother Nature dumped a lot of snow on the ground that day. The reason why there were a lot of trucks on that stretch of the highway was that truckers were required to "chain up" before proceeding. Chaining up is the process of putting chains on the truck tires in order to increase traction when driving on an icy, snow-covered road. DOT agents require chaining mostly in remote mountainous areas, because the stretches of highway in those areas do not get deiced promptly when there is icy rain. Roads within city limits get deiced fairly quickly, but often that's not the case in remote areas.

Chaining up is a seasonal thing, done only during the winter and in certain parts of the country. Many truckers are regional drivers, and some probably never in their careers go through states or drive on highways where there are signs directing them to chain up and DOT agents looking around to make sure that every driver complies. When I was training with Jacob, we drove a lot in snow and icy rain, but we never stopped once to put chains on the tires. I never saw a "chain up" sign anywhere in the Midwest. But on the other side of the country, the requirement for truckers to chain up makes sense, for safety reasons.

Being safe and doing everything that was necessary to stay alive on the road was paramount for me; I was not ready to die. Given that I was doing a dangerous job by all measures, I had to follow to the letter all the highway safety rules and regulations.

I pulled over to the side of the highway. There were several other drivers there putting chains on their tires. I got off my truck and put my gloves on. I disentangled the heap of chains in the back of the tractor. There were a dozen of them. I extricated them one by one and started putting them on the trailer tires, starting from the rear. Even though I was wearing gloves, my hands and fingers were hurting from the combination of the severe cold and the weight of the chains. It was so cold that even with the gloves, I was not feeling the blood flow in my fingers.

After all the chains were on, I got back in the truck, put it in gear, and started driving. As I was going down the highway, there was a DOT agent who glanced at my tires. He was to make sure that I was compliant with the chain ordinance for truckers that day. I could hear the sound of the chains as I was moving. I stepped on the brakes lightly to make sure I would indeed be able to stop the truck when I needed to. The gentle push that I gave the brake pedal reassured me that the braking system was working as it should despite all the chains on the tires.

As I was rolling down the interstate, I could feel the ice on the road cracking under the truck's weight. Despite the perilous state of the road, I saw some drivers speeding along as though the road conditions were normal. I was not impressed by their bravado. For me, safety was more important than showing off.

After a few miles, the road surface seemed better, and it was no longer necessary to keep driving with chains on the tires. I got off the highway, parked the truck, and took off all the chains. I arranged them in an orderly fashion and placed them in the back of the tractor.

After going through Idaho, I crossed the state line into Washington. Not far from Washington's eastern border, just a few miles ahead, was Spokane, a city of about 215,000 inhabitants. Spokane is mostly known for its Native American heritage. From there, it's about 280 miles to Seattle. Once I was outside the city limits of Spokane, heading toward Sumner, it was like driving through a desert.

At this point, I was still about four and a half hours away from my final destination. For several minutes, I did not come across anyone on the interstate. It was as if the highway was dedicated to me, just me. I saw neither trucks nor cars in either direction, eastbound or westbound. It was one of the moments when one feels the loneliness associated with the job of a truck driver. My only companion was the radio. But unfortunately, when I tried to scan radio channels in the area, there was almost none to tune to. Both the radio and telephone signals seemed weak. All I was left with was contemplation of the scenery. I had been doing that since I started the job. I came to appreciate the beauty of what I was seeing.

Eventually, as I was getting closer to my journey's end, I saw other vehicles on the highway, sporadically. It was not until I was about two hours from my destination that I started seeing some traffic. It was my first time in Washington, and given that my delivery location was very close to Seattle, I intended to do some tourism there. After a weeklong trip, I thought dispatch would give me at least a couple of days off before my next load assignment.

CHAPTER 14

The Rewards of the Job

After six days on the road—from Virginia to western Washington—I finally arrived at my destination in Sumner, Washington. I had just traveled across the entire United States from east to west. What an experience that was! I made my delivery and headed to the Swift terminal in the area to have a rest and wait for my next assignment. As I was going to the terminal, there was one crucial thing that I was yearning to do: take a shower. In fact, the last time I'd showered had been four days earlier, when I'd made a stop at my apartment in St. Louis. That was the first time in my whole life that I had gone that many days without bothering to wash myself. The subsequent stops I'd made were for other purposes; none included shower time. I was not very proud of my sketchy hygiene, but the reality is that it is part of the nature for over-the-road truck driving.

For the first time in four days, at the Swift terminal, I was inside a shower. It was a good feeling. The sensation of the water gushing out of the showerhead, cleansing my skin of all the impurities that had accumulated over the past few days, was utterly refreshing. I vowed that day not to spend that many days without taking a shower—at least once between pickup and delivery. It was easier said than done. It did not take me long to realize that not showering for days might just be my new normal; it's typical in that line of work. A trucker I met at a truck stop one day confessed to me his shower routine. It was a confession that raised my eyebrow. He showered once a month at most. And he was not even shy about telling me.

There are many things in life that are easier said than done. There is a Japanese proverb that goes "Beginning is easy, but continuing is hard." The job of a truck driver requires a lot of discipline. Given that I was driving a truck—a dangerous job in itself—to save money for college, discipline and a high dose of inspiration were what I needed. I was a student of the martial art of wushu for several years when I was a teenager, and I regularly practiced until my early twenties. I needed to channel again the discipline that I had embraced when I was that student and apply it to my present life.

At a juncture when I was looking for something to inspire me, it was opportune that I was now so close to making the pilgrimage I'd planned to Bruce Lee's grave in Seattle. During his life, Lee embodied discipline. He applied it to his life in a way that took him to heights never seen before. Fortunately, Seattle was only about 40 minutes north of Sumner, where I had just delivered my cargo. I knew it would be at least two days before I would go on my next assignment. Therefore, I set a day aside for my excursion to Seattle.

Given that I did not know much about the area, I thought that the best thing to do was to rent a car so that I could move about more easily in the city. I secured a car and planned my day. In my opinion, doing any sort of tourism in Seattle without visiting the Space Needle would be pointless. For that reason, I started there before heading to the Lake View Cemetery. The influence on my life that Bruce Lee has had—a man who was dead and gone long before I was born—is worth sharing.

I was seven years old when one of my cousins, Lance,* took me to the movies to see *The Way of the Dragon*, a Bruce Lee movie. Before watching that film, I had seen other Chinese martial arts movies, but I had not really been captivated by the action or the fight scenes I'd seen on screen. Sometimes there was too much screaming, and the fight scenes were disorganized. Some were good, but some were not.

Everything changed when I saw Bruce Lee on-screen for the first time

---

* Some names have been changed.

that day. His style of fighting looked applicable in real life to me. The techniques and styles he used were clearly different from what I was used to seeing. I had seen fight scenes that were without doubt choreographed to be pleasing to the eyes. They showed a lot of jumping, too, which in real life would be impossible to accomplish during an actual duel.

Even at a young age, I knew that Bruce Lee's fighting style could be used in real life. At times during the movie, he used a signature weapon, the nunchakus. I had never seen anything like that before. The way he handled and utilized it was masterful and breathtaking. What style of fighting he was using, I couldn't tell. All I knew was that it was different from everything I had seen before. Almost all the martial arts movies I had seen prior to *The Way of the Dragon* featured Chinese actors. It dawned on me then that there must be something between China and martial arts. The style of fighting that I knew of was kung fu. As I would later learn, I was right about China and its history with kung fu.

In fact, martial arts in China could be traced back several thousand years. Some of the styles best known to the rest of the world are wushu, tai chi (popularized on the silver screen by Jet Li), wing chun (demonstrated by Donnie Yen in movies like the *Ip Man* installments), Shaolin, monkey style (practiced by Jackie Chan in his movies), cricket style, and shuai jiao. To the novice, the styles may look similar, but they are different in form. Some styles seem to be more efficient than others. Each style is geared toward defeating the opponent in a particular fashion.

Although there is some fiction to the action scenes in martial arts movies, Chinese films in particular, the different styles and fighting techniques used are well known and even documented. Some techniques, though, are not even formally documented because of the secrecy surrounding their teaching. For simplicity, I will refer to the Chinese martial arts as kung fu.

For the Chinese, kung fu has almost always been part of their tradition. For centuries, there have been schools that have taught the art. Getting into those schools is very selective, and each school is headed by a master, or *sifu*, who is an expert in one or more particular styles. Some fighting tactics or styles are not indiscriminately taught to students but are handed down from father to son or from a master to a single protégé or a select few of his students whom he deems worthy of learning them. In other words, a kung fu student can spend years at a school and leave without learning the "crown jewel" technique at that school.

For generations, China was closed off to the world. Even afterward, when it came to the teaching of kung fu, martial arts schools did not accept foreigners as students. Whether inside or outside of China, the martial arts instructors would not teach those they perceived as foreigners. The reasons are several. For instance, Chinese instructors did not view foreigners as disciplined enough to learn. Moreover, some of the techniques or styles are lethal. Therefore, it behooves the *sifu* to ascertain that the knowledge of some techniques does not fall into the wrong hands. In addition, China has also been a very conservative country, which could be another reason for the reluctance to accept foreign initiates.

Bruce Lee, born in San Francisco, challenged that deep-rooted tradition of not teaching kung fu to foreigners. Although born in the United States, Lee was raised in China, where he of course learned kung fu, especially wing chun. He returned to the United States to study at the University of Washington and opened a martial arts school in Seattle where he took as a student anyone wanting to learn. He did not discriminate, and as a result, brought some unwanted attention to himself. He was also worldly, and that was something I came to like about him as a person.

Upon learning that there was a Chinese man teaching kung fu to locals—including Caucasians—some in the Chinese community in Seattle, particularly other martial arts instructors, urged Lee to close his school or face serious consequences. These Chinese instructors believed that Lee, as a Chinese man, should know that teaching kung fu to people who were not of Chinese descent was not acceptable.

As he drew the ire of that community of instructors and faced pressure to close his school, Lee stood his ground and did not yield. History has it that he was challenged to a real fight with another martial arts instructor. The agreement was that if Lee lost the fight, he would have to close his school. Lee's wife was present at the duel. From the account of those who witnessed the fight, it lasted under three minutes. Lee's challenger, overwhelmed, started running around and finally surrendered. Lee won the fight. As agreed, he kept his school open.

These anecdotes have fortified me since I was a very young man. After my near-death experience on the road with Jacob back in Missouri, for a while I became apprehensive whenever we went out for deliveries while it was snowing. I had good reason to be concerned, but I remembered one of the most powerful quotes I had learned from Bruce Lee: "A good martial artist does not become tense, but ready. Not thinking, yet not dreaming. Ready for whatever may come." Pondering that quote from the movie *Enter the Dragon* gave me the courage to go out there and do the job, and not think too much about the danger I might face daily. If I thought too much about the risks of the job—fatal accidents in particular—I might see more of them happening in real life, to the point where I could become a victim just the way I'd envisioned it.

Lee started as a student of wing chun, trained in Hong Kong by a master named Ip Man. Lee drew from his knowledge of wing chun, combined with styles derived from other disciplines like karate, tae kwon do, and boxing, to form his own style of fighting: jeet kune do. It means "the way of the intercepting fist."

Me at about age 14, when I was a student of kung fu

119

Anyone who has seen a Bruce Lee movie will have noticed the particularity of his fighting style. After I watched *The Way of the Dragon*, in which he faced off with Chuck Norris, I did not need any more motivation to start learning Lee's martial art. There were not many instructors of jeet kune do around the world. They were Lee's former students, and his art was known to very few upon his death. After his passing, those students carried on his legacy. In fact, hardly any legitimate jeet kune do instructor could be found outside the United States when he passed away. It took years before dojos (martial arts studios) teaching jeet kune do appeared elsewhere around the world.

When I was still a very young man in my native country, there was no dojo where jeet kune do was taught. However, there were dojos for karate, judo, tae kwon do, and shotokan. These forms of martial arts are mostly of Japanese origin, except for tae kwon do, which was developed in South Korea. Their accessibility probably reflects the fact that Japan and South Korea opened up to the world long before China did. Thus, my options were limited in terms of the style of martial art that I could study. I began karate, but I only practiced it for a short period because it did not have the beauty in form, style, and strike that I was accustomed to seeing in Chinese martial arts movies—the kung fu style, the Shaolin form—where there is more fluidity, and every single part of the body seems to be involved. The seamless coordination of mind and body is fundamental to the success of any martial artist. I have come to realize that it applies to driving as well.

Even though I stopped devoting time to karate, my passion for martial arts did not subside. I binged on traditional Chinese kung fu movies and observed the fighting styles and skills used. When I returned home from the movies, I tried to duplicate by myself the actions I'd seen. Some of them were quite challenging to me; others were easily mimicked and perfectly executed. At a young age, I had a very sharp memory, which allowed me to remember almost every fight scene and, most importantly, the fight choreography. That was what I tried to mimic. In this way, I learned a lot about the art all on my own.

Over the next few years, as I saw more of Bruce Lee's movies, I came to admire the man not only for the martial artist he was, but also for his acting skills, and most importantly his philosophies. He was very good in front of a camera. It was not until the mid-1990s, when I was about 12 years old and saw Lee's Hollywood-coproduced, most-acclaimed movie, *Enter the Dragon*, that I really decided to formally learn kung fu. Up to that time, I had been practicing martial arts as a pastime. *Enter the Dragon* gave me a greater impetus to learn kung fu. Before watching *Enter the Dragon*, I had seen another one of Lee's movies, *Fist of Fury*, which had taught me at an early age the importance of fighting for honor, respect, and dignity. The settling of scores has its own merit that should not be overlooked, as it creates a deterrent against any future insult or disrespect.

Aside from being a martial artist, Bruce Lee was also a philosopher. In his televised interview with Pierre Berton in 1971, Lee said:

> Empty your mind, be formless, shapeless, like water. When you put water into a cup, it becomes the cup. When you put water into a bottle, it becomes the bottle. When you put water in a teapot, it becomes the teapot. Water can flow or it can crash. Be water, my friend.

As someone born under the sign of Aquarius—the only zodiac sign with the water symbol—I have always tried to adapt to every situation I find myself in. The above is probably Lee's best-known quote. It pretty much summarizes the essence of the art that he developed. Most styles have limitations. For this reason, martial arts practitioners should not be slaves to one and only one art. They should use their skills learned from one art and bring in their own knowledge. "Be formless." Every fight is different, thus every opponent is different. An opponent may initiate a real fight, in a different combative way. Therefore, one should adapt and respond to each combative way differently. Water is the ultimate fighter in the entire universe.

Lee's water philosophy transcends the realm of martial arts. We, as humans, need to learn to adapt to every circumstance surrounding us. Otherwise, we are doomed to failure or disappointment. It has been shown that the human body is composed of about 60 percent water. Thus, we human beings are in essence water. Therefore, our actions should reflect the "water" that we are. Being mostly made up of water, we are inherently adaptable creatures. And for our own survival, we shall adapt. Water penetrates rocks over time.

This is the same philosophy that I believe can be applied to knowledge. There is no denying that as individuals, we have different abilities and skills. But anyone can acquire and learn any new knowledge or skill if he or she truly understands the "water" philosophy. Water has three powerful characteristics, or characters, I should say, that every human being should channel in life: patience, steadfastness, and determination. I believe that success is hardly elusive in any area of life if a person embodies these three inherent characters of water.

Before going to the Lake View Cemetery, I stopped by a florist in downtown Seattle to buy some flowers. What good would it be to travel all the way to the cemetery without offering some flowers to the late hero? At the florist's, I asked for advice. I did not know exactly what type of flowers to buy. Even though I had some idea of what they should look like, I wanted to be sure. I bought appropriate flowers upon the florist's recommendation.

In Chinese culture, one pays respect to a dead person not only by offering flowers but also by burning incense. So I found a store in the Seattle downtown area that specialized in Asian goods and purchased some incense as well.

The cemetery was just a few minutes away. I decided to park my car outside and enter on foot. As I was walking, I didn't know exactly where Bruce Lee's grave site was, but I had seen its picture on the Internet, and I knew I would recognize it when I saw it. The cemetery was one of the most well-maintained I had ever seen. It was quite easy to get a broad view of the entire cemetery from any corner. It was simply beautiful. I knew that there were other celebrities buried there, but it seemed that the most famous person there was Bruce Lee. I spotted the grave and started walking toward it.

At that point, there were a lot of emotions going through me. Knowing that I was very close to finally standing before Lee's tombstone, being there at his grave site—for much of my life, I had thought about that. When I was younger, practicing martial arts, I had toyed with the idea, but I never thought it would one day come true. At first, I always imagined Lee was buried in China. It wasn't until my late teenage years, after I saw a documentary about his life, that I learned that even though he died in Hong Kong, his widow flew his body to the United States to be buried there. I have to confess that that day, when I visited his final resting place, was probably among the most emotional days of my life.

The grass surrounding the grave was well kept. There were two tombstones: one for Bruce Lee and the other for his son, Brandon Lee. Tragically, Bruce's son died in an accident on the set of the movie *The Crow* in 1993. A photo of Bruce Lee was encased in his own tombstone. Across from the graves of Bruce and Brandon, there was a stone bench to allow visitors to sit down. On one side of the bench was conspicuously engraved "The key to immortality is first living a life worth remembering." On the other side, the bench read "Husband and father, son and brother / You are always with us—Linda and Shannon." (Linda is Mr. Lee's widow, and Shannon is his daughter.)

At the grave site of Bruce Lee at the Lake View Cemetery in Seattle

I sat down on the bench for a few minutes to soak it in. I still couldn't believe I was there. I had thought about that moment since I was a boy. There I was at the burial place of the person whose movies I'd seen and who had influenced me in embracing martial arts in all their forms, especially kung fu wushu. Beneath his name and birth and death dates on the tombstone, the engraving read, "Founder of Jeet Kune Do."

As I sat there on the bench, scenes from Bruce Lee's movies that I'd seen years earlier were playing in my head. I realized what a force he was.

A couple who had arrived to visit the grave of a relative of theirs nearby kindly agreed to take my photo as I paid my respects. I laid the flower that I had bought on the gravestone and then knelt down. I got out the incense, lit a stick of it, and bowed my head and my body three times. In the Chinese tradition, each bow carries a meaning. The first is taken to acknowledge heaven. The second bow is for Earth, and the third is for mankind. I took the three bows and then said a few words thanking Lee for the inspiration he has been to millions of people around the world, and to me in particular. His story of breaking taboos and breaking barriers has fully resonated. On the one hand, he put his life at risk to teach kung fu to non-Chinese. He went against all odds, threats, and intimidation just to teach kung fu and his own fighting philosophy to anyone who would study it, regardless of race, gender, or ethnicity. On the other hand, his message was about mankind—suggesting that we are all one family under the sky.

It was amazing how in death, even decades after his passing, Lee was still receiving that kind of respect and attention from people from all over the world.

It was getting a little foggy inside the cemetery. The sky was losing its clear-sky blue. I felt that I needed to leave before Mother Nature surprised me. As I was watching the incense stick burn, I stood up and one last time bowed in respect before Lee's gravestone and his son's. Then I left.

After leaving the cemetery, I headed to a restaurant for lunch. Over the next few hours, I wandered around Seattle. I knew my tour of the city wouldn't be complete until I went to the Redmond area to see the Microsoft campus.

I remembered that in college in Benin, during a class in my freshman year—History of Computer Sciences—Microsoft and its cofounder's name, Bill Gates, had come up often. Bill Gates has always been an inspiration to me. If my memory serves me well, it was in the late 1990s when I first learned that Gates was ranked the richest man in the world. The news came as a surprise to me, because I had always believed that the richest man on Earth must be one of those princes from an oil-rich nation in the Arab world. When I was growing up in West Africa, the ostentatious display of wealth and fortune that I saw on television was often that of royalty in the Middle East showing off everything from gold-plated china to cars and toilets adorned with precious metals. Bill Gates has remained a fascinating person to me ever since.

Back then, I wondered what it would feel like to become and be universally known as the richest man on the planet. Gates's name usually came to my mind when there was news about an upcoming release of a new Windows version. It would have been great to go see and be in the presence of that man that I have admired for not only his contribution to the computer industry, but also his philanthropic work through his Bill & Melinda Gates Foundation.

My circuit of the outside of the campus concluded my Seattle tour, and I headed back to the Swift terminal, where I'd parked my truck. There, I found out that my next pickup and delivery assignment had been issued. It was time to get back to work.

⌒

I had been on the job for a little more than a week since going solo, and I had to admit that I liked it a lot. There are hundreds of major cities in the United States. I thought to myself that I might not get the chance to visit all of them, but if the opportunity arose to make a delivery in one of those cities I had always longed to know, I could replicate what I'd just done in Seattle if I had extra time.

After about four days spent in Washington State, I received an assignment that would take me to the state next door: Oregon. I got a load assignment to the city of Eugene. Oregon had never been on my radar as a place I would like to visit, but I was curious to see what it might look like. I had heard a lot about Portland. It has a professional basketball team, and I am a basketball fan. The Portland Trail Blazers have been good ambassadors of that city.

Eugene is only about two hours south of Portland, so I knew I would be at my next destination soon. I was glad that I'd be traveling in the daytime. That would give me the opportunity to contemplate the views from my truck cabin. Shortly after I crossed the state line and entered Oregon, I started seeing a change in scenery. But as I proceeded south along the highway, I came upon the most beautiful coastline I had ever seen in my life. Even though I did not stop the truck to get out and savor the view, I knew I was seeing something special. The main expressway heading south does not run far from the shore, so it is relatively easy to see much of the beauty of the coastline from a distance: lagoons, lakes, sparkling dunes . . . It felt like a paradisiacal garden. At one point, I couldn't resist the temptation of pulling over the truck to gaze at that marvel of nature right here in the United States.

CHAPTER 15

The Lifestyle Over the Road

As a truck driver, naturally, I was always on the road. Most of the time, I was on so tight a schedule that pulling over to go to a restaurant and have a decent meal felt like a waste of time. As most of the truck drivers out there do, I first started filling my truck with junk food, cookies, soda. Inside my truck's cab, there was a very small refrigerator. I stored some food in that and also kept some items right next to me or on the passenger's seat so that I could reach them while driving. During my first few months, my diet consisted mostly of junk foods. Once in a while, I went to truck-stop restaurants. Some of the major truck stops have restaurants that are very trucker-friendly. Most truck drivers, I believe, like to go to those truck stops to take their federally mandated breaks, but sometimes there might not be one of those facilities along the route when the driver needs to shut down the truck and have a rest. The only food he or she can rely on as a dinner at that point is whatever happens to be in the truck.

Eating at restaurants three times a day can also be costly, which is another reason why many truck drivers, including myself, tried our best to limit our restaurant stops. But it didn't take a lot of time before I realized that the junk food I was eating was not doing my health any favors. I knew I had to change my diet, but how? When a driver stops at some point to eat at a restaurant, he might spend about an hour. An hour is a lot of time for a truck driver, because the maximum amount of time that a driver can stay behind the wheel legally is 11 hours of "pure driving" time in a 14-hour period.** However, that on-duty period allows the driver to do 3 hours' worth of other things, such as having meals, taking rest breaks, and refueling the truck. The 14 hours begin to count down as soon as the driver does his pre-trip inspection before setting out. The Federal Motor Carrier Safety Administration (FMCSA) is expected to announce changes to the hours-of-service rules that will take effect in 2019. So, the current regulations that appertain to truckers working hours may have changed. Because of body fatigue, it is a challenge to max out the 11-hour driving limit once the clock starts.

To me, it was particularly challenging because of my truck's programming not to exceed 55 miles per hour. It's hard to cover much distance under those circumstances. And of course, the truck doesn't go 55 miles per hour for many hours straight. Intermittently you're slowing to go through towns, or you find yourself in traffic jams. For those reasons, maximizing my time on the road—with the vehicle actually rolling—was very important. I found my answer in a small portable cooker.

It was the best money I had ever spent on an appliance.

Small enough to fit in my truck, the portable cooker was made to consume between 6 and 12 volts, so I bought a surge protector with multiple plugs. As I was looking at the device that I had just bought, I knew I would be doing a lot of cooking inside the truck. The idea of cooking a meal on the go was very entertaining to me. In other words, I wouldn't have to park my truck somewhere, wait while I was cooking, and resume my trip after I finished. It was a game changer.

Now, with my new stove on board, I needed to buy groceries. I headed to the nearest Walmart. Besides food, I also bought a lot of trash bags and disposable plates, spoons, and forks. I didn't want to resume my trip without at least seeing how the stove would perform. In the same Walmart parking lot, I decided to cook some rice and beans and make a soup to accompany it. With only the one stove, I elected to cook the rice and beans first. I

** There is an exception that allows for 16 hours on duty if the driver is on a single-day schedule and departs from and returns to the same terminal.

poured some water in the stove and mixed it with rice and beans. Then I plugged the stove into the battery charger plug below the dashboard. The stove was sitting right next to the driver's seat. It was important to keep the engine running while cooking; otherwise the stove might drain the truck battery. I headed out to my next destination, with my rice and beans simmering while I was driving.

After a few minutes, I figured that the rice was done. I pulled the truck over, emptied the rice from the stove, and quickly mixed canned tomatoes and fish to make a soup. I plugged the stove in once again and resumed my trip while the soup simmered. Because the stove was right by my side, when my surroundings were clear of any other vehicle, I would once in a while open the lid a little bit and glance inside to see if the food was ready.

Soon the soup was ready. With my rice and beans already prepared, and now my soup, I couldn't fight back my hunger anymore. I found a place where I could safely park the truck and test-drive my first cooked-on-the-go meal. I had everything I needed in my truck: water, soda, fruit, disposable plates, forks, spoons.

While I dished out my meal, I reflected on my journey thus far in America. First of all, I had never thought in my wildest dreams when I left my native country that I would one day be driving a commercial vehicle. Secondly, turning the inside of my truck into a kitchen on wheels was not only one of the funniest episodes in my life as a truck driver thus far, but also a proof to me that I was determined to find every way to survive under any circumstances and reach my goals. Knowing very well the reason why I was doing all this, I had plenty of energy to keep going.

Driving a truck is a lifestyle and a life-altering job. All alone in my semi, I turned on the radio and tuned it to a music station, then sat on the cabin's lower berth and ate my own version of a "meal on wheels." The stove had done a wonderful job. The soup was delicious, and the rice and beans were very well cooked. At that point, I started entertaining the idea of buying another stove, which I did the following day. With two stoves in my truck, there would be no need to wait for one dish to cook before preparing another one. I could do both simultaneously. By cooking inside my truck, I saved not only time but money. It was one of the most efficient meal-cost-cutting decisions I ever made as an over-the-road truck driver.

One of the harsher realities of being a truck driver was the time spent away from home. When I started going solo in early 2008, I did not get a break for two months. In other words, I stayed out for about 60 days before I was able to return home to St. Louis for a few days of rest. But when I did get back home, I was not only proud of the experience I'd had but also eager to share my experience with my friends. Most of them had not been anywhere else other than the neighboring state of Illinois. They were in awe of the places I had visited. My description of each part of the country, especially the Oregon coastline, took their breath away. Those among them who had thought that I couldn't do the job a few months ago started showing me some respect. Yes, I'd earned it. And I had a trove of pictures to show them.

In a matter of eight weeks, I had been to more cities and states than I'd ever thought possible. I had seen much of the country and had formed an idea about each state I had visited.

Up to that point, I was still renting an apartment. So, who was living in my apartment all that time I was gone? Nobody. Before I'd left St. Louis to go to Memphis to pick up my service vehicle, I had paid my rent days in advance because I knew I wouldn't be in town when rent came due. When I was on the road and realized that I wouldn't be home by the time my next rent was due, I called a close friend of mine in St. Louis, Christian, and arranged to transfer him some money through MoneyGram to pay my rent.

I was probably in New Mexico at the time. After that experience, it became clear to me that it might become a bit difficult in the future to honor some of my critical appointments if I had to go home for certain reasons. And that was exactly what happened a few months later, when I missed a doctor's scheduled consultation because the company didn't honor my time-off request despite my having asked for it weeks in advance. In fact, this is something that happens a lot in the industry. It is a situation that creates anger, frustration, and resentment among drivers toward the companies they work for. It is very frustrating, given that some drivers miss important family days.

For me, continuing to pay the rent for an apartment that I did not live in became a nuisance and a clear waste of money. After my first home time off, I came to the conclusion that I would not renew my apartment lease. I decided to put all my belongings in a storage unit and pay $70 to $80 per month instead of the $500 I was paying for rent at the time. Based on my projected estimate, it was a move that should save me thousands of dollars. I came up with the idea that I could just live inside my truck, and when I came to St. Louis, I could stay at a friend's house for two or three days. I followed through on that decision. A post office box was now my address.

It was another excellent decision and quite a relief. I knew that it would accelerate my college saving goals.

For the next two years, I rarely went to St. Louis. The reason was simple. I was not married, and I didn't have any children at home to see. I was not like the other drivers, married with children, who had family responsibilities and spousal duties to fulfill. I was my own family. I was only living for the job. I had come to really enjoy the freedom that truck driving had given me. Though it was all good, I never lost sight of my purpose in working that hard and tirelessly: making as much money as possible so as to save as much as I could for college expenses, and possibly to start a small business. When I did go to St. Louis for time off, I stayed at a friend's house for just two or at most three days. It came to a point where I saw going on break for even a few days—the way most drivers with families do—as a missed opportunity to make money. My attitude was, what will you be going home to St. Louis for? I no longer had an apartment, and to be quite honest, I didn't like staying at another person's place, even though we were friends.

In the fall of 2008, I was in Dallas, Texas, when my cousin Alicia called me to ask whether I would be going to St. Louis for Christmas. She was inviting me to come home so that I could spend that day with her and her family. I thanked her for the invitation, but I politely told her that I didn't plan to go to St. Louis.

During my years as a truck driver, I spent both Christmas Days and New Year's Days either at a truck stop in the company of other drivers or on the road somewhere on my way to a pickup or delivery. My most memorable New Year's Eve was the one I spent at a truck stop in the state of Georgia with other drivers. As soon as the clock hit midnight as we watched on live TV the pyrotechnics indicating that we had just entered a new year, we hugged each other and wished all the best to one another. We ate together in that little TV room that night, swapping stories and good-natured banters.

Those holidays were just more working days for me. I was wholeheartedly dedicated to the job. My dedication didn't go unnoticed. One day my driver manager observed that I had not requested a home time off for almost three months. She asked me if I was not interested in taking at least a few days off to go see my family. I was pleased by her attention, but I replied that I did not need it. She commended me for my dedication to the job and promised to "keep [me] busy and rolling." That was all I wanted to hear.

CHAPTER 16

Temptations, Traps, and Dangers

Truck drivers do have a tough job, and besides that, their marriages and love lives are not the most desirable in the world. There are certainly other jobs out there that keep partners or spouses away from each other for days, weeks, and even months at a time. But, to put it bluntly, relationship-wise, trucking is a lifestyle that sucks. I have stories to share in that regard.

I was in Arkansas one day in maybe August or September of 2008 when a windstorm advisory was announced on the radio. I sought a safe place to park my truck, because the wind was becoming very strong. I saw that there were two other trucks parked there, so I felt safe to stop there and rest. It was around 7:00 in the evening. I was not running behind schedule, so I thought I might just as well spend the night there and resume my trip the following morning, after the storm had calmed.

About 20 minutes after I pulled in, it was getting dark outside, and I was already lying on my berth and ready to sleep when I heard a knock on the driver-side door. There had been almost no one in sight outside when I'd parked the truck, so I was a little bit startled. I'd heard stories in the past about truckers being robbed, and even killed. So, I was a little bit nervous and on guard.

I did not want to become another statistic, but I also knew that for anything terrible to happen to me inside my truck, I would have had to open the door first and let someone enter. The doors to the truck are so well designed that it would be a challenge for someone to get in without the key. By the time I decided to get up and see who it was, I heard another knock. I moved to the door and drew aside the curtain to look out the window. Outside was a woman who waved at me, smiling. Before I could even react, she lifted her tank top and flashed me her breasts. She shook them left and right, with both hands holding up her top. Still smiling, with both breasts exposed to me, she cupped her left breast and began circling her tongue around her nipple. It didn't take a lot of thinking or guessing to figure out who that lady was. She was a sex worker looking for a client.

I smiled back at her as she motioned for me to roll down my window to see her closer. I had to admit that at that very moment, it was a little bit hard to take my eyes off her assets. She was a young woman, probably in her early twenties, and very attractive. She sensed my hesitation to roll down my window, or open the door to let her come in. She was not deterred. Instead, she turned around, lifted up her skirt, and gave herself a slap on the buttocks. It was like a scene straight out of a pornographic movie. I was not prepared for all that, and I even found it funny, entertaining, and, frankly, exciting to have a sex worker enticing me that way.

By way of information, it had been months since the last time I'd had sexual relations of any kind. The truck-driving gig had done a "good job" of disrupting my quest to form a new relationship after I'd split with my girlfriend back in St. Louis. So the prostitute's offer was not without its temptations. For a second, I thought to myself that all I had to do was chat with her and invite her inside my truck, but I quickly came to my senses right there, realizing I wouldn't want to do that. Still, the urge to give in was almost overwhelming. I do not condone prostitution, and paying for sex with a complete stranger was never something I thought I would want to partake in. So, although she was very inviting, I waved her off and indicated that I was not interested in her "product."

She didn't leave immediately. She stayed around for a few more seconds, expecting me to change my mind. But I quickly lost my smile and put on a poker face. She got the message. She understood that I was not going to change my mind. She left a little bit disappointed. I slid the window cover back on and then went to sleep. With my head resting on my pillow, both hands intertwined under my nape, I looked up at the ceiling and relived in my head what had just happened.

Truck drivers, in general, know that there is something like that out there, but contrary to popular belief, it is not something in which that the majority of them engage. The woman who'd knocked on my door trying to sell me her sexual services looked very young. One thing I know about prostitution is that there is a darker side to it: human trafficking. Sometimes those young women do it under threat. They could be the victims of a kidnapping, or sometimes they're foreign women who are promised a better life in the West. They arrive in the country, their passports are seized, and probably with no marketable skills, they succumb to threats and are forced to sell themselves. Others are American women who are drug addicts. Some have been denied steady, legitimate employment because they cannot pass a drug test. Still, others do the work simply because they have fallen on hard times.

Regardless of why some women resort to that method of earning a few bucks, it's both unwise and unsafe for a truck driver, or anyone, for that matter, to have dealings with a lot lizard.

Though *prostitute* is a generic term, sex workers who cater to truckers at truck stops are known in the industry as lot lizards. The term is appropriate, because they go from truck stop to truck stop to offer their services. Even though direct solicitation by knocking on windows is their most common way of procuring customers, they also rely on the CB radio that truckers use to communicate among themselves. At a truck stop one night, I had heard a woman—clearly a pimp, or a madam—asking drivers through the CD radio if they wanted a professional massage.

The woman on the CB insisted that the massage was for gentlemen only. She added that any gentleman interested in the service would receive special and undivided attention from the masseuse, and that the masseuse would be satisfying all the customer's needs so that the latter could be 100 percent ready for his next trip. Though the service was being advertised as a massage, the woman's wording and innuendo clearly indicated that it was a solicitation for sexual services. There was no question about it. The pimps do that because in case their messages are intercepted by law enforcement, they cannot be accused of explicit solicitation.

As I was listening to the madam seeking clients for her so-called masseuses, the temptation to reach out to her started growing in me. But in my soul-searching, I quickly convinced myself that it was absolutely not a prudent or wise way to appease a carnal appetite. I resolved just to continue listening to the madam through my CB radio for entertainment.

My second experience dealing with a lot lizard was when I was headed for delivery in Dallas. I was still a few hours away from my destination. Along highway I-30, I decided to pull over at a small rest stop and get some sleep before continuing on my route the next day. The place where I parked my truck was not a particularly big truck stop. It was more like a makeshift rest area for truckers along the interstate, in one of those areas with no major businesses around. There was hardly even any pavement—just dirt.

After shutting down the engine, I got out to do a post-trip inspection. The sun was setting. The sky appeared to have been set on fire. It was a combination of yellow and orange on the horizon. The weather was great. It was Texas, after all. Dallas was about one and a half to two hours away. There were about five other trucks already parked there when I first arrived. I got back inside my truck, served myself the meal I'd cooked earlier with my stove, and grabbed a book to read for a while, as I always did before closing my eyes.

I was reading the book *The Secret*, by Rhonda Byrne. I was absorbed in my reading when all of a sudden, I heard two simultaneous knocking sounds on my windows—both the driver-side and the passenger-side window. It did not occur to me what that might be. I put down the book and drew aside the curtain on the passenger-side window. As I looked out, I saw a young woman who was casually dressed. She motioned for me to roll down the window glass so she could speak to me. She was carrying a large purse and holding a small bottle in her hands. I could not from my cabin read the label on the bottle. I rolled down the window. At that point, I was just curious about the product she appeared to be selling. The purse she was carrying did not appear to contain a lot of items.

I greeted her from my cabin. She raised the bottle and said that she was selling perfume. To draw my attention further, she sprayed a little bit of the perfume on her left wrist and sniffed it. She touted it as a great product that I would certainly like. She was casually dressed, so I did not suspect that she was a lot lizard. Why was she trying to sell a bottle of perfume to a truck driver at a truck stop? It was strange to me, but once I collected my thoughts to answer that question for myself, it made sense to me, because truck drivers do not shower often. A perfume might be useful to conceal body odors, especially for those drivers who shower maybe once a week or even less frequently. So, I thanked her for showing me the perfume but said I wasn't interested in buying any. She invited me to sample it for myself, hoping I might like the fragrance and buy it. I stood my ground and politely said no with a smile.

She quickly put the perfume back in her purse and asked me if she could come inside my truck. That was when I realized her ruse. She was indeed a lot lizard, but was using the sale of perfume as a cover to get customers. She was very polite. She wanted to know where I was headed. She was playing with her hair, exposing more and more of her cleavage. I had gone through that kind of solicitation experience in Arkansas. As I was talking to her, I still had my book in my hand. I said to her that unfortunately, I was not going to accept her services. I mentioned to her that I was reading a book and that not only was I tired, but I was not in the mood for the type of services she was offering. I rolled the window back up as she stood there outside, speechless. She turned her back and left while I was closing the curtain.

As I mentioned earlier, there were two who'd knocked on my windows. When I was chatting with one, the other was there all the time, on the other side of the truck, but I didn't know for sure if she heard my conversation with the first woman. After I had waved off the "perfume merchant," no sooner had I sat on the berth to resume my reading than I heard another knock on the driver-side door. Clearly, I knew it must be one of those hookers again. I didn't want to ignore it, because when they know that a driver is in his truck, they keep knocking until he comes out. This second hooker, too, looked like she was in her early twenties. She had more makeup on than the previous one. When I uncovered my window to look out from my truck cabin, she already had her right hand buried inside the waistband of her skirt. The movement of her hand from below her navel clearly suggested that she was rubbing and caressing her genitalia in a very inviting and seductive way. While doing so, she had her left thumb in her mouth to make it even more titillating. Even though I knew I wouldn't be consuming her "product," I told her that I was not interested in her services, but I would like to know what else she had to offer. I was curious how much these women charged and what services they were willing to deliver. I got her attention. She thought that she might have me as a customer.

All this was happening while I was still inside my truck. She quickly withdrew her hand from her skirt, revealed her breasts, exposed her nipples, cupped them with both hands, and softly shouted to me, "It depends on what you want, sweetheart."

"I want you for a few hours," I fibbed. I didn't know at the time that they charge in increments of 30 minutes or per hour. The minimum service she would provide if I hired her was 30 minutes or one "round," whichever came first, for $200. There was also the option of $300 per hour, or even an all-nighter for $1,000—unlimited "rounds"—if I wanted her company until 5:00 in the morning. As she was telling me her rates, I was not only amused but also confounded. She was candid in listing for me what she would agree to do and what she wouldn't. I remained silent for a moment. I could feel a turmoil inside my head.

Truth be told, it's a temptation that can be difficult to resist. It's during such a moment that the idea of having a first experience germinates inside your brain and you ask yourself if you really might want to give it a try. Though the biological need was awakened in me at that instant, I did not envision myself spending "quality time" under those circumstances. At that moment, I was searching my mind for a stroke of spiritual guidance that could inspire me to remain steadfast. I found it. Proverbs 29:3 in the Bible: "A man who loves wisdom makes his father glad, but he who keeps company with harlots wastes his wealth." I had to devise a way to send her off.

For a few moments, I lost the ability to utter even a single word. She took notice of the uncertainty on my face and went ahead to reassure me that her service fees were negotiable and that I should counteroffer with something. It was already dark outside. The area was sparsely lit. There were about a dozen other trucks there at that time. I had gotten the answer that I wanted, but given that I had no real interest in buying her services, I had to find a way to send her away quickly so that I could go back to my reading. I counteroffered $5.

After a few minutes of going back and forth, she sensed that I was not as interested as I'd appeared to be earlier when I'd inquired about her rates. I thought that after my ridiculous counteroffer, she would just storm off hurling insults my way, but to my utter astonishment, she didn't do that. She became more hell-bent on convincing me to buy her services. She made me a last and final offer of $90 for a 20-minute sex session. I was looking for a humane way to end the "bargaining." My eyes were wandering. I took a deep breath and let her know that I did have the amount she wanted to charge, but that I was not willing to part with my $90 in that fashion. She raised her eyebrows and moved a step closer to my window. She reaffirmed to me that I was passing up a lifetime opportunity by not being with her to see how well she would treat me and cater to all my fantasies.

Twenty minutes and one "round" with a complete stranger at a truck stop was definitely not going to be enough to satisfy all my carnal desires, lust, and fantasies. I had too many of them to rush-fit and pack in that short amount of time.

I decided to end the conversation by telling her frankly that I appreciated her offer, but I was not interested. My curiosity to find out how the lot lizards did their "business" revealed to me something about their activities, service fees, and so on. I took pity on her and even thought about giving her some food and money, but I was not sure if that would have been a right move. She later asked me to just give her the money that I had, but even though my heart was in the right place, I was reluctant even to give her a handout. What if we were being observed? What if she was a decoy? What if she was an undercover cop? If the latter had been true, the simple act of handing money to her for any reason whatsoever could put me in serious legal trouble. At that time, if any criminal charge were to be brought against me, I wouldn't have been in the position to hire a good lawyer, because I might not have been able to afford it. In addition to that, my employer, the trucking company, would have gotten wind of it, and termination of my employment would have ensued immediately. I had heard cases of truck drivers who were caught patronizing prostitutes and who lost their jobs. Soliciting a prostitute is a criminal offense, either misdemeanor or felony depending on whether the prostitute is a minor, and it is one of those charges and convictions that can ruin a person's life for good.

When the hooker walked away from my truck after I refused her services, she went directly to knock on the door of another truck parked catty-corner to mine, a few feet away. I watched the whole scene from my cabin to see how the other truck driver would react. That other driver obviously knew for what he was being solicited. After a few seconds of back-and-forth between the two, he invited her inside his truck. I shook my head in disbelief. But a little part of me was happy for her because she managed to find at least one customer that night.

From an outsider's perspective, driving a truck for a living may seem not too challenging in the sense that truckers just sit in the comfort of their vehicles and drive. But in fact, as I mentioned previously, truck driving is one of the ten most dangerous jobs in the United States. According to a recent article by David Johnson in *Time* magazine, there were more than 900 fatalities among truckers in 2016. During that same year, 51 police officers were killed in the line of duty. In the same article, Johnson noted that the fatality rate among truckers was 24.7 deaths per 100,000 workers. That's a lot. This is the kind of figure that, when published, should bring people's attention to the danger associated with the profession of a truck driver.

July 14, 2008, was a day that will stay in my memory for a long time. What happened that day was something that all truck drivers dread: an accident. On July 13, the day before, I left home after a two-day hiatus from work and set out toward the city of Jackson, Missouri, where I was expected to arrive in the afternoon to pick up a load. After two hours of driving, I made it there and picked up the cargo, which was scheduled for delivery in Savannah, Georgia. I headed straight to Atlanta, where I planned to take a rest at the Swift terminal in order to replenish my focus and energy before continuing my trip the next day. I pulled up at the terminal very late at night, tired from the long drive from Jackson, and slept for a few hours.

The next day, the 14th, I ended my break at 1:00 p.m. *Let's move this truck and make some money,* I said to myself. After performing a routine pre-trip inspection on my truck, I was ready to head straight to Savannah to deliver the load. It was very beautiful outside; sunny sky. The temperature was about 85 degrees Fahrenheit. I spent about 20 minutes in the traffic before leaving the Atlanta city limits. As I was departing Atlanta and heading south on I-75, the traffic got better. By then, I had already reached the exit for Jonesboro, which is a small city in Clayton County, about 15 miles south of the Atlanta city center.

To kill the boredom, I was nodding my head in sync with a soft rock song playing on the radio. I was traveling in the far-right lane at about 40 to 45 miles per hour. I was way behind the minivan in front of me.

All of a sudden, the van driver began slowing down. All the other drivers in front of him were doing likewise, and to me, it was obvious that they were all trying to take the next exit. I-75 at that point is a four-lane highway in each direction. Cars, small trucks, and SUVs in the other lanes were moving at full throttle. The minivan driver seemed to have come to a complete stop on the road. I put my left turn signal on to make a lane change. My immediate left lane was clear, and it was safe for me to move over. I safely changed lanes.

I had rejoined the pool of through traffic, and everything seemed to be as it had always been until the minivan driver turned upside down what was supposed to be a routine day of work on the road. Clumsy, reckless, inattentive, and disorderly, as I would describe his behavior, he started backing up on the highway because, I believe, he felt that the lane he was in was not moving fast enough. I was in the next lane to the left. Without putting any turn signal on, he veered into my lane, trying to cut in front of me. Being at a higher level relative to the vehicles around me, I did not notice him until I realized how close he was to the front of my truck. He was in my blind spot.

It was clear that he was in a hurry to go somewhere. Most trucks wear a big yellow sticker on both sides of the vehicle that clearly reads: "You are in my blind spot—I can't see you." It is a message intended for cars in particular and is self-explanatory.

The minivan driver, in an attempt to quickly squeeze in front of me, darted his car left along the passenger-side flank of my truck. My facial muscles tightened. My right foot instinctively hit the brake pedal to make way for him to cut in. But before I could make room, I heard a screeching sound coming from outside, followed by a loud noise. The driver-side rearview mirror of the minivan, and the body of the car were scratching the passenger side of my truck, leaving behind a trail of scrape. I felt a nudge inside the cabin, as if my truck had been hit by a sudden wind gust. Fortunately, the minivan's momentum was not strong enough to push me out of my lane. But the impact rocked my tractor. I floored my brake pedal, jamming it all the way down in an attempt to just let that madman through. A truck with a fully loaded trailer in tow is not a vehicle that can stop on a dime. It takes longer for the truck to come to a complete stop after the driver hits the brake.

When the minivan driver hit my truck, he became "glued" to my tractor. I felt that he was sort of trying to nudge me out of my lane. I tried to move over to the left a bit to make room for him. As I slowed down, the van was able to barge his way in front of me before quickly switching lanes again to the right. I couldn't believe what I was seeing.

At that same moment, there was another driver in a red rental car who was also trying to switch lanes in an attempt to move from the left to the right. That was when that car and my truck came into contact. I heard another loud sound. The impact was inevitable. The front part of my truck hit the red vehicle's rear bumper. Behind the wheel of that car was a shocked woman. I could only imagine what was going through her mind. She quickly stopped on the highway. I did likewise, so that when the police arrived, they could piece together what had really happened. The minivan driver who'd caused the accident moved his van to the side of the road.

I got off my truck and went to check on the lady. Fortunately, she looked fine. The van driver's eyes wandered around in disbelief. He'd gotten out of his car and was standing by his unrecognizable vehicle. The minivan's driver-side door was pushed in, the side mirror was hanging by a thread, and the hood was mangled because its driver had ended up rear-ending another car. The minivan driver and I made eye contact as I walked toward his car to make sure that he was all right. He seemed embarrassed to look me in the face. He knew he'd caused all that had happened. He looked mortified, and at the same time panicky. I was very angry with him, but there was no need to confront him. Per Swift Inc. policy, when a driver is involved in an accident, he or she must check on the welfare of the other parties. The truck driver is also required to secure the scene with reflective triangles, notify law enforcement, and take photographs for proof. I did all that.

I dialed 911 to call the police. The lady in the red car had gotten out. Glancing at her, I saw that she was on the phone with her arms akimbo. I assumed she was calling 911, or she might be talking to the car rental company or her insurance agent.

When I was on the phone talking to the police, I realized that the traffic was backed up for 300 yards or more. Traffic was oozing past my truck very slowly.

The police arrived at the scene. From a distance, one of the several responding officers motioned for me to move my truck off the road. I got back in my truck and moved it to the shoulder.

The police collected information from the other drivers, including witnesses. One of the responding officers approached my truck and asked for my driver's license. I handed it to him. He left and went back in his patrol car without asking me any questions about the accident. Meanwhile, the minivan driver, the rental car driver, and other witnesses were being questioned. I stood outside my truck expecting my turn so that I could give my account of what had just happened. Astonishingly, it was an opportunity I wouldn't get. A few moments later, as I was playing again in my head everything that had just happened, the officer who had taken my driver's license came back. To my utter astonishment, he handed me two citations to sign. I told the officer that the minivan driver was at fault, and asked him why he had not asked my version of what happened before issuing me two citations.

"You can come to court and fight them if you want to," the officer responded. I told him right there that the citations he had just handed me were a travesty and that I would certainly be going to court to fight them.

For the police, it did not matter who else was at fault. Given that I was the truck driver, it was easy to blame everything on me. According to the statistics, more than 97 percent of the accident reports involving truck drivers find them at fault at the moment of the incident, before they can go to court to argue for the charges to be expunged. Most people think and believe that an incident or accident involving a tractor-trailer has to be pinned on the driver of the truck. It is extremely rare for a truck driver not to receive any citation after an accident, whether or not he or she is at fault. It's rooted in people's minds that truck drivers are always the bad guys. The minivan driver who caused it all left without any citation. His account of what had happened was heard, and the lady in the other car gave her account as well. A couple of other witnesses were questioned, too. But not me.

According to the citations I was given, I would have to go to a court in Atlanta to fight the charges.

I called my dispatch to inform them of what had just happened. I recounted my ordeal. Dispatch was supportive and advised me just to be safe out there. That accident that day was another reminder of the inherent nature of the job that I was doing. I had been warned several times while I was in driving school that distracted drivers were what I should watch out for the most. After the accident, I started to wonder seriously if I could summon enough courage to get behind the wheel again and drive. If yes, for how long? After the scene cleared, I was by myself, and it had just dawned on me that there could have been loss of life as a result of that accident. Thanks to my alertness and vigilance, there were no deaths. I assessed that I had just shown an expert display of skill that had saved lives. I convinced myself that I would continue to do the job.

I asked myself, *What would have happened if things had gone the other way, and someone had lost their life?* There was no question in my mind that I would have been blamed for it, and depending on the situation, the law enforcement might have brought manslaughter charges. That's usually how it happens.

The company gave me some post-accident instructions, and I left the scene. Before my court date was due, I hired an attorney in Atlanta. The lawyer represented me in court a few weeks later to help me fight the charges. After the judge reviewed the case, I was simply ordered to make sure that I didn't receive another citation for at least six months. Going to court was well worth it for me, because I wanted my side of the story to be heard.

⌇

The road conditions during the winter season were another situation that I found very dangerous. As we all know, every winter brings its own share of inclement weather conditions. Most of those conditions, especially snow and black ice, each year leaves a trail of accidents and fatalities. When I was a trainee based in Moberly, Missouri, I experienced firsthand how dangerous and treacherous our roads can be during the winter season. Everyone has seen on TV at least once a slew of cars that were involved in a chain-reaction accident and formed a messy pile in the middle of the highway as a result of a slippery road. I have seen a lot of those. I was lucky enough never to be involved in such a pileup, but I came close back in December of 2008. To be specific, it was December 26—the day after Christmas.

As a matter of fact, I had just spent Christmas Day inside my truck. Like many other truck drivers that day, I had stayed on the job rather than going home to celebrate Christmas with my family and friends in St Louis. The year before, I had spent Christmas with my cousin, her husband, and her children. It was a very enjoyable atmosphere. This year, although Alicia had invited me again, she knew the type of job I was doing and understood when I let her know that I would not likely be present to break bread with her and her family. I spent almost that entire Christmas Day on the road, driving. I was probably on a load assignment from Tennessee to Chicago. I was routed through Indiana on my way up north to make my delivery. After a long driving day, I decided to take a well-deserved rest in Lafayette, Indiana.

Soon after I parked the truck, I did my post-trip inspection, then cooked a meal with my stove and spent the rest of the evening reading until I fell asleep. Meanwhile, a light snow was floating down outside. It snowed a lot in the Midwest, and there was snow everywhere. The rest stop where I'd parked was littered with heaps of snow. The markings for parking spots on the pavement were barely visible.

I woke up the following morning shortly before 4:00. By the time I got ready to head to Chicago, it was 4:30 a.m. Even though Chicago was only about an hour away, I wanted to leave a little early to allow for unexpected delays in traffic.

When I'd woken up that morning, I had noticed that my truck's windshield was completely ice-covered. The same was true of the rearview mirrors on both sides. I deiced all the glass, got everything cleaned off, and was ready to set out. The ice on my windshield was an indication that some sleet or freezing rain had fallen during the night. There would be black ice on the interstate, but I knew that cities are usually prompt about dispatching their maintenance crews to clean up and deice their roads.

From where I was parked, I could see the traffic on the highway. I glanced at the interstate and saw that there was good traffic flow both ways. My assessment was that it would be safe to drive.

I left the rest stop and headed on to Chicago on I-65. I was about 15 minutes into the trip when I saw a car in front of me moving with all its emergency lights (four-way flashers) blinking. The car was going very slowly, but at the same time, there were other vehicles driving faster and passing us in the left lane, as though the road conditions were normal. As usual, I was riding in the right lane. I had to reduce my speed considerably to stay behind the car in "distress," but soon I would be practically tailgating. The driver was going about 15 to 20 miles per hour.

I quickly tested my brakes to make sure I had traction. At that point, I didn't suspect that anything was wrong. I was still a few feet behind the car when I did my traction test. I was convinced that I had traction, because the truck did slow down when I hit the brake. It was time then for me to pass the car. There was no other vehicle in the left lane. I put my left turn signal on and initiated the pass.

When I got in the left lane, I felt that the truck was trying to veer farther left. I tried to correct it a little bit by moving the steering wheel to the right. I got a sudden jolt of panic when I realized that the truck kept moving straight, and started failing to respond to any of the steering wheel commands. I tapped on the brake pedal a little to check if I had traction. What I found was no surprise: I did not have traction. None whatsoever!

The truck was simply gliding over a miles-long layer of black ice. I tried again to step on the brake to see if I would have any chance at slowing down. When I touched the brake, I did not feel the tractor stopping, but instead, it tended to skid sideways. From the passenger-side rearview mirror, I could see the entire trailer swinging, straddling both lanes and trying to form a V shape with the tractor. If the trailer got closer to the tractor, that would be a jackknife scenario. With almost zero traction, I was at the mercy of whatever was supposed to happen. It's a cliché, but my life flashed before my eyes. I was convinced at that point that the truck would undoubtedly crash, and I would die inside. In those types of situations, panic clouds good judgment. I did not know what else to do.

The truck was veering wildly left and right as it barreled along down the interstate, but I held on to the steering wheel and tried to control it to stay on the pavement the best I could. As I mentioned before, it was cold that day, but in a matter of seconds, I started sweating as though I had been running a marathon for hours. The images of my parents, sisters, and friends started going through my mind. I honestly thought that could be the end of me. A crash in the ravine seemed inevitable.

I had gone through a similar feeling back in Missouri, when Jacob was the driver. Now, it was just me. All of a sudden, I was wisdom-struck. I regained my lost poise, took a deep breath, and completely removed my feet from the brake pedal. Instead of holding tightly onto the steering wheel as I had been doing, I eased up on it a little bit. The truck made a jerky forward movement. It was darting toward the right shoulder of the road. Instead of hitting the brake pedal, I kept my foot off it, exhaling very slowly as I said, "Oh Lord, oh Lord!" I moved the steering wheel to the left a smidgen, trying to get the truck back on the highway. I had lost hope. From my cabin, I glanced down the drop-off on the right. What I saw was even scarier. The ravine on that side of the highway was deep and steep. For a second, I pictured that it was undoubtedly where I would die, inside that truck. There was absolutely no way I would survive if my truck plummeted into that ravine.

As I steered the wheel to the left, the truck did respond inexplicably to stay on the highway, but now I was heading to the ditch on the left side of the road. I did another slight adjustment to the right. Miraculously, the truck was finding a little bit of traction just before the extreme edge of the asphalt. Fortunately, there was no other vehicle close behind me.

After having exhausted all the skills I had—in a matter of just under two minutes—to stay alive, I came to a stretch of the highway that sloped downward. The truck was now going downhill with almost no traction. As I started the descent, I saw that there were three cars flipped over in the ditch to the left, and two other cars off the road to the right. Of the latter two vehicles, it appeared one had probably rear-ended the other. There was also a police officer at the scene. I began thinking that I would soon join them. My heart started pounding hard again in my chest. My hands started trembling. I took a deep breath in an effort to regain my composure.

With my truck going down the slope, I knew that braking would only have precipitated my demise. It was tempting, but I kept my foot completely off the brake pedal. To me at that point, there was nothing else I could do other than say my last prayer. In a last-ditch effort to slow the truck, I thought maybe tapping on the brake pedal a little bit would do something. I did try, but it was a vain effort. The rig was now skating straight toward the right-hand ravine. I looked around me as if I were saying good-bye to this world.

For one more time, I took an instant to admire the nature around me: the trees, the grass, the sky, the snow, the road I was driving on, even the very same black ice that had put me in that uncomfortable situation. I took that short moment to start thinking about my goals in life, the plans that I had but wouldn't be able to fulfill now that I was about to die. I felt a little sad. I thought about my mother, who had cried two years ago at the airport when I'd left. I thought about my dad.

With all those thoughts going through my mind, as my truck had become unstoppable and was taking me straight to where I knew I would inevitably die—there in the ditch—I uttered a few words as my last prayer. With sadness and defeat in my face, I said, "Lord, my Heavenly Father,

I haven't led a perfect life. Forgive me for my sins. I am putting my life into your hands now. Please have mercy on my soul. In the name of Jesus. Amen!" As someone who was born and raised in a family of Catholics, I'd had the habit of praying in times of distress drilled into me. By the time I finished the last words of my prayer, the truck was almost at the bottom of the descent on the highway, where the asphalt leveled off. But the truck was only about one to two feet away from heading down the ravine. There was nothing I could do. When the truck's passenger-side tires got off the pavement, I don't have a recollection of exactly what happened.

What I do remember is that the truck just came to a complete stop as if I had stepped hard on the brake, but I was convinced that I had not done that on purpose. All I knew was that the tractor and trailer both came to a complete and sudden stop less than a foot away from the right-hand ravine. I was dumbfounded. I did not know how to explain it. Due to the close proximity to the ravine, I waited a moment to make sure the ground didn't shift under the truck. The vehicle had stopped awkwardly with the trailer still on the slippery pavement and the tractor a few inches from the ravine. All of that brought back the memory of when Jacob and I had been in a similar situation.

I was processing what had just happened. I looked around myself to make sure that I was indeed still alive. I pinched myself on the arm and on the chest to check whether I felt some pain. I breathed heavily inside my palm to ascertain that air was indeed still coming out of my lungs. Clearly, something had just snatched me out of the jaws of death. Again! I could not believe that the truck had not crashed into the ditch as I'd foreseen it a few moments ago. I cupped my head in the palms of my hands and started saying a prayer of gratitude.

Moments after my truck inexplicably—miraculously—halted at the very edge of the ditch, a police officer in his patrol car pulled up next to me and motioned for me to roll down my window.

"Is everything all right?" he asked me. I looked to my right, gazed at the ditch for a moment before looking at the officer, and then replied, "Yes, sir!" The officer looked at me, shook his head in disbelief, and then proceeded on his way.

The reason why the officer stopped to inquire about my safety was because he'd been behind me the whole time that I was wrestling with the truck to keep it on the road. He'd seen all the wild swaying of the vehicle left and right on the asphalt. He'd probably kept a safe distance behind me to see how everything would pan out. He, too, certainly must have been thinking that the truck was going to go into the ditch. The road's surface was nothing more than a layer of thick, very slippery black ice. The officer had probably seen several crashes that early morning, and no doubt had thought he was about to witness another one. I believe the way my truck had suddenly stopped, less than a foot away from the ravine, had surprised him, too. I incontestably escaped death that day. I was grateful that the angel of death had missed an appointment with me at that moment.

Even after the truck had come to a complete stop, my nerves didn't settle down for a while. The close proximity to the ravine was making me very uncomfortable. I was so uneasy, I could no longer stare at the abyss the way I'd done earlier. I might not be out of the woods yet. I was hauling a fully loaded trailer. I began to pray that the ground underneath the truck did not shift. If it did, the truck would flip over and cascade down to the bottom of the slope.

In an effort to extricate myself from harm's way, I slowly, cautiously, meticulously steered the tractor just a little bit to the left, back onto the icy pavement. Remaining inside the truck, I turned on my CB radio to see if there was any ongoing discussion about road closure in the area. I also tuned the AM radio to a local station in search of news about the weather and road conditions. I didn't hear anything about the specific stretch of highway I was on, but there were warnings about other nearby road closures. I used my CB radio to alert the drivers in the area about the road conditions they should be aware of.

It was around 5:00 in the morning. My delivery was scheduled for 6:00 a.m. After the near-miss misfortune I'd just had, no amount of money would have convinced me to get back on the road and make that delivery. Absolutely no way. I thought at that point that the best thing to do for my safety was to stay inside my truck.

Through my truck's onboard Qualcomm device, I sent a message to my dispatch and let them know that I was not going to make the delivery at the assigned time, and why. As a courtesy, I also called the recipient in Chicago. The person there that I got through to was very kind, advising me not to rush and to just come when I was ready. It was still a bit dark outside. The truck's thermometer was still showing an outdoor temperature way below the freezing point.

I stayed in my truck for about four more hours. At 10:00 a.m., the sun was shining brightly. I had waited that long to resume my trip because I knew that maintenance crews would have deiced the road by then. I was also aware that the authorities had shut down the highway for a while. By the time four hours had passed, I felt confident that it would be safer to drive.

Hardly had I gotten back on the road—I'd gone maybe a mile—when I saw a scene of chaos along the highway.

On both my right and left, I saw ambulances, police cars, paramedics attending to injured people, mangled cars, people being carried on stretchers and gurneys, semitrucks flipped upside down—with tires still spinning—scattered debris from broken taillights, bumpers lying on the pavement. It was mayhem. Part of the scene that particularly caught my attention was a car that I saw almost entirely buried in a pile of snow. The car's position with respect to an exit ramp suggested that it had fallen off the road and nosedived into the heap of snow at the bottom.

I made it to the customer later that morning. I was glad to be alive.

Many of us have had moments in our lives when we've felt defeated and resigned to the fact that we might not survive to see the next day, or the next minute. There are cancer survivors who, at the time of their diagnosis, never would have believed that they would live longer than three months, six months, a year, or whatever the case may be. But against all odds, some do beat cancer and go on to live longer than expected.

When faced with the possibility of a threat or danger to one's life, we go through a lot of emotions. Sometimes we are overcome with fear; sometimes we're surprised. It is not a good feeling to have even a slight thought that you might be put in a casket soon and be buried in a cemetery somewhere. Most of the time, life-changing decisions come out of those near-death circumstances. Over the course of 14 months since I'd started that job, there had been at least three situations when I'd thought the inevitable was coming my way. I escaped all of them, every one. I had been prudent, and also very lucky. But I did not know how much more luck was in store for me. After that scary experience in Indiana, I started seriously thinking about an exit.

The new year of 2009 was around the corner. I was still saving toward school tuition. But I needed to stay on the job for a couple more years to reach that goal. I started making resolutions, setting my exit strategy in motion. I decided to shorten the three-year period that I'd initially intended to work on that job before returning to school.

CHAPTER 17

Preparation for the
Next Chapter after Trucking

For years, I had not been comfortable with the prospect of returning to college and starting from scratch as if I were straight out of high school. I had gone through the exercise of degree equivalency and validation of academic course work from abroad, and I had not been satisfied with the result. Meanwhile, I'd had plenty of time to think about a degree program that would fit me best and that I would need to pursue. One way or another, as we were entering a new year, I decided that it would be my last as a professional truck driver.

The way I saw it, when it came to my future career, I was at a fork in the road: I could take the scholarly turn and return to college, or I could veer another direction and start a business of my own. Each route had its appeal.

Having always had strong aptitudes for the sciences, mathematics, and all things computer and electronics related, I knew that a degree in electrical engineering would be a good fit.

I began visiting several universities' websites to investigate their curricula. Since I had always wanted to go to MIT, I started with its site and was pleased with the content of the electrical engineering curriculum at that iconic school. From there, I moved on to assess other perennially well-ranked institutions, such as Stanford, Caltech (the California Institute of Technology), Princeton University, and the Georgia Institute of Technology. After a few days of research, I was convinced that majoring in electrical engineering not only would bring me satisfaction in terms of my aspirations but would also be relatively easy for me because of my mathematical skills.

To secure enrollment in any school, I was aware that I would have to pass entrance exams. I knew I had to study for them. But how could I study while on the road? The job of a trucker was too demanding. I would have to find time to learn and prepare for those tests. After 8 to 11 hours of driving, I was usually tired. Spending more time in my truck studying would be even more challenging. Nonetheless, I devised a potential study plan, figuring I'd have to set aside at least 2 hours each day to read and prepare.

And yet the idea of starting a business was still on my mind. My savings account had just begun to grow a bit since I'd freed myself from renting an apartment and had put all my belongings in storage. Should I pour my savings into starting a business later, or should I use the money for school? For weeks and months, I'd been torn as to which way to go. It was a dilemma that I needed to resolve.

If I was going to open my own business, I wanted something that could at least rival, and hopefully exceed, the yearly income I was making as a truck driver. There was also a risk associated with becoming a business owner. I was ready to take that risk, but I had no safety net in case the business failed.

As a starting point, I entertained the idea of a franchise. A convenience store, a gas station, or something of that nature seemed best. But even those franchises required down payments that I could barely afford. For some, the deposits would have devoured most of my savings.

The freedom from day-to-day supervision that I enjoyed as a trucker fueled my desire to be my own boss. Even though I still had an employer and had to make my deliveries on time, no one in the company was dictating anything to me.

Of course, there's nothing wrong with working for a company or being an employee. At the end of the day, someone has to work for someone. But the ultimate success comes with owning something. There is a sense of pride and accomplishment that ownership brings.

Still, after much consideration, I decided that returning to school to complete a degree would be the better choice for me. I believed that studying electrical engineering would broaden my knowledge more, open up more opportunities, and pave the way to starting a tech company one day, which was something I had thought about often. After all, this was the degree program I had wanted to enroll in back in my native country, but I hadn't done it because the curriculum there had not appealed to me. Now that I'd found myself where everything I had wanted academically was available, there was no way I would pass up that opportunity.

Attending a school with a nationally or internationally recognized name does look good on a résumé and boosts one's ego for sure, but it is not a guarantee of success. I looked at the state universities in Missouri and was not disappointed with what I found. My home state has excellent schools with very strong engineering programs all around, such as Washington University in St. Louis and the University of Missouri System.

To prepare for the admission test, I had to find a way to study despite my hectic schedule as a truck driver. By that time, it had been more than three years since I had really invested myself in any type of academic studies.

My English and mathematics levels were already good, but I did not want to be too cocky and show up for a test without any preparation. It was early 2009. We had just entered the new year. I had made my decision and carved out my plan. I knew exactly what to do to pass the tests in order to get back into academia. Instead of prematurely quitting my job as a trucker to study for the college entrance tests, I decided to prepare for them while still on the job. I would take along the necessary books and dedicate two hours a day to studying after I'd finished driving.

After a few days of mulling it over, I requested some time off from work to go home to St. Louis and rent a few books from the library near where I used to live. I hadn't decided yet where—to which school—to apply. I was just ready to get started with the preparation.

At the library, I took out SAT, TOEFL, and GRE prep books. I also bought some books at a local Barnes & Noble store. With my truck now filled with test preparation books, the reading of any other book just for pleasure was out of the question. I needed to stay focused and study hard for the admission test. I started with the SAT book and quickly finished it. It was way beneath my level. Over the next few months, I dedicated a lot of time to reading the books, practicing, and testing my own knowledge about what I was learning. For months, I stayed true to my commitment. As time went by, I knew I was doing the right thing by preparing myself. -Given that I was still legally a resident of Missouri, I would be paying in-state tuition fees if I decided to go to any of the University of Missouri System schools. I was on a budget, so staying and studying in Missouri was the best decision I could make.

When I decided to enroll for the fall semester of that year at the universities of my choice, I had missed their deadlines. I did not want to wait longer. I felt I should at least start somewhere.

There was one option available to me that required just some of the documentation I had ready at the time: It was the St. Louis junior college. After a few days of reflection, I grew convinced that enrolling in a junior college for maybe a year or a year and a half would be a good starting point. I could always transfer my course credits later to a four-year college. With my decision made and a clear academic plan mapped out for each of the next four years, I was now ready for the next chapter of my life after trucking.

I scheduled an appointment to take the St. Louis Community College's placement test, which was reputed to be difficult and would require several hours to complete. I already knew what I would be tested on: English and mathematics. In the comfort of my truck, all across the country, I had already read as many SAT, TOEFL, GMAT, and GRE prep books as I could. For the placement test I was scheduled to take, my preparation had been overkill. I had also read and practiced with the additional mathematics books I'd bought, and had even gone a step further and bought a few CDs from The Great Courses. These lessons were some of the best investments I made in preparation for my return to college.

It had really been challenging being a full-time truck driver and studying for the test in my spare time, but as the day of the placement test drew nearer and nearer, I felt more and more confident. Though the exam loomed large, I felt ready.

Having taken time off from my job to be in St. Louis for the test, I reported to the facility ahead of time and was ushered into a room where I would sit alone, face-to-face with a computer. The proctor explained the ground rules. Most were about disqualifying acts or behaviors, and how to request assistance if needed. I agreed to the rules and then was given the green light to start the exam.

The test was indeed similar to the SAT, TOEFL, and GRE—sort of like all of them combined into one. When I'd finished, I was given the option of submitting the test for grading or not. Of course, I chose yes! I left the exam room and sat outside while the test was scored. A few minutes later, the proctor who'd ushered me in earlier emerged to congratulate me and hand me the transcript of all the different sections of the test I had just taken. I had passed them all.

Later, I officially enrolled in classes. My trucking years were coming to an end. I knew it. About two months before school was to start, I called my dispatcher and also sent a message to my driver manager about my impending resignation.

The moment that I informed dispatch and sent a courtesy message to Kirsten,* my driver manager, I knew that there was no going back. I started reliving in my mind everything that had transpired over the past two years on the road. The training, the accident, the brutal winter seasons, the states I'd crossed, the camaraderie among truckers at truck rest areas, the pickups, the deliveries, the interaction I had had with customers all over the country, and, last but not least, the magnitude and beauty of the United States of America, with all its breathtaking sceneries.

My driver manager was very sad, but she was also happy to hear of my decision to return to school. Often, while I was on a trip assignment, Kirsten used to send me messages to inquire about my well-being. She would make sure I was getting enough pickup and delivery appointments so that I could stay busy and keep driving and keep making money. She wished me all the best but asked me to come and see her in person before I

---

*   Some names have been changed.

left. My last assigned delivery was in the Kansas City area. After I made my delivery, I took the truck to the Swift terminal in Kansas City. There, I saw Kirsten one last time. We talked about family, hers and mine, and especially my future plans after trucking. She hugged me, and I held her in a warm and long embrace. I then surrendered the key to the truck. I, too, was a little emotional on my last day as a truck driver for Swift Transportation.

CHAPTER 18

The Long-Overdue Return to School

When I returned to a college campus in the winter of 2009, I felt right about the decision that I had made to study again. With discipline and perseverance, I would graduate in four years. Four years can seem long, but one has to remember that time goes by quickly. Before I enrolled in school, I knew exactly when I would be graduating. Under no circumstance would I take more than four years to complete the degree I was seeking. The only concern I had at the time was my parents' health. For years, my father had been suffering from diabetes, and my mother was often confined to bed due to her own health issues as well. If anything serious were to happen to one of them, I would have no choice but to suspend my studies and return home to take care of things. I had them in my prayers all the time. I prayed for their well-being more than I prayed for my own. In fact, I don't recall praying for my own well-being that much.

I had saved some money when I was a truck driver. After all, that had been one of my primary goals from the outset. I used that money to pay for my education to start. I enrolled in St. Louis Community College in Florissant, Missouri, as a full-time student and saddled myself with the maximum class load that I could possibly take. Being in school as a full-time student, I did not have any other source of income. The money I'd saved from my trucking job was all I could rely on to tide me over for as long as it could. I planned to find a part-time job somewhere eventually. And I made sure to move to an apartment that was not too far from campus.

During the first semester, I was lucky enough to have all my classes in the morning. By 2:00 p.m., I was usually at home. In some of my classes, I was surprised to see not only young students but older ones (midtwenties and up) as well. At first, I'd thought that most of the classrooms would be full of young men and women in their late teens, wearing shorts, T-shirts, and sandals. I was surprised to see students visibly around my age and even older than me.

As months went by, I became comfortable with my schedule and the number of credit hours I was taking. I made a lot of new friends in my first semester. Classmates who turned into friends: something that was not realistic when I was a truck driver.

In my calculus class, I met Dr. Rokhaya Ndao, also known as "Daba." She not only knew her subject very well but also had an excellent teaching method. Her heuristic approach to imparting the concept of every mathematics subject that she taught was like nothing I had experienced before. The in-classroom practice exercises that she selected undoubtedly gave the student an epiphany moment about what the lecture was all about. She was certainly one of the best mathematics teachers I have come across. Personable and approachable, Dr. Ndao was well-liked by many students who at every semester rushed to sign up for her classes. She was always professional in her appearance, and I have to say, her sartorial elegance was something not commonly seen on college campuses.

After a few months, with no other source of income, my savings were dwindling. I had to find a part-time job to bring something in to replenish my bank accounts. In fact, I had begun looking for a part-time job about two months after I'd started school, but I was not finding anything that would fit in around my class schedule. At one point, I stopped looking for a job altogether. Eventually, though, perseverance paid off a few weeks later when I went to a job fair held at the Forest Park campus, not far from my school, to interview for a part-time position with a parcel delivery company. It was a job that fit my student schedule perfectly.

With Dr. Ndao in St. Louis at the Phi Theta Kappa honor society new members' dinner

Even though I was not desperate for it, it was a relief knowing I would be doing something to bring in some income again. With the job in the bag, I now had to find a way to balance both endeavors. I would be going to school in the morning and working in the afternoon. I was a full-time student, so I knew there would be some challenges ahead. But I was ready for it. After I started working, I was able to mesh work and school pretty well. One semester, some of the classes I enrolled in coincided with my work shift in the afternoon; I quickly requested a shift change at work. The company accommodated me, and I was very grateful for that.

Despite spending a lot of hours working after class, I was able to maintain a good enough GPA to make it into the Phi Theta Kappa honor society. The school organized a gala in our honor.

In the spring of 2011, the tutoring center expressed the need for a mathematics and physics tutor, and a faculty member passed my name along as someone knowledgeable enough in both disciplines to tutor in them. I was flattered. Although I already had my part-time job, I decided to apply for the tutoring position. I was doing it not for the money, but for the fulfillment that comes from helping other students demystify math and physics. Hopefully, they would get good grades thanks to my tutoring. That would mean a lot to me.

One of my best memories is of one of the students who was having serious troubles with physics. His challenge was the equations governing the motion of a particle in two and three dimensions. He confessed to me that even though he attended the lessons, he hadn't retained much. I understood what he was going through. His grades hadn't been good thus far, and he told me he was considering dropping the class. The whole concept had just become mysterious to him, and he needed another voice besides the one he heard in his regular class. From the outset, I knew I was going to be doing a lot more than just helping him with his homework. After all, how could he even tackle homework without nailing down concepts and steps for solving physics problems, especially mechanics?

To begin, I took the time to learn personally about him. We swapped life stories and got to know each other better. I wanted to take the strict formality out of our meetings, even though the subject matter about which we met—physics—required academic discipline. He appeared not to be someone who smiled a lot. He was still undecided about what major he would choose. However, the physics class was one that he had to take. He was a bit frustrated, but it was my job to make it easy on him.

My introductory advice was that discipline would make him successful in much of what he would deal with in life, including physics. We took turns defining to each other what the word *discipline* meant. Then I explained to him that in solving a physics problem, a certain set of steps is necessary, and that those steps should become a discipline to follow whenever he was facing a physics problem: (1) identification of the concepts, (2) setup of the problem, (3) execution, and (4) assessment of the result. The result obtained should tell you a story. At this point, you have to pause for a moment and make sense out of the result.

After that, I went through the idealized model steps with him, just to give him a great picture and show him what he needed to be doing next when he grappled with a physics problem. Using visual aids, I explained how to interpret and derive each equation one by one, from the velocity equation all the way to the position equation, under any conditions. We tackled a few basic problems, then worked out more-challenging ones. After just two sessions, I saw immense progress in his understanding of the concepts. He later revealed to me that he had caught up with his lessons and felt very confident every time he stepped in the physics classroom. I had helped impart to him the fundamental concepts and procedures he needed to feel less intimidated by physics. For me, the experience was very fulfilling.

By the end of that semester, I had taken action to transfer to a four-year university where I could complete the degree I was seeking. During my third and last semester at St. Louis Community College, I started applying to schools I wanted to attend. The two out-of-state schools I was interested in were MIT (the Massachusetts Institute of Technology) and the University of Illinois at Urbana-Champaign. Missouri University of Science and Technology was the only in-state school I was interested in, because not only had a previous instructor of mine graduated from there, but also its curriculum catered well to what I wanted. Having taken some classes in Missouri, I assumed that the two out-of-state colleges might not allow me to transfer some of my classes. I was right.

One day I sat down and made a cost comparison among all three schools. My budget didn't allow for out-of-state tuition fees. I still had a little money left to pay for my education, but for affordability's sake, an in-state school was the best option for me. The Missouri University of Science and Technology, also known as Missouri S&T (or MST), was just under two hours from St. Louis. I applied and sent my transcripts to the school.

Still, I had always wanted to go to MIT, or at least the University of Illinois at Urbana-Champaign, which was next door to Missouri. That would require supplemental effort (documents and tests), and the prospect of retaking classes and graduating later than I had planned made a convincing case for me to complete my degree in Missouri. I got an answer to my prayers a few weeks later, when Missouri S&T sent me an acceptance letter for the upcoming school semester. I was thrilled. I would be studying in my home state of Missouri.

CHAPTER 19

The School Years at Missouri S&T

In the summer of 2011, I moved to Rolla, Missouri. By the time the academic year began, I had projected the financial commitment needed for me to stay in school and finish my degree. The part-time job I'd had near the junior college had been just enough to help me cover the rent and buy fuel for my car. When I decided to move from the St. Louis metro area to Rolla, I had to resign from my job with the package delivery company. Rolla is a small town. The university was the largest employer there. Jobs on campus were not that easy to get, and jobs off campus were even more scarce. I knew before going there that I might not find a part-time job opportunity like the one I'd just left. I still had some of the money I'd saved from my trucking days, but there was absolutely no way I could live off those savings alone and cover tuition for the next six or seven semesters.

I stringently budgeted everything over the next two years, and the money was still coming short. The only solution left was the one I had dreaded and spurned for years: student loans. There was no way around it if I was to finish the engineering program in which I'd enrolled. At St. Louis Community College, I'd been able to cover the tuition out of pocket. The circumstances at MST were different. So, I had to adapt. Nevertheless, I would be taking very minimal loans and tapping into my savings once in a while for my rent and other expenses.

When the financial aid that I applied for went to the university to pay for my tuition, there was money left over. The school deposited the surplus in a checking account that I opened for school expenses. The costs that a student faces while in school go far beyond just tuition, which I believe is why the financial aid that students receive is usually more than enough for tuition alone. It makes sense, because a student who lives off campus needs to pay rent and utilities, buy food and books, and either keep a car fueled and maintained or pay for public transportation. Normally—advisedly—the loan money is to be used only for educational purposes, such as tuition, books, and maybe dormitory lodging (room and board), but the lender—be it private or the federal government—does not enforce that. Once the borrower—the student—takes the money, the only thing the lender cares about is that at some point, the borrower will start paying back that money with interest, just like any other loan. That first experience in taking loans to pay for school was an eye-opener. Going forward, I would still have to dip into my personal savings to cover some tuition fees for the sake of reining in student loans.

When thousands of dollars hit your account just like that, the temptation to spend it becomes great. I was not immune to the urge to spend the money. But I knew that if I ever had a money problem, there was absolutely nobody I could turn to for help. I was not like one of those kids from affluent families who knew they could turn to a parent, grandparent, or uncle when they misused their loan money. I had heard of grandparents using their social security money to help their grandchildren. I didn't have that luxury. In any unforeseen circumstance that might arise in the future, I would have to rely on myself 100 percent. I was already a mature person. I was inching toward my late twenties. Could I afford to squander money? Absolutely not!

When I started my first class at the university in Rolla, I was very pleased with the sizes of the classrooms. They were neither too big nor too small. Most had a capacity of 25 to 30 students and usually were not full. Very few of the classrooms were amphitheater-style. The teacher-to-student ratio was very attractive. For that reason, I knew the students would get the opportunity to interact better with the instructors.

I started the autumn semester in August of 2011. I had just settled in Rolla. The following month, with school in full swing, I had another important thing to take care of back in St. Louis: my naturalization ceremony. In the spring of 2011, I had become eligible to apply for citizenship. As soon as I became eligible, I had applied through the US Citizenship and Immigration Services (USCIS) when I was still living in St. Louis. For years, I had looked forward to this. When the time actually came and I knew that I was eligible, there was no point in waiting any longer. It was a process that I knew would take months before I was invited to take the Pledge of Allegiance—a pledge that would make me officially a citizen of the United States.

A few days after submitting my application, I received a learning kit in the mail. The packet comprised a booklet, a CD, and other documents, and a list of questions and answers to help the applicant prepare for the citizenship test. I was impressed by how the US government goes to great lengths to help applicants prepare. In fact, local public libraries also have books and resources on how to study for the US citizenship test. They are worth reading, because they teach certain aspects of the nation's history.

Years before I even became eligible, the very first books I'd read when I'd immigrated to the country were history books. Even though I had known some US history, it was important for me to learn more. For every person who moves to a new country or any society, for that matter, it is extremely important to learn about its history. That way, you understand the culture and the behavior of the people. Most of the time, the people's behavior and the social interaction among them have roots in the nation's history.

Initially, I handpicked the topics I was interested in, such as governing institutions—how the federal judicial system works, how a bill becomes a law, and how the US Senate and House of Representatives and the presidency function. I also read about capitalism, the news media, political parties, and voting laws. (I was shocked to learn that voting is more a privilege than a right.) Another subject that intrigued me was the American Civil War (1861–65). I had overheard a few things about it here and there, but before arriving in the States, I hadn't read any serious material about this war. A book entitled *1863: The Crucial Year* gave me more insight into the genesis of the conflict and what it was all about.

I was already relatively well versed in American politics and history way before I even enrolled in college. Thus, I felt ready for the citizenship test. But I also knew that I didn't know everything. There were things that I needed to learn. So, when I received the immigration test kit in the mail, I started reading it immediately. The questions were not difficult, and the companion CD was very helpful. A few weeks later, I received a letter from the USCIS inviting me to go to its offices in Downtown St. Louis for my citizenship test.

The process was speedy. After a staff person took my picture and fingerprints, I was face-to-face with an immigration officer who asked me a few questions from the questionnaire I'd received in the mail. The officer pulled out my Form N-400 to make sure she was dealing with the right person. Once I had given her all the correct answers, she stopped and handed me a document to sign, and that was it. I'd passed the test. My next appointment would be to show up for the naturalization ceremony.

A few days later, I received in the mail an invitation from the USCIS to attend the ceremony. According to the invitation, the event was scheduled to take place at the United States District Court Eastern District of Missouri in Downtown St. Louis in September. The process of gaining citizenship took four months, from the date I'd submitted my Form N-400 to the date when I took the Oath of Allegiance at the naturalization ceremony.

The event was in September of 2011. I arrived early. We were a total of 55 applicants scheduled that day to take the oath. There was an eclectic mix of applicants coming from every corner of the world: Bosnia and Herzegovina, Germany, India, Jordan, Kuwait, Mexico, Moldova, Nepal, Nigeria, Peru, Poland, Spain, Switzerland, Thailand, Turkey, Ukraine, the United Kingdom, Vietnam.

The ceremony kicked off with a welcome note from the National Park Service, followed by the opening of the court with the deputy clerk, David L. Braun. After his welcoming speech, the vocalist Maribeth McMahon graced us with "America the Beautiful." There was enough noticeable presence during the ceremony to make it feel very official. For instance, the guest speaker was the Honorable Richard B. Teitelman. He was the Chief Justice of the Supreme Court of Missouri. Most of the folks in attendance were accompanied by their friends and family. The International Bible Study instructors from the Fee Fee Baptist Church were in attendance to cheer me on. We were all well dressed to mark the occasion.

As I sat, I was thinking about all the years leading up to that day, from the very first day I'd arrived in the United States through the port of entry of New York, up to that particular day when I was about to take the Oath of Allegiance. I was doing an assessment of where my journey had led me, and of what I could be proud. Even though I knew I still had a lot to accomplish, I was very pleased with the path I was on. I had made an effort to learn the language and much of the culture of the country. I was enrolled in school, and I was on target to complete an engineering program. Summing up the host of things I had already done and was planning to do gave me a sense of belonging and accomplishment. I was pleased.

The official business of the ceremony got under way when we welcomed the presiding judge: the Honorable E. Richard Webber. He ruled favorably on the motion to approve the citizenship applications of all the applicants in attendance. A round of applause ensued. No one was denied. As one would imagine, it was a matter of formality. But there could have been cases in which the presiding judge during a naturalization ceremony had rejected a motion. I have never heard of that happening, though. For us that day, our collective motion to become new citizens was accepted. Afterward, the deputy clerk invited us to stand and take the Pledge of Allegiance. The ceremony concluded with the national anthem and the presentation of certificates of citizenship. Each of us took time to introduce himself/herself to the audience. Soon after the ceremony ended, I rushed back to Rolla.

My first semester of class at MST was not too challenging. Most of my classes were continuations of the basic classes I had taken the semester prior at St. Louis Community College. My Circuit Analysis II class was the one that stuck with me the most. The diversity and depth of the chapters covered reinforced the foundation I had built upon to take on higher-level classes. Circuit Analysis II for me was one of those classes that help the student assess whether he or she can become successful in the field of electrical engineering.

I participated in a group project with two other classmates in which we had to do some research about a particular form of renewable energy and explain thoroughly how it works and how it can be deployed. We were assigned to do research on wind energy.

The project for us was appropriate. It was one of the best learning experiences I have had. Before working on this project about renewable energy, it had not been something to which I'd paid much attention. Of course, I knew that those technologies were out there, but I had always thought of the most popular and traditional ways to deliver power. While I was working on that project, I realized that renewable sources of power—solar, geothermal, wind, biofuels—were definitely the way to go for a cleaner environment. I explored a little bit of each of them during our project, but given that our assignment was wind-focused, that was where we spent most of our research. Personally, I was intrigued by solar energy.

What appealed to me about it was not just the opportunity to harness energy from the sun, but also the physics that make it possible. Physics had always been one of my favorite subjects in school. So, when I decided to explore solar energy more to better understand it, I quickly realized that I was venturing into a territory in physics known as quantum mechanics. The basic knowledge that one needs in order to understand photovoltaic (PV) cells doesn't go beyond an introductory class in electricity. However, a designer of a solar cell, or the manufacturer of PV devices, must have a grasp of the laws of physics that make creating a PV a reality. My research took me back to 1887, when the German physicist Heinrich Hertz discovered the photoelectric effect. But it was Albert Einstein who conducted a thorough study of the subject in the early 20th century.

One essential characteristic of solar panels is that they are all tilted to face the sun. The angle has to be such that the top surface of the panel receives the maximum amount of radiation, or wave energy. An incorrect tilt could reduce the panel's efficiency. So the panel's designer has to calculate its slant so that the panel is perpendicular to the Poynting vector (named after the English physicist Henry Poynting, who introduced the concept in 1884). The Poynting vector,

$$S = \frac{1}{\mu_0} E \times B$$

is a physics quantity of which the magnitude is expressed in watts per square meter.

Several industrialized nations around the world are already producing part of their electricity from renewable energy sources. Fossil fuels will still be around for a long time, but the demand for them will decrease over time. Harnessing the force of nature for the production of energy is no longer something that we can afford to neglect or belittle. The investment in alternative energy has gained steam over the past few years. There are even some cities across the world that have challenged themselves to convert to 100 percent renewable energy to power homes and businesses. These are efforts that merit support, but it is important that they enjoy favorable policies at the local, state, and federal levels in every country in the world.

Classroom projects are a formidable method of prodding students to do research and learn by themselves. In my circuit analysis class, renewable energy was not one of the subjects that we were to cover during that semester. But the instructors knew that there were some among us who would probably specialize in power engineering. Also, the project for each of us was a way to apply the electrical circuit concept we had learned in class. It was like a hands-on experience so that we could see how the theory and the ideas that we had learned in class applied in real life.

Standing at the entrance hall of Missouri S&T's
Department of Electrical and Computer Engineering

Electrical engineering, just like medicine, has several branches. A student pursuing a degree in electrical engineering can later focus on optics, electronics, telecommunications, radio frequencies (RF), computer system design, power engineering, or electromagnetics. During my first semester at Missouri S&T, I hadn't yet decided which branch would be my focus. I had many more semesters ahead. So I knew that as time went on, I'd gain more information to help me make my decision.

That said, I was leaning toward electronics. I had developed a passion for the subject when I was little. Because my father bought and sold electronics components, I knew the names and functions of some of those parts even before I entered junior high school. Moreover, the design side of engineering was the area that I wanted to go into; for instance, how to go from the conception of a device all the way to assembling the parts that go into it. But I still had to take other classes before ultimately deciding. As the semester was winding down, registration for the next semester's classes opened. I selected my courses and went to see my advisor, Professor Moss, to discuss them. I had the prerequisites for all the classes I'd chosen.

Of those classes, the one in electromagnetics has remained one of the most challenging and eye-opening classes I have ever taken. It's challenging because of the myriad of nonintuitive, abstract, and bizarre concepts and arcane mathematical equations that might drive an already mathematically challenged person to dementia. And eye-opening because it was a class designed to make the student better understand circuit-analysis theory, as well as how the world around us works.

I was very pleased with the way my first semester at MST had gone. I had made new friends, I had learned new skills, and the classes I'd taken had broadened my knowledge. I was pleased with the move to Rolla that I'd made to attend school. At the end of my first semester, we went on Christmas break. The next semester wouldn't begin for another month, but I had to be ready by then, by all means.

I knew what I had to do: start reading the books that would be part of the upcoming semester's course work and reinforce my knowledge of the prerequisite subjects for those lectures. The Engineering

Electromagnetics class was one that I knew I had to brace for, given the myriad of abstractions that its course content dealt with.

When the semester started, with Rolla gaining back its temporary residents, I was prepared. I had spent only three days off in St. Louis in late December and had quickly returned to Rolla as soon as Christmas was over.

The spring semester started very well. Most of the instructors shared their syllabi with us and got down to business. One instructor in particular, Professor Cheng-Hsiao Wu, welcomed us to his class—Engineering Electromagnetics—and wished us much success with the semester. Professor Wu is a graduate of the University of Rochester, where he earned his PhD in the early 1970s. He clearly warned us from the beginning that the class he would be teaching over the next five months would probably be one of the most challenging and difficult classes we had ever taken. He advised each of us to be very attentive and diligent, and to ask as many questions as we needed to when a concept didn't make sense to us. The reward for paying attention and doing well, as he put it, was that the class would give us an epiphany and sharpen our minds to develop more discernment and understanding of not only circuit analysis but also most other subjects in the realm of electrical engineering.

Solving a microelectronics problem

Now that we'd gotten the message, all we had to do was rise to the challenge. I really appreciated that Professor Wu was forthright about the material he would be teaching us. The classroom was almost full at the beginning of the semester. I would estimate that there were forty or fifty of us. But as weeks went by, the class size dwindled to the point where, if I'm not mistaken, there were fewer than ten students by the semester's end. Where did everyone go? Well, clearly, the majority dropped out of the class. It was predictable but also shocking that many students just stopped coming for some reason. To be honest, the reason for the exodus was not that hard to guess. The class did live up to its challenge. It was like being fired upon from all corners. For me, self-discipline was the key. As Professor Wu was going through the lessons, I was attentive and also had to make several consultation appointments with him in his office outside of class for a better one-on-one discussion of certain concepts. I had very good engineering discussions with Professor Wu, especially ideas pertaining to the transmission of wireless power.

Our conversation on charging cell phones wirelessly was one of those discussions between instructor and student that I have missed the most in the years since college. Some of the concepts that I learned from that class opened my mind to the possibilities that are out there when it comes to radio waves' power-carrying capabilities, for example.

The fact that our cell phones lose battery power and we have to find a power outlet to recharge them is something that I have always found frustrating. The course material of the electromagnetics class gave insight into alternative ways to power our devices wirelessly.

My desire to go into design engineering grew stronger as we progressed through the semester. There is no shortage of ingenuity, but not all ideas are convenient or easily implementable. Dr. Wu's class opened my mind to thinking outside the box. In fact, it's a critical trait to have for someone looking to go into designing electrical circuits. One of the thoughts I had was that we, as humans, are bombarded with radio waves everywhere—inside our homes and out. Everywhere. It would be great to harvest all those tiny "flying powers," amplify them and reuse them for other purposes. I soon realized the challenge that would arise in the design of an antenna and amplifier that would make that a reality. Exploring engineering ideas does give a person "wings." Sometimes you think about an idea, only to realize that someone else already thought about it years or even centuries ago. Nikola Tesla was one of the great minds I just want to salute en passant.

My most memorable moment in Professor Wu's Engineering Electromagnetics class was when one of the students, who was Chinese, asked the instructor if he could clarify in the Chinese language the concept he was explaining. Upon such an unusual request in a class taught in English in an American classroom, there was a deafening silence in the classroom. As a matter of fact, Dr. Wu himself is of Chinese descent. Obviously, being an instructor at a US university, he delivers his lectures in English. This particular student believed that sharing a mother tongue with the instructor gave her the right to ask him to explain the lesson to her in a language other than English, in the presence of all of us. Dr. Wu did not honor her request. What he did instead was slowly go over the same concept several times. When he first explained it, I did not fully understand it, either. But, when he expounded on it again and again, I finally wrapped my mind around the abstraction.

That day's lesson was about the Smith Chart and how it is used in the design of transmission lines and antennae. A Smith Chart is a graphic mathematical tool used mostly by radio frequency/microwave engineers to solve problems related to matching circuits, transmission lines, and waveguides. The treatment of the mathematical set of equations that govern the Smith Chart is a feat in itself, and also a beautiful sight to behold.

Throughout the lesson, the classmate I've mentioned struggled a bit as she asked Professor Wu other questions that suggested that she still was not out of the woods. The instructor, as he always did, invited and welcomed to his office those who might need one-on-one attention. It could be that Dr. Wu honored her request to explain the concept to her in Chinese when she went to see him in his office outside of regular classroom time. There is nothing wrong with that. The student and her sister were among the ones who had been steadfast enough to stay until the end of the semester to finish the class. We had earned each other's respect by the semester's end.

Amidst the excitement, the challenge, and everything else that was going on academically that term, the specter of my not finishing the semester was looming over me. Beginning in about the middle of the semester, I started receiving text messages and phone calls about my mother's degrading health conditions that made me very anxious.

She was more than 6,000 miles away. It was not like I could just hop in my car and drive to see her in the next town or city. The only thing I could do at the time was to support her to the best of my abilities from afar and hope that she recovered. I prayed a lot during those difficult weeks as I was receiving updates about her health. Because I am her firstborn and her only son, the weight of responsibility for support and decision making fell automatically on me. Even though my father was still around, I was expected to make my presence felt, even from thousands of miles away.

My prayer at the time was that if anything bad were to happen to her to the point where all hope was lost, it would happen after my semester was finished. Dropping out of all classes in the middle of the semester for family reasons is not something any student would want to go through. Dropping classes after the deadline for doing so has passed is even more serious, especially in light of how it would look on one's transcript. In addition, if it came to that, I would be graduating at least a semester later than my targeted graduation date. With no way of knowing how things might pan out as far as my mother's health was concerned, I resorted to prayer and meditation.

Drawing from what I had read in the book *The Secret* about three years before, I filled my mind with positive thinking in an effort to emit as much positive vibration and energy into the universe as I could. One meditation exercise I did was to picture my mother in good health, as though she had never felt ill before. I pictured her smiling, singing, and dancing with joy. I imagined her doing all the good things that she liked to do. Positive thinking carries a lot of weight and eases our stress. In addition to meditating, I fasted and prayed, hoping that her failing health would soon improve.

In the middle of my mother's health issues thousands of miles away and my own efforts to focus on and navigate through the challenge that my course work in school presented, meditation also certainly helped me concentrate on my academic duties. And soon after I plunged myself into prayers and meditation, I started getting promising news about my mother's health. I was thankful that the treatment she was receiving was having positive results. As always, she would tell me over the phone not to worry too much about her. She always promised she would recover and get back on her feet soon.

After a few days of intensive medical treatment, my mother regained her health, to my delight. It was around the same time that I was preparing for the semester's final exams. The news of her recovery definitely gave me a huge mental boost and allowed me to focus more on preparing for the tests. That semester turned out to be one of my most successful.

Three weeks after the spring semester finished, I was already on my way to Texas A&M University in College Station, Texas, where I'd been selected to participate in a summer research experience for undergraduates. Sponsored by the National Science Foundation (NSF), it was a 10-week program that brought in students from all over the country. It felt quite special to be among a select group of students who had shown brilliance in their respective schools.

A day marking the end of the research experience at Texas A&M was set aside for a symposium poster and presentation. All of us participated, and we had to explain what we'd done before a jury of faculty members. Among more than 200 students, three who were deemed to have created the most outstanding posters were recognized and awarded prizes. My poster didn't make the top three, but I finished the research experience and left Texas that summer with very good memories and an invaluable learning experience.

A year before my graduation, as was required of all of us, I focused on my senior design project. As its name suggests, a senior design project is a design endeavor undertaken by a group of students that allows them to apply in real life the academic concepts they have learned in the classroom. Students are encouraged to come up with novel ideas or work on the improvement of an existing project. It is an opportunity for students to show their creativity. During my senior year, the design group that I was part of spent the penultimate semester brainstorming. Each of us in our group of four was tasked to come up with an idea for a project that we could work on together.

Thanks to the design project, I was able to take the formulae that I had learned in the classroom and apply them to designing something that could be used in real life. I knew that once I started applying for jobs later, this would be something that I could put on my résumé and leverage during job interviews. I wanted to become a designer of circuits in my field of engineering. Our senior project was to be like a debut for me in the field that I wanted to go into, and therefore, I had to invest my all in it. We called our project the Flood Warning Device. It was the effort of a very dedicated group of classmates: Danny, Daniel, John, and myself, with the input of our advisor, Dr. Kosbar.

At the Gamma Theta induction ceremony at Missouri S&T

In the design's executive summary, we stated that the purpose of the Flood Warning Device was to indicate potentially dangerous water levels that could cause structures to become flooded. We added that the project would be modeled to operate on a bridge that was constructed above a stream or river. For our system to complete its intended task, we outlined three important stages: (1) The system must indicate and process water-level status a certain number of times per day. (2) Then, the system would transmit the water-level status signal within an unlicensed frequency band, and (3) the system would operate all its devices from a self-sustaining power supply, to ideally provide a maintenance-free apparatus. The advancement of electronics in communication systems has given marvelous power to the Global Positioning System (GPS). Our project was conceived primarily for rural areas where some GPS devices cannot determine flood status. In a nutshell, the Flood Warning Device can determine if the water level below a bridge is approaching flood levels, and then send a warning signal to a distant location so that early warning actions can be made. The project was a very good learning experience for me.

Before our final semester officially ended—a few days before the graduation ceremony—two of my group members had already had job offers. I did not have a job offer going into graduation. A few weeks earlier, I had declined an offer I'd received. In fact, Missouri S&T does a good job of inviting employers on campus to recruit students. At least twice per semester, several companies came on campus to interview students and hire some of them. During my senior year, I signed up for one of these events. Dressed in business attire, several of us from the school went to meet the headhunters there. Of all the companies present, two of them in particular caught my attention, given the field in which they operated: aerospace and defense.

I could have majored in aerospace engineering, but I purposely chose electrical engineering because I knew that it would give me more skills to attain my goal of becoming a design engineer. At the hiring event a few months before my graduation was scheduled, I spoke very briefly to a few recruiters, but only two of them had my attention. One was recruiting for its office in a small town in Alabama, and the other was seeking personnel for its facility in Hawthorne, California. The latter was SpaceX.

California was one of those states I had always entertained living in, but I would do it only if the conditions were right. That Hawthorne was in the Los Angeles area sounded good, but the picture of housing affordability and cost of living there were not enticing to me, especially for someone who would be getting an entry-level job. Moreover, by my own assessment, the position that the company was hiring for was a good fit for me, but not a great fit. But I kept my options open to consider it later.

The auditorium that was hosting the recruiting event was very crowded that day. Some of the recruiters had students in line waiting to speak to them and hand them their résumés. The line waiting to speak to recruiters from SpaceX, for instance, was the longest I saw during the event. I guess a lot of students were interested in being part of the marvels and the mission that SpaceX founder Elon Musk had been working toward. Elon Musk is one of the entrepreneurs I have come to admire and respect for their ambitions.

The job offered by the other company that I was interested in sounded very good to me and was in fact what I had wanted. My conversation with the recruiter went very well. It all seemed good, but there was one hitch: I had already made a list of my preferred states, least preferred states, and do-not-consider states in which to live. Alabama was one of the states on my do-not-consider list. As much as I valued the opportunity to land a job that I wanted, I was not too eager to live and work in that part of the country. The company's recruiter corresponded with me for a few days after the interview and eventually sent me a formal offer of the position, but after much reflection, I decided to turn it down. My preferences were states on the coasts, followed by some states in the Midwest, and finally a few select states in the southern parts of the United States.

As an OTR truck driver years before, I'd had the privilege of seeing the country from north to south and from east to west and had developed an affinity for some areas more than others, based on geography, economy, and culture. Affordable housing, cultural landscape, education, school system, and crime rate were the determinants to which I gave heavy weight in choosing what part of the country I could comfortably settle in. Wherever I would be working, I assumed there would be a chance to set down roots and raise a family if I was blessed with the opportunity. I value my human dignity, and clearly I wouldn't be happy about living and raising my family in an environment with a high crime rate or where my loved ones and I might not be welcome because of the historically entrenched or rising clannishness—with its tentacles of intolerance or what have you—associated with that place. There are not many places in the US that are immune to some of these situations and demeaning deeds, but at least I could make an informed decision about where I would be taking my talents and where I would be living. The country is big. There is no shortage of where to live, and I was glad to have a plethora of options.

I am also an optimistic person. I do not live my life meeting trouble halfway. I am of the belief that keeping a positive mind-set, being optimistic regarding, and not clouding one's thoughts with the woes that life brings are good for sound mental health and overall well-being. That being said, I was also not naive to the fact that I was not living in a fantasy world. We live in a society with certain realities. In some states, there are public places with the Confederate flag still flying high, and counties where minorities, especially black Americans, are literally excluded from jury duty. It is a practice that is rampant across most of the Southern states, but in many other areas as well, even the ones that have forged the perception to be liberal and progressive. As a person who has a live-and-let-live attitude vis-à-vis my fellow human beings and who is also forward-thinking, why would I choose of my own volition to live in a place that fears acceptance or that is hostile to change? The Civil Rights Act of 1875 banned racial discrimination in jury selection, but despite that, the practice in the justice system—at least in some states—has never ceased. In 2011, when I was still in school, there was a class action lawsuit brought forth in Alabama pertaining to discriminatory practices in jury selection in several counties. I followed the story, and I was nauseated by the claims and evidence produced by the plaintiffs. The narrative surrounding the case undoubtedly put a damper on my considering relocating there. Most of the time, attorneys prefer all-white juries. This kind of biased jury selection is a cowardly tactic employed by some lawyers (probably endorsed by their communities) who use their position as a leverage to do so. It is nothing short of psychological warfare against non-whites living in those counties. The ramification of this kind of prejudice, its origin and all that it's begotten have been touched on by the author Michelle Alexander in her book, *The New Jim Crow: Mass Incarceration in the Age of Colorblindness*. Counties where those discriminatory practices—though unconstitutional—are practiced routinely by the very same officials who are to enforce the law might not be good places for minority groups to live.

This creates a dehumanizing climate that reaches into every nook and cranny of people's lives. I can only imagine how degrading that must be to receive a summons for jury duty in the mail knowing beforehand that ultimately, you will not be chosen to serve just because you are deemed a person of color. However, in a civilized society, those aggrieved by these regressive practices can always muster their voices as one to challenge that type of systemic discrimination. My citizenship might fall short of the eligibility to run for the presidency of the United States, but the least what I should expect is to be given a chance to serve on a jury in any county, city or state if I meet the legal requirements.

When I think of a man like me living in one of those areas of the country, I wonder what his quality of life might be and how he might fare if he were ever to become a defendant or even a plaintiff in any court case, civil or criminal. Either way, that individual won't likely benefit from an equity in justice. The wheels of justice will probably turn differently for him, and he will in all likelihood be at the receiving end of a biased judgment and the most draconian punitive measures possible. These are things that can be very depressing and unnerving to people, and when housing discrimination is thrown into the mix, it becomes even more infuriating. Fortunately, the past few years have ushered in the passage of a wave of equal opportunity housing laws that have made the latter less blatant than it once was.

Although declining the position in that city in Alabama meant that I went to graduation without a guaranteed job offer, I was not concerned at all. I was convinced that I would find something soon.

A few weeks after the job fair, my graduation day arrived. Several of my friends attended, having made the trip all the way from St. Louis to Rolla. I looked back and reflected on the journey I had embarked on a few years before. The time had gone by so fast. I had completed everything on schedule, exactly as I had set out to do. I was proud of myself that day, and I had already set my sights on more challenges ahead. I had just closed a chapter and was ready to begin a new one.

CHAPTER 20

The Career Begins

Two weeks after my graduation, I got the type of call I was waiting for. It was from a communication systems company headquartered in Alburnett, Iowa, a city located a few miles north of Cedar Rapids. I was in my apartment in Rolla when I received the phone call. It was a phone screening, and it went technical very quickly. I liked that, because the company wanted to make sure I had the knowledge that I claimed to have and had put on my résumé. My conversation with the recruiter was a bit long. But before hanging up, the recruiter asked if I would be open to going to Alburnett for a face-to-face interview. My answer was an unambiguous yes.

Thus far, I had turned down a few job opportunities because either they were not in the sector I wanted, or they were not in one of my preferred geographic locations. Iowa is immediately north of Missouri. It was not on my list of preferred destinations, but it wasn't on my do-not-consider list, either. I'd grown familiar with the state in some respects during my trucking days. It was not a place known for some of the things that I look down upon, and the folks I'd met there years before had seemed to be polite and hardworking, welcoming, and minding their own business. The state has an excellent school system. It is evidently not a very ethnically diverse place, but that didn't bother me at all. I knew I could take a chance living and working there as opposed to some of the parts of the country that I had put on my do-not-consider list. So, for me, the idea of going to work and live in Iowa was appealing. I was open to that new phase of my life if the company that was bringing me in for the interview decided to hire me.

During the phone screening, the recruiter asked me to prepare a PowerPoint presentation about myself before coming to the interview. That was how I would be introducing myself that day. I found the idea very original and intriguing. The following day, the company e-mailed me information about my plane ticket from St. Louis to Cedar Rapids. As a matter of fact, they sent me a full package: airfare, hotel, and a rental car. In addition, the company offered to reimburse me for fuel and food expenses incurred during my two-day stay there. It is not uncommon for companies to do that to attract talent, but for me at the time, it was unbelievable.

At that time of year, Rolla was almost empty. The semester had ended about three weeks ago, and most of the students had left town. I started putting together a PowerPoint presentation about myself, as the recruiter had asked. As I had done before in anticipation of job interviews, I also did some research into the company and its products and services. By the day of my departure for the interview, I had finished creating my PowerPoint introduction. I was ready to go.

My flight put me in Cedar Rapids at about 3:30 p.m. Once there, I picked up my rental car, and off to my hotel I went. It had snowed the night before. The sky looked gray.

My interview was scheduled for 8:00 the next morning. Before the interview, I was expected to have breakfast at my hotel with the company's appointed ambassador. Yes, the company put at my disposal someone who would be there to answer any questions I might have about the city of Alburnett and its surroundings. The ambassador was an Alburnett resident who obviously knew the area very well. She was there to give me some historic facts about the city and fill me in on matters like housing, schools, and leisure activities.

At around 6:30 a.m., I met with the ambassador, Susan Cooper,* a woman in her mid-, maybe late fifties. When I first caught a glimpse of her in the breakfast room adjacent to the hotel lobby, I knew that it was she. Professionally dressed and well coiffed, she was wearing a pearl necklace and had a warm smile on her face. I felt like a VIP. She also knew as soon as she saw me that I was the one she was expecting to meet there.

After we introduced ourselves and sat down, Susan handed me a welcome package that held a stack of thick brochures. Inside, there was information about the seasons, sporting activities, tourist sites in Iowa, and upcoming events. While we were eating, she gave me a brief history lesson about the company she represented and spoke to me about the state taxes and a host of other things. It was an interesting conversation, and I enjoyed talking to her and learning more about the company and the state as well.

After more than an hour there in the breakfast room, it was time for me to report for my interview. When I arrived at the company's facility, Clayton Stone,* one of the hiring managers, was there at the entrance door to greet me and usher me to a small conference room. By 8:10 a.m., the conference room was full. I had plugged my flash drive into the computer on the conference room table and had my presentation open and ready to go. The interviewers took time to introduce themselves to me one by one, then turned the floor over to me to introduce myself. The PowerPoint presentation I had prepared contained about 12 slides. In it, I covered my previous work experience as a semitruck driver, my work as a mathematics and physics tutor, my summer internship, my years in school, my hobbies, my senior design project in school, and lastly my knowledge about the job I was being interviewed for. The presentation went well, by my own estimation and the overall impression and vibe inside the room.

During the presentation, I fielded a lot of questions, especially pertaining to my role in my senior design project. I answered all the questions; I was on top of it. What stood out to me the most that day was

---

*   Some names have been changed.

that the interviewers had many questions for me about the last slide of my presentation: the slide pertaining to the area of radio frequency (RF) engineering. I talked a little about filters, receivers, and transmitters in general. The presentation was well received, and I got nods of approval. It was a good feeling. My presentation lasted about an hour. Afterward, some of the interviewers left the room, and I remained with only two of them. That was when I sensed that the rest of the interview would be very technical. To be honest, that was what I had always wanted: to be tested on knowledge about the job for which I was applying.

In the conference room, there was a whiteboard on the wall. One of the two interviewers stood up and drew a circuit diagram on the board as he talked to me about a common design problem relating to power amplifiers, and then handed the marker to me and asked me to describe how I would solve that type of problem.

First, I explained to them how to approach the problem given the unknown variables. Then I wrote down a set of equations and formulas that could be used. (Recalling my third-grade experience at a classroom chalkboard, the reader may be relieved to know that I did not count on my fingers on this occasion.) My answer went over well. What stood out to me the most was how deep they wanted me to explain—at the atomic level—the functioning of both the bipolar junction transistor (BJT) and the metal-oxide-semiconductor field-effect transistor (MOSFET), their practical applications, and how they can be put together to perform specific electronic tasks in the realm of high radio frequencies. The microprocessor in your computer, the memory chip that you carry around are made of MOSFET. With the marker still held tight between my fingers, I elucidated all the concept and step on which both men wanted me to focus. Several other questions about electronics theories and problem-solving principles and skills ensued. I satisfactorily answered all the questions one by one. I was very pleased with my performance thus far.

I spent about 45 to 50 minutes with the pair of interviewers. They thanked me for my time, and I thanked them, too, for taking the time to interview me. After both men left, I remained in the conference room

alone for about 5 minutes, and then another pair of interviewers, Glenn*
and Clarence,* came in. They were part of the group that had attended
my presentation earlier. They reintroduced themselves to me. My time
with these two men, I believe, was the most testing. I spent more than
an hour with the pair. Their questions spanned three areas of electrical
engineering: circuit analysis, microelectronics, and control systems.

They kicked off their series of questions with a few meant to gauge
my understanding of the functionality of an operational amplifier in a
circuit. An operational amplifier (also known as an op amp) is an integrated circuit that functions as a voltage amplifier. It is characterized by
a high-input impedance (infinite resistance) and low-output resistance.
Its use is widespread in devices for instrumentation or measuring tools
such as digital multimeters, headphones, calculators, and televisions.
Clarence drew a circuit on the board with an op amp included and
invited me to derive a mathematical expression of the output voltage in
terms of other components in the circuit. It was not that difficult a problem to solve. In fact, it was beneath me. I explained to them the function
of the circuit, and then I proceeded to write equations that would solve
the output voltage problem. It took me just a few seconds to give them
the answer.

Given the rapidity with which I had dispatched that problem, the least
I could expect was to receive a more challenging one. And that was what
happened. Clarence modified the circuit a bit and asked me to solve the
problem with the new parameters. To me, it didn't matter how much the
problem was reformulated or how much the electronic circuit was al-
tered or tweaked. I'd been taught in school the steps to follow in order to
successfully solve problems like that. I was well trained and proud of my
alma mater, Missouri University of Science and Technology.

As I looked at the circuit in its new configuration, I knew the type
of application for which it could be used. The new exercise took me a
little longer to complete, but in the end, I did solve it. Both Clarence
and Glenn congratulated me. They were convinced that I knew my way

---

*   Some names have been changed.

around solving a circuit problem. No sooner had they given me a nod of approval than they segued into the branch of control systems. Their knowledge-check questions tapered off after the latter.

We started discussing topics related to the work that they were currently doing, as if I were already their colleague. Before they left the room, as their allocated time was running out, they started asking me behavioral and routine questions like why I had applied for the job. They concluded the interview, wished me good luck, and asked me to stay behind in the room once more to wait for another set of interviewers.

Thus far, I was enjoying the process. It was a job interview like I had never done before. To be quite honest, I had had the feeling that I would be asked a few questions here and there about my knowledge, but I was not expecting that level of rigor. I embraced that style of job interview wholeheartedly. Given that the pair left the room wishing me well, I realized that I would probably be facing each one of the engineers who had attended my PowerPoint presentation.

I was mulling over what had happened so far when another pair of interviewers walked in. I recognized one of them as part of the group that had been in the room for my introductory program. His name was Thomas.* The theme of this next round of questions was data link, a term used in telecommunications to refer to ways in which two or more distant locations can be connected to each other. The goal for such connections is the safe transmission of digital data from one point to another. For example, an aircraft in the air needs to send information not only to the airport control tower, but also to the airline company under which the craft operates. That information can be radar communication, aircraft black box information, aircraft location, and transmission of data and information between two buildings. My knowledge about the functioning of antennae and radar was put to the test.

During the interview with both men—Thomas and his assistant—their questions necessitated that I draw some diagrams on the whiteboard in order to demonstrate my knowledge of telecommunications. After about

---

* Some names have been changed.

20 minutes answering those questions, the men invited me to sit down. The next round of questions was more of a discussion of ideas.

We talked mostly about radar—its design and function, and a host of other topics. The radar class that I had taken in school and the radar altimeter design I had participated in had given me the nomenclature and the ease to answer their questions as they were expecting.

Before Thomas and his assistant left, Thomas informed me that somebody would be coming shortly to pick me up for lunch. Having sustained three consecutive rounds of interview sessions, I did deserve a lunch break. While waiting for the next person to enter the room, I reflected on how I'd performed. There were some questions that I thought I could have expounded on better. Even though all the interviewers I'd faced that morning had told me they liked my answers to their questions, I still had a slight doubt in my mind. Could it be that they'd said that just to be kind and diplomatic? Anyway, I was their guest that day for an interview. I felt welcome, I was treated well, and the preparation and interview process as a whole had been a valuable experience. For me, that was all that mattered.

I was munching on my thoughts when the manager who'd first welcomed me when I'd arrived earlier that morning, Mr. Stone, entered the room. He invited me to grab my winter coat and come with him to lunch. He thanked me for my patience. I replied that it was an honor for me to be invited for an interview in the first place. There were probably dozens or maybe hundreds of other applicants for the same job. Being invited for an interview meant a lot to me. I was thankful for that.

After lunch, Mr. Stone took me on a tour of the company. I visited a few offices, and he introduced me to some other engineers. I took the opportunity to ask him more questions about the company. Later, we returned to his office, where we discussed further the job I was applying for and the projects I could be involved in if I were to be the one selected for the position. At that point, I sensed that I had one foot inside the company; I felt close to being hired.

I left Alburnett later that afternoon very confident. I was not persuaded I would be called back with a job offer, but I knew I had done the best I could during the interview. At home in Rolla, I spent the next two days not even trying to apply for another job. By then, I had submitted several applications already. Four days after my interview, I received a call from the company in Alburnett. The recruiting managers believed that I was the right candidate for the job. I was offered the position. I was very pleased with the news. I had just landed my first job right out of college. I felt triumphant. The human resources person who phoned me with the news gave me an offer and asked me when I would be ready to start. I requested two weeks so that I could get my things in order.

There are very few moments in our lives that we can reflect upon and say to ourselves that we are proud of what we did. Just a few years before, I had been living like a nomad—a truck driver—going from city to city, state to state, not knowing exactly where I would have dinner or where I would sleep. Years earlier, I'd been hesitant to start school over again at the freshman level when my credits wouldn't transfer. When I was laid off, I'd decided to become a truck driver for the sake of job security so that I could save money for school. I had studied for college entrance exams wherever my truck and I landed, and I'd set the goal of returning to school to complete the type of degree I had always wanted. And now I was a new graduate with a decent job offer in a tech company with a position as a radio frequencies (RF) design engineer.

To me, that was success, and I was looking forward to this new chapter in my life up in Alburnett.

CHAPTER 21

A New Beginning

Soon after accepting the job offer, I moved to Alburnett. I had already made arrangements for housing. My belongings in tow, I drove from Rolla—approximately a six-hour journey—and arrived four days before my job was to start. I felt enthusiastic about this new venture. But it was a bittersweet moment, because I knew that I would have less opportunity to see Rebecca,* whom I had been dating for two years in Rolla. One month before our graduation, she got an outstanding job offer from a pharmaceutical company in Massachusetts. My attempts to secure a position in or near Boston were not successful. Though we both were happy about my job offer in Iowa, we knew that it might complicate things, especially given that Rebecca had mentioned several times that she loved the East Coast and not so much anywhere else.

My first day on the job began with a five-hour orientation session, at the end of which Mr. Stone, Clarence, and Thomas came to welcome me. I was excited to be there. I soon realized that I would be joining Stone's team of engineers. At the plant, Clarence, with whom I would later work on a few projects, ushered me to my new cubicle. Given that there were many projects being worked on, it didn't take long for Mr.

---

* Some names have been changed.

Stone to assign me one. He gave me ample time to conduct my own research as needed, and we agreed that I would give him periodic updates on my progress. My assignment was part of a bigger design project under way, so I had to interact a lot with other engineers to meet our deadlines.

Adjusting to my new life in Alburnett was a bit challenging at first, because I didn't know anyone. But I quickly made new friends. Most of them were colleagues with whom I developed friendships. In the area where I lived, there was not much to do.

I have always liked contributing to my community and doing things to make me feel more part of it. I started attending local churches in Alburnett. I was born and raised in the Catholic faith, but on Sundays, it did not matter to me at all to which church denomination I went. I attended nondenominational churches, Baptist, Lutheran, Latter-Day Saints. Most of the churches that I went to in Alburnett were almost full on Sundays. I made a few friends at those church services. I liked the escape that attending services gave me. In fact, I do not consider myself a religious person. But, for my entire life, I have tried my best to live by the Ten Commandments as prescribed by the laws of Moses in the Old Testament and have treated others as I want to be treated. I value respect a lot. I give it without preconception and expect it in return. However, any sort of disrespect toward me is hardly something I forgive or tolerate.

Amidst my hectic work schedule and the weekend outings with my friends and colleagues, I started missing Rebecca a lot. When I first moved to Alburnett, we talked on the phone frequently, but as months went by, the many miles between us were not helping our relationship. She took on a management role at her job and therefore was constantly traveling, both domestically and internationally. There was a possibility that she might move to Alburnett after much coaxing from me, but no job in her field in that city could match the salary and perks she was earning in Boston. Eventually, it became clear that there was no longer any real hope of our being together.

Once Rebecca and I parted ways, I began seriously thinking again about starting a family. My move to Iowa had put a strain on that long-distance relationship. I now lived in Alburnett, and for that reason, I needed to think local.

In my search for a partner, I met Lisa,* an accountant for a large law firm in Marion, on the outskirts of Cedar Rapids. She first struck me as somebody I might not be involved with in a romantic relationship. She had a serious demeanor that could intimidate anyone. After getting to know her a bit more, I realized that she was nice and in fact more out-going than I'd initially thought.

I made a move and invited her out on a date with me in Iowa City, which boasts a myriad of very nice restaurants and a vibrant nightlife. We met for dinner. Lisa arrived for the date conservatively dressed and wear-ing minimal makeup. She was a brunette woman who by all appearances, seemed to work out at the gym a lot. She had tone and long arms, and to my surprise, was carrying over her shoulder a large Gucci handbag. She wore very big prescription glasses that rested perfectly on her pointed nose, and she was in high heels that reminded me of Meryl Streep in *The Devil Wears Prada*.

During that dinner, we learned a lot about each other. She was an Iowa native. She confessed to me that she had lost her father the year prior. She shared with me a lot about her work as an accountant. The date went very well, and we knew right away that we would be an item. As we were talking, I started seeing in her something I hadn't seen at first. I didn't hold back my compliments to her. Her reactions indicated to me that she was receiving them well. We hit it off.

By the end of that evening, we could sense that we would be seeing each other more and more in the future. There was no point in hiding our intentions toward one another. As our conversation was going on over plates of spaghetti Alfredo, sirloin steak, salads, and glasses of wine, I start-ed caressing the fingers of her left hand. She was single, so she was not wearing any ring. I paused for a second, lifted her left hand, held it in my hand, and asked her why there was no ring there. She looked at me and

---

*   Some names have been changed.

smiled. I stared at her in the eyes, waiting for an answer. She looked around the room. There were other patrons in the restaurant. I don't think that anyone was paying attention to us. I didn't care. I have never shied away from showing my affection in public. I have always done it that way. I was still holding her hand in mine. As if she was a little bit coy, she looked down, took a sip of her wine, and stayed mute for a while.

"I can buy one and put it there if I want to," she replied.

"That's not the way it works," I said. "I guess men around here in Iowa must be too blind to see a treasure like you in the open." On that note, I made it clear to her the type of relationship that I wanted. We left the restaurant late that night. It was getting close to midnight. We agreed to see each other again. We each went home knowing that something had just begun between us.

Over the next few weeks, Lisa and I continued to see each other. We were officially a couple. She introduced me to her mother and the rest of her family. I felt welcome, and I liked it. Meanwhile, my schedule at work had become very hectic. My project there was taking a lot of my time. Besides that, I had started working on my own business projects. Even though I had a job, my intention was not really to devote 30 or 40 years of my life to working at a particular company until I retired. If it has to be the case, maybe that's destiny, but having another source of income besides my main activity was something I had thought of very seriously and was taking steps to make a reality.

Even though I have always brought my best to my workplace, I also like to spend my spare time developing or working on something personal. I like to keep the entrepreneurial spirit alive in me. The remainder of my free time I spent entertaining myself and hanging out with friends and colleagues, or with Lisa.

She and I started spending a lot of time together. Because we both had professional careers, we were busy during the week. Once in a while, we would manage to see each other after work and certainly during the weekend. As our relationship developed, the conversation about getting married and starting a family became unavoidable. It was a topic that cropped up now and then. We were both already in our thirties. When it came to building a family together, I thought it was promising that Lisa liked to be around children and loved to babysit her cousin's son. I felt that she and I were ready for a life in common, but still, I did not want to rush things. We had managed to keep the relationship exciting. We always looked forward to doing new things and going on adventures.

Lisa breathed into me something typically Iowan that I truly came to like: shopping at farmers' markets. Whenever there was a farmers' market on the weekend, Lisa would drag me with her. Agriculture and farming are huge in Iowa, and sales events organized by farmers are not only plentiful but also well publicized. Very often, we went shopping at farmers' markets in different cities around the state. Going to these markets became something I looked forward to doing with her. She was someone who had traveled to other parts of the world and liked interacting with folks from different cultures. She once even did volunteer work in Malawi. It was fascinating to hear about her experiences there. It can be quite a challenge for someone who was born and raised in Iowa and spent all her life there to stay for a while in such a different part of the world.

Sometimes we didn't agree on certain activities to do together. For example, I am a country music fan, but she was not. She always found it very weird that I listened to that genre of music. When we would be riding together in a car listening to the radio, she was quick to change the station when a country song came up. Sometimes we fought over that. In September of 2014, the country music legend Loretta Lynn (part of whose life story was portrayed in the film *Coal Miner's Daughter*) was scheduled for a concert at the Paramount Theater in Cedar Rapids, not too far from where we lived. Weeks in advance, I informed Lisa that I had bought two tickets to the concert and that I expected her to come with me. Her facial expression in response sent a clear message that she was not at all interested in going to that concert with me. Her answer was unequivocal. She would go with me to any other show or concert, except a country music performance.

In life, we all have different tastes in things like foods, clothing, movies, and music. When a person doesn't like something that you do enjoy, it is always polite and good to understand why that person feels that way about what you like. First, Lisa did not have a flattering view of country music singers and especially of the type of rural life that they seem to depict in their songs. Second, the customary themes of country songs bothered her, and she often described country singers as "less educated" or lacking sophistication.

The themes she brought up were the stereotypical ones, such as pickup trucks, beer, girls, guns, horses, and farm equipment. I mean, the typical rural setting. I understood her opinion and respected it but I was initially also puzzled given the fact that she was born in a rural and small town. The Loretta Lynn concert was postponed, but when it was rescheduled later, I went by myself. We joked a lot about it. We had been together for a while, and we had learned a lot about each other's likes and dislikes.

Things were going pretty well between us, barring a few occasions when her mood swings could be very difficult for me to cope with. Sometimes she was pensive; at other times, she had a volatile temper. One day I summoned the courage to ask the reason for her sporadic and untimely outbursts. In a relationship, there are things that you can hide from your partner for a period of time, but it is very hard to hide them forever. As I pressed for an answer, Lisa let me know more about her medical conditions. Before some of her revelations to me, there had been signs in her behaviors that had led me to guess what the issues might be. But I had exercised restraint, because not only was I not a medical doctor, I didn't want to jump to any conclusions. She was a woman I cared for, and I wanted the best for both of us.

It turned out that she had chronic depression. I had seen her taking antidepressant medications. As a medical condition, depression used to carry considerable stigma, but this is less the case nowadays. For fear of losing me, Lisa had not wanted to reveal her condition. She confessed to me that she thought I would run away upon learning what she had been battling, healthwise. Of course, I didn't run. I cared about her and wanted her to be well. At the same time, I wondered whether in her case the antidepressants were truly helping. Though I had never suffered from depression myself, I had had an experience of my own with the side effects of an antidepressant that a doctor had prescribed for me years before.

For the short story, years earlier, when I was still living in St. Louis, I went to a health center for a consultation about unexplained headaches I was having. After diagnosis, the doctor prescribed an antidepressant. At first, I thought that the pills would alleviate my headaches. It was only when I went to buy the medication and read its usage that I realized it was an antidepressant.

Based on the commercials I'd seen on TV, I understood depression to be some sort of prolonged sadness and downheartedness from which people suffer. I was not having that problem. I was puzzled by the doctor's diagnosis of the symptoms I'd brought to his attention, but I followed his recommendation and started taking the medication every day. I was supposed to take it for, I believe, a month, or perhaps longer. After just a week, I stopped taking it, because I was convinced that it was having a negative impact on my health, especially my mental health. I started feeling hopeless and sad. My energy level dropped, and suicidal thoughts started coming into my mind. For about ten days or so, I didn't recognize myself. Yes, I believed that the antidepressant was actually causing depression in me. For the first time, I felt what it was like to be depressed. I threw the rest of the pills away. As soon as I stopped taking them, I felt normal again. I regained energy. The suicidal thoughts completely vanished. Since that moment, I vowed never to swallow a single antidepressant pill again, even if it was prescribed to me. The antidepressant I had tried took me to a very dark place in my mind that I don't want to experience ever again.

I had suspected Lisa's depression issue for a while, given some of the medications that she was occasionally taking. But there were other pills and tablets in barely marked boxes that I used to see in her house, and I couldn't quite figure out for what they were. If I had known the names of those medications, I certainly would have researched them to understand the health condition they were meant to cure. Those drugs were hidden in plain sight; she had removed their identification labels for some reason. At first, I thought that they were vitamins, but they were not.

Given that there was nothing about her health that could be contagious to me or compromise my health directly, there was no reason for me to just end the relationship, I thought. I took that opportunity to become closer to her than before. It wouldn't have been right to just walk out on her. So I stayed, and we became closer. As she opened up more to me, I understood her more. I became very supportive. Things went back to normal between us.

Soon, my life was about to change.

CHAPTER 22

Dashed Expectation and Tragedy

One day at work, I got a call from Lisa. She used to send me text messages when I was at work; that day in particular, she called. I picked up the phone. It was around 10:00 a.m. Normally, we called each other around lunchtime. We had been together earlier that morning, so I thought she just wanted to hear my voice. She asked me how my day at work was going, and I replied. Then, there was silence. I knew she was about to tell me something, but I didn't know what that could be. At last, she dropped the news: she was pregnant.

"Wow! That's good news. Are you sure?" I said. She had taken the pregnancy test several times, and therefore she was certain and confident about the test result. I could hardly contain my joy that day. Given that I was at work, surrounded by the cubicles and offices of colleagues, I didn't want to make too much noise. I had been preparing for this news for a while.

All kinds of emotions ran through me. I was very excited to go home and see her. At the end of my shift at work, I rushed to her house, where I was now staying because I'd been spending less and less time at my own home. We had been talking about conceiving a child together, and now it had happened. The 30-minute drive to her house seemed like an endless trip. I was in such a hurry that I was barely paying attention to the speed limit. The only thing I was thinking about was getting there as soon as I could to start kissing and caressing that belly of hers.

When I arrived at her home, Lisa was already near the entrance door waiting for me. I hugged her, and we held each other for close to two minutes before I could let go of her. Then I started staring at and caressing her belly, even though it was of course not visibly apparent that she was pregnant. It was too early for that.

She held my hands as we walked to the bathroom, where she performed the pregnancy test about three times in front of me to assure me of the positive result. I was convinced that she was pregnant and we were expecting a baby. While she was still sitting on the toilet, she looked at me and asked if I was indeed ready for all that—that is, a baby. I was unequivocal in my answer. It was something we had been talking about. I found her question a little bit strange, because it was not that we weren't ready for it. In fact, we had planned it. I was even surprised that it had taken so long.

As we were having dinner that night, Lisa informed me of her plans to go see her gynecologist for confirmation of the pregnancy. It was a step that I welcomed. At that point, she had been pregnant for about four weeks. To mark the news of her pregnancy, we had a memorable night. A night of love and passion. A few weeks prior, she had attended the baby shower of one of her closest childhood friends, Laura.* Even though Lisa had been to other baby showers before, she told me that that shower was different in the sense that she felt she could be the next person having one. We joked about it and hoped for that to happen.

I was soon to become a father for the first time. I needed to be prepared. But how? To do that, I turned to one of my favorite things to do: reading. I started reading everything I could on the Internet about first-time parenting. Then, I decided it would be better to read actual books about first-time fathers. I made a trip to the nearest Barnes & Noble store in Cedar Rapids and bought two books: *How to Raise an Amazing Child the Montessori Way*, by Tim Seldin, and *The Everything Father-to-Be Book: A Survival Guide for Men*, by Kevin Nelson.

Meanwhile, Lisa and I had started talking about the baby's future. I

---

* Some names have been changed.

was all in and ready. Lisa was talented in music and knew how to play the piano. She told me that she would love to instill the passion for music into the baby after the birth. At that point, we didn't know the baby's gender yet. She hoped to have a girl. As for me, it didn't matter. I told her I didn't really care about the gender of the baby. All I wanted was to become a dad soon and start teaching the baby calculus, economics, and languages.

For a few years, Lisa had worked part-time at a day care center before starting her job as an accountant at the law firm. Having worked with young children in the past, she claimed that she knew more about parenting than I did. I never tried to argue with her on that. She did view my parenting approach as extreme. There were several reasons for that: (1) I told her that I would make sure that my child would know every English word—both in the Merriam-Webster and Oxford dictionaries—before the fourth grade. (2) I told her that I would expose the child to university physics, calculus, and at least one computer programming language by the fifth grade, or before he or she left elementary school. (3) He or she would receive extensive French lessons from me in order to be at least bilingual. Beyond that, I would give the child the incentive to pick a third language to learn. French is one of my native languages, and being fluent in it would make it easier for the child to communicate with my extended family. Lisa and I each had our position, but we knew we would work things out when the time came.

It had been about a month since she'd announced to me that we were expecting. So, she had been pregnant for two months. She had already started decorating one of the rooms in her house. From that point on, I was in money-saving mode. I had started putting money aside and taking steps to make cash available.

There was one thing, though, that I had to address before the baby came. We were not legally married when she became pregnant. We were just cohabitating, although I had already asked her to choose an engagement ring. In fact, I had gone shopping for a ring myself, but Lisa had told me that she didn't want me to go buy a ring that she might not like. She proposed to choose the ring herself, or both of us could go find the perfect ring together. Up to that point, I hadn't known that a couple could shop for an engagement ring together. I had always thought that it was up to the man to go out there by himself, buy a ring, and surprise his future wife with it.

Instead, as Lisa wanted, we then went together to visit a few jewelry stores in the area, and in one of them, she pointed out a particular diamond ring in a catalog. But we didn't place an order at that time.

After she became pregnant, I brought up the idea again. We were already living together, but I wanted to do things right. I thought "putting a ring on it," as Beyoncé suggested in one of her songs (Put a Ring on it), would be the right thing to do. When Lisa's belly started growing, I wanted people to see a ring on her finger so that at least they would know that she did have someone in her life. She agreed that we could go out ring shopping again.

But this time around, the mood was a little different. Since she had become pregnant, her mood had changed. I already knew that she struggled with severe depression and regularly took medication for it. It seemed to me that now that she was pregnant and entering her third month, she was not enjoying being a mother-to-be. I was then at the full mercy of her mood swings. She had become an entirely different person. The house was unkempt. There was a display of anger all the time. I tried my best to be very supportive and stoic.

As we were together one night after dinner, Lisa informed me that she had been thinking about getting an abortion. I was in shock. It was news that hit me like a rock in the face. The reason she offered was that her depression had worsened since she'd become pregnant. She also added that her hormones were not in correct balance.

At first, I did not know to whom to talk. I hadn't shared the news of her pregnancy with anyone else. I had an idea about what depression and the consumption of antidepressants can do to a person's psyche: despondency, dejection, dispiritedness, and moroseness are what's on the mood menu for that person. But could that lead a pregnant woman to have thoughts about terminating her pregnancy, just to get some relief from being medically depressed? I didn't know. I needed some answers. The two people who first came to my mind were my mother and my sister who had already given birth twice. I thought both of them would give me more insight into what a woman feels when she is pregnant.

I turned to my mother first. She shared with me that at times during all her four pregnancies, she had felt exhausted, but most of the time she had been in a good mood. My mother also said that she had never suffered from depression or any mental illness before any pregnancy, and therefore, she could not relate to Lisa here. When I spoke to my sister, she told me that barring the lack of energy and the back pain that had ailed her during her pregnancies, she also had always been happy to be pregnant. Both of them were very supportive.

The situation between Lisa and me deteriorated quickly, to the extent that she didn't want to see anyone around her, including me. It came to the point where I had to pack my belongings and leave the house. She claimed that she wanted "some space alone." I didn't know to whom else I should turn. She refused any assistance and even shunned her own mother and closest friends. She reiterated to me that abortion was the only solution she could think of in order to regain good mental health.

It was one of the most challenging times in my life. When a woman who chronically suffers from depression gets pregnant, is that what always happens? Does pregnancy trigger a hormone imbalance in women suffering from depression? Those were some of the questions swirling around in my head. Lisa wanted to regain her health quickly, and for that to happen, she believed that she needed to have an abortion. To do that with peace of mind, she wanted me to consent to her doing so.

As she continued to ask my permission to abort, I repeatedly refused and discouraged her from doing so. A part of me at the time viewed my stance as an effort to rescue my child who was in danger of losing his or her life. I just couldn't stand by and let Lisa have her way. Even though the baby was still a fetus inside the womb of my girlfriend, I was ready to do anything I could to save his or her life. I started brainstorming about what I could try. How else could I convince Lisa not to have an abortion? I didn't know for sure if I could legally force her to carry the pregnancy to term, and just take the baby away from her after delivery. I started investigating whether I could do this.

Because I believe that life begins at conception, abortion is something I frown upon, but there are exceptions that I might go along with, when the life of the mother is in danger. As far as Lisa was concerned, she was not in danger of losing her life. Therefore, I categorically opposed her getting an abortion. In a last-ditch effort to win me over to go along with her plan, she convinced me that the dosage of antidepressants she had been taking might have already caused great harm to the fetus anyway. "You are stubborn, Herve. Why would want a baby with infirmity or malformation?" she asked. "It doesn't matter to me, Lisa. I will take care of the baby and surround it with the love and attention it deserves," I answered.

In fact, she had doubled her recommended intake of antidepressants during the pregnancy. She was exceeding the daily dose that her doctor had prescribed. My opposition to her reckless intake of these medications was what indisputably angered her to the point of asking me to leave her house and give her some "space." I packed up and left. She truly believed that indulging in antidepressants would lessen her suffering. Even though I had learned through my own research that antidepressants could have a negative effect on a baby in the mother's womb, it didn't bother me unduly. I didn't care whether the baby would be born with a defect, anomaly, or anything of that nature.

I started doing research online about how to legally prevent someone from having an abortion, but my search results were not satisfactory. As a matter of fact, I knew beforehand that abortion is not illegal in the country, and I was well aware of the landmark United States Supreme Court ruling of January 22, 1973, known as *Roe v. Wade*. In a nutshell, it was the Supreme Court decision that made abortion legal. Before the ruling, some states had restrictive laws about abortion. But after that ruling by the highest court, abortion was no longer criminalized. Therefore, for some, seeking abortion was the same as seeking a medical treatment like any other. Even though I was aware that it was the law of the land, I decided to hire an attorney to see if there was any legal avenue I could use.

I contacted a family lawyer in Cedar Rapids who agreed to meet with me, and I explained the situation to him. The meeting with the lawyer turned out to be more like a session of advice and life lessons than a consultation about any legal action I intended to take. The attorney applauded me for such an effort, because he had never been involved in a case like mine, in which somebody tried to legally prevent a partner from having an abortion. I was determined to do so. Unfortunately, there was nothing that the lawyer could help me do. According to the law, a woman has the right to her body and therefore can do with it whatever she likes.

The lawyer gave me a lot of advice. It was like a father talking to his son. I almost burst into tears in his office, but I did not want the lawyer to see tears in my eyes. I tried my best to contain my emotions. He advised me to let everything go and just move on. Yes, in fact, he was right. There was nothing I could legally do to stop Lisa from having an abortion. I thanked the lawyer and left his office.

As I was leaving, I felt powerless. I pictured the baby in Lisa's womb asking me not to stop fighting to save it. It was as if I was hearing the baby's voice from a distance. What else could I possibly do? As I was thinking about what to do next, I received an unexpected e-mail from Lisa. At that point, e-mail had become her preferred mode of communication.

In summary, the e-mail was about how things were getting out of control and about her plan to go ahead and seek the abortion without my consent. After all, it was her body, and she could legally do as she pleased. She had already mentioned to me during one of our previous conversations that she was a Western woman and therefore had the absolute right over her body. To me, it felt like a punch in the abdomen. Upon hearing those words, I felt paralyzed from head to toe. I felt dizzy, vertigo-struck. How could I have reacted to that statement? She was blunt with the assertion, but she was also right that she could do with her body as she wished, regardless of whatever life might be growing inside her. She claimed that the reason I was so against her having an abortion was because I was born in a country where women probably didn't have that absolute right over their bodies. But here in the United States, they do.

She clearly knew very little or nothing about the laws that governed abortion in my country of birth, but I didn't hold that against her. Even in the Western Hemisphere, there are several nations that restrict abortion. It would have been pointless to have that debate with her anyway. However, I pointed out to her the then US senatorial candidate Joni Ernst. It was mid-2014, when the Iowa Senate race was heating up—a race that would decide whether Joni Ernst (Republican) or Bruce Bradley (Democrat) would represent the Hawkeye State in Washington, DC. I was following the race closely because I was registered to vote. The antiabortion/pro-life statements from Mrs. Ernst were clear and unequivocal—and she is a "Western woman." When I brought Lisa's attention to the Senate candidate's view on that issue, she was not too pleased. Her opinion about Mrs. Ernst was not flattering, either. "She has never gone through what I am going through," Lisa replied.

After reading Lisa's e-mail, I made her an offer that I thought might dissuade her.

I offered her $7,000 in cash. It was about the amount of money I had readily available at the time and was the emergency fund I had kept in case I might need fast cash. I thought the idea might entice her and maybe she would up the ante to, say, $10,000. In that case, I would likely go to withdraw more money from my bank account to meet her demand. Besides that, I offered to bear all the medical costs and any pregnancy-related expenses she might incur. Moreover, I offered to take the baby from her upon birth and raise it myself.

After that, I didn't hear from her for about two days. I guessed that she was pondering the idea and my offer. Meanwhile, I stopped reading the books about soon-to-be fathers that I had bought a few weeks earlier. It had become too painful for me to continue reading them, because I had the gut feeling that she would not have the baby.

The way things were going had me very puzzled. Not long ago, we had been the perfect couple. We were doing everything together. We went ring shopping and had plans to get married. We planned to start a family. She became expectant, and now her depression, resurgence of mental illness, and determination to abort the baby were all our conversation revolved around. It was a mess.

First, her reply to my offer of $7,000 was that she was not interested in the money. Second, she informed me that if she were to carry the pregnancy to term and give birth, she probably would not give up the baby and relinquish her parental right to me as I'd suggested. A week went by during which I heard nothing from her. As it turned out, she had started failing to report to work.

Shortly after she had become pregnant, I'd learned that she suffered from mental illness beyond depression. I started connecting the dots, and everything began to make sense to me. I had a flashback to the day when she'd pulled a kitchen knife on me. She had quickly put it down, but the look on her face was something I am not ready to forget. Some of her mood swings at times were channeled into verbal skirmishes with me from which I did everything I could to stay away. I don't like that kind of verbal exchange. When that happened, I just stepped out of the house. I had come to understand why some of her prescription bottles had their labels torn off. She knew that I would look up the names of those medications. She didn't want to take any chances.

A few days later, she invited me back to her house to help her bring some order around the house and for us to have a dialogue. I accepted. I had always wanted to be around her; she was the one who elected to be alone. We agreed to meet on a Sunday afternoon. I got ready and headed off to Newport, where she lived. When I entered the house, an unpleasant smell assailed me. As a matter of fact, Lisa had missed work for a few days, and the house was a shambles. The dishes had been piling up in the sink for days. Every room was in disarray. All those were things I used to help her with when we were living together in that house.

For hours, I did my best to clean up. It could have been that the depression had taken a toll on her. In addition to that, wrestling with the thoughts of whether to have an abortion did not prove helpful to her mental state. Before leaving the house, after I finished cleaning, I again offered her my help with any chores that she might need to do inside and outside the house.

My help that day was not in vain, because Lisa later "rewarded" me with the ultrasound pictures of the pregnancy. For the first time, I learned that she was pregnant with a baby girl. I had mixed emotions running through me as I looked at the ultrasound images: emotions of happiness and sadness at the same time. Happiness because there was a marvelous life inside her that I had helped create. Sadness because I knew that that life was in danger because its mother wanted to get rid of it to regain her mental health.

All I knew was that I was not ready to give up on both of them, especially the baby. But I believed at that point that there was not much else I could do. Although I was not a medical doctor and not trained to diagnose illness in people, the research that I had carried out had led me to surmise that she had a case of psychosis. I became even more concerned, because I was dealing with someone who was living in another reality. What could be going on inside her head? She had been forthright with me a few weeks earlier when she'd confessed to me that she was hearing mysterious voices inside her head. Where could I find qualified professional assistance to help silence those voices and bring her back to reality? I was on a personal quest to find her some help, but she had already expressed that she didn't want to see me or anyone else. I could only see her upon her request.

A severe case of postpartum psychosis was what I dreaded for her. I would later be proven correct.

At one point, Lisa informed me that she was contemplating suicide. I started losing hope that there was anything else I could do. In an attempt to give me a pulse of hope, she later confessed to me that she had been thinking about the offer I'd made to pay her and take care of the baby. I reiterated to her that it was still an option on the table. When she kept insisting that she might not have the strength to endure it all for a few more months to come, I became convinced beyond doubt that she would proceed with her plan, and therefore, for my own sanity, I should forget about negotiating any monetary enticement with her. My unyielding refusal to give her my consent—which she didn't need anyway—to abort the baby might have exacerbated things, but I didn't want to endorse in any way the termination of that pregnancy.

During one of our go-rounds about her intent to abort the baby, she told me about an article she had recently read online in a British newspaper about a British woman who had gone through the same situation Lisa was going through. According to the article, the woman was convinced against her own will to give birth. The alleged British woman did finally have the baby, but shortly afterward, she killed the baby by drowning it in a bathtub. As Lisa recounted the story to me, I just remained silent, looking at her. I didn't know what to say. I never even bothered to ask her to show me that article. I knew that with her, I was dealing with a very strange situation. She clearly had turned into someone I did not recognize. I fought back tears. For me, it was like being tortured as I was listening to her telling me the story. "I can do that too, you know," Lisa said. She claimed that she had been dealing with confusion like she had never experienced and was hearing strange noises inside her head.

In another attempt to get closer to her, I pleaded with her to let me be by her side so that I could help her find adequate care to address the issue. She declined again. She reaffirmed to me that the voices she had been hearing inside her head had convinced her that she should stay alone, avoid contact with anyone else, and get an abortion. Therefore, she was going to follow those humming and strange and ghoulish voices inside her. From there, I just fell back on meditation and prayers and gave it all up for Providence to deal with. Up to that point, I had played my hand the best I could. I had no other ace up my sleeve.

Finally, I decided to share with my mother the predicament I was in. As a matter of fact, when I had first talked to my mother earlier, I had not revealed that my girlfriend was contemplating having an abortion. I had withheld that information and had only spoken to my mother about Lisa's depression and some of the health discomfort she was having being pregnant. Once again, my mother told me about her own experience with being pregnant. She had never experienced what Lisa was claiming. But, to my utter astonishment, my mother suggested I let Lisa do as she pleased, but also advised me never to verbally or in any way give her the permission to go get an abortion.

From my mother's words, I recognized the fervent Catholic woman speaking. "Let her go, and just move on." That's what her advice was. Those words echoed what the lawyer had said to me a few weeks earlier. I did just that. I was convinced that just having an abortion would not make Lisa's mental health issues go away. But Lisa was convinced otherwise. As I was advised to do by both the lawyer and my mother, I decided to just get out of her way. By that time, she was about three months pregnant.

On January 14, more than two months after she'd announced that she was pregnant, Lisa phoned me late in the evening to inform me that she had scheduled an appointment at a clinic where she would have the abortion the following day. The late-night call was clearly an attempt to learn my reaction. I reiterated my opposition to it. But at the same time, I reminded her of the exact words she had used a few weeks before, about being a Western woman in this part of the world that recognizes her full right to her body. "After all, it is your body, as you said. What else can I do?" Those were my last words to her.

"You're right," she replied. We ended the phone conversation right there. From what she told me, her mother would be accompanying her to the clinic for the operation. After I hung up the phone that night, finding sleep was very difficult for me. Knowing what was going to happen to that baby was hard for me to bear. It was about 10:20 p.m as I was lying in bed. After hanging up the phone, I got up and went to turn on my computer to look at the ultrasound picture that she sent to me days before. I had the picture saved on my desktop. As I was looking at the picture, I stroked my computer screen. I moved my hand over the pixelated image of the fetus.

I was emotional. I knew that the end of something was coming. With my hand still on screen, staring at the ultrasound picture I said, "I am sorry!" I bowed my head as though I had just been defeated in a fight, because I knew with no shadow of a doubt that Lisa would go through the procedure the following day. Depending on how far along the mother is in the pregnancy, the abortion process itself is nothing short of barbaric. The fetus is taken apart piece by piece in a way that is more like a slaughter. Sometimes, if it is at just a few weeks of gestation, modern medical technologies can carry out the process in a more humane way by just sucking the fetus out of the womb. It is a procedure that can be very graphic at times.

On the day that Lisa was scheduled to undergo the abortion, I sent her a message to inquire what she was doing. It was around 9:00 a.m. It was too late.

She replied that she had just had the procedure done hours earlier. I was devastated, but I was not surprised. She also told me that I should stop contacting her immediately. In my response, based on a conversation we'd had earlier, I reminded her that a postpartum psychosis might come roaring at her in a way that might not be easy for her to deal with alone. She wrote back to me, "Leave me alone!" From then on, it was over. We could each go our separate ways.

Despite my grief over the baby, at the same time, I felt a sense of relief, because I had been mentally drained by guessing whether or not Lisa would go through with the abortion. Given the poor state of her mental health, and after everything that had transpired, I had nothing to reproach myself for. On the day of my last impassioned plea, what I saw in her facial expression was something I do not have the words to describe.

I also believe that Providence saved me from a much more harmful and chaotic situation that could have been lurking ahead for me if things hadn't ended in that fashion. There is a popular French proverb that goes: *Les voies du Seigneurs sont impénétrables*. This would translate in English as *The Lord moves in mysterious ways*.

Two days went by. I was still emotionally reeling from what had just happened, but I decided to refocus on my job and the future. I thought that Lisa and I had just said good-bye to each other forever. It was time to move on.

⌒

Four days later, I was on my lunch break and away from my desk at work when I missed a phone call from someone within the company. The other employee left me a voice mail and also sent me a message through my work e-mail account. The messages were from one of the firm's security agents.

The agent was trying to reach me to inform me that the police had been there earlier looking for me, and that I should contact the county sheriff's office as soon as I could, at the phone number provided. I was baffled. I knew it could not be something criminal. Otherwise, the police wouldn't have left the premises until they'd seen me in person. I was searching for answers. I came to the conclusion that it must have to do with Lisa, but there was nothing I knew of that would have necessitated the involvement of law enforcement. She had already had the abortion, and I assumed that she would have nothing more to do with me.

I called the phone number I'd been given. On the other end of the line was a police officer. He told me that he would like to meet to give me some court documents. I did not have any legal case pending at the time. Once again, I was stunned, searching for answers. What could that be? I had no idea. Whatever it was, I had to find out. The officer and I agreed to meet at a nearby convenience store. I got into my car and rushed there to meet the police officer. As I arrived, the officer was already present, waiting for me. Before heading out, I had given him a description of my car so that he could recognize me.

Hardly had I pulled up in a parking spot in front of the convenience store when the officer approached my car and handed me a document. It turned out to be a temporary restraining order. The officer explained what the document was about and also pointed out to me the scheduled court date for a hearing for the parties involved. Per the officer's words, I had to avoid any type of contact with the plaintiff and stay a certain number of feet away from her.

I knew what a temporary restraining order was. At that point, I knew that it could only have come from Lisa. Anything coming from her wouldn't surprise me at all. I skimmed the document. The restraining order was temporary, not full. For the court to grant the petitioner a full restraining order, the plaintiff and the defendant have to appear before a judge. The judge has to hear both parties to make a final decision as to whether there is merit to grant the plaintiff a full restraining order. But I was also not naive, and I knew that in those circumstances, the court system usually sides with the petitioner (especially if she is a woman), regardless of the basis of her claim.

There had never, not even once, been an instance when I had made any physical threat toward her. On the contrary, I was the one who at one occasion had a knife pulled on me. For that reason, I was stunned. It was something I hadn't seen coming. And yet, she had already confessed to me that she would follow everything that the voices inside her head prodded her to do. It should sound scary, because there was more that she could do.

When I received the papers, I immediately started looking for an attorney. It was not easy to find one who would take my case. Nevertheless, I persisted. My perseverance paid off. I was able to find an attorney in the area who was willing to hear the story. According to the papers, the court date to appear before the judge for a hearing was just two weeks away. Therefore, I had to prepare my defense. There was absolutely no basis for the restraining order, but for some reason, Lisa thought that doing so would guarantee that I wouldn't bother her again. For me, there was no need for it. I had already erased from my phone by then almost all the photos that we had taken together. I had done it so quickly. But, fortunately, I had not deleted her phone number yet. I turned over to my lawyer all of our e-mail exchanges and text messages, and any other pertinent information that I had.

I believed that shortly after Lisa had gone through the abortion, things had gotten worse for her in a way she never saw coming. But, for me, it was a choice she made. My lawyer reassured me that he did not see the basis for the restraining order against me based on the evidence I had presented and that I should not worry about it. The only thing I had to do was not initiate any type of contact whatsoever with her. Doing so could put me in legal trouble, and even in jail if I dared. No text messages. No phone calls. No e-mail communication. Our houses were at least 30 minutes apart, so I had no need to worry that I would inadvertently go near her house.

Nine days passed. Our court date was about four days away. I was ready. Meeting Lisa in court would have been the first time we'd met since she had gone through the procedure. To my extreme surprise, it was a court meeting that would never occur. What had happened?

Here is the twist to the story. I was at work when my attorney called me on the phone. Upon seeing his name as the caller, I thought that maybe he was calling to obtain some more information before our court date. I answered the call. To my amazement, my lawyer told me that he had just received a message from the court. As it turned out, the court clerk had informed him that Lisa had just withdrawn the restraining order and therefore, there would be no hearing. Case closed. It was stunning. With the phone glued to my ear, I was speechless. It became clear to me that Lisa was acting on impulse and things might have gone badly for her after the procedure. The so-called voice in her head that had urged her to go make up a story for the judge in order to file a ludicrous restraining order was probably the very same one that had asked her to withdraw it. Or could it be that she had just temporarily come to her senses? Frankly, I didn't know what to believe.

Two days before the scheduled court date, I received in the mail an official court hearing cancellation letter. I did not know why all of a sudden Lisa had chosen to withdraw. I had had no contact with her in two weeks. But for me, it did not matter, because everything that had transpired between us was just a testament that we were not meant to be together, and that Providence had saved me from something. All that seems bad on the surface might not always be horrible, after all. I had also concluded that it was even good for my welfare and safety to stay away and cut ties with her completely, as I had previously been advised to do. Although I had urged myself to put that episode behind, I could not stop thinking about what would have been if Lisa had had that baby. I would never know what the little one might look like and whom it might take after; I would never have the chance to hold the tiny hands of the baby and say to the newborn, *welcome to the world, my princess*. Her warm embrace is something I would never feel. At times, these thoughts made me pensive. I had resorted to meditation to stay grounded.

I had already picked a name for the unborn child: Mackenzie. I contacted the local Catholic church and requested a series of masses in her memory.

After Lisa's withdrawal of the temporary restraining order, I thought that we would never hear from each other again. What a relief for me it was. It was like a burden lifted from my shoulders. With that ordeal behind me, I started focusing on work and my projects. For the first time in weeks, I felt free and well. The smell of air became refreshing again. I felt great. Life goes on. That was my mantra.

A week later, after Lisa had inexplicably abandoned her court case, I was at home around 8:00 at night when the doorbell rang. I was not expecting any visitor. *Who could that be?* I asked myself. I stood up and went downstairs to see who it was. I often got visits from Jehovah's Witnesses or young missionaries from the LDS Church who came to my house to share the Scripture with me. It's always a pleasure to have those people at my residence to lift my spirits. I went downstairs to open the door.

To my utter astonishment, I saw Lisa there on the doorstep. There are probably no words to describe how I felt. Shocked? Stunned? Bewildered? I thought I was staring at a ghost. We greeted each other, but I kept my distance. I knew she was mentally unstable, and for that reason, I didn't want to take any chances. I observed that she was not carrying a handbag or purse in which she could have concealed something like a knife or firearm. A quick eye scan around her hips did not reveal any bulge or protrusion that could have indicated that she was carrying a weapon.

I was very suspicious of her, and I was extremely uncomfortable standing in front of her. I also took the time to look carefully around her face, eyes, cheeks, and arms to make sure that there were no bruises or any sign or mark of affliction. I did that so as to protect myself against any false accusation of battery on her part, because I was of the belief that the authorities certainly would have taken her word against mine. She had already proven to me that she was capable of anything. I was well aware of the dynamic between the two of us. My feeling at that moment was that I had already spent hundreds of dollars in lawyer fees over her bogus claim. I was afraid of another false and vengeful accusation that could damage me financially and even professionally.

She repeatedly asked to come inside my house, but I refused. I wanted her to tell me what she wanted. She started pleading. When she began crying and continued begging to come in, I let her in.

With tears in her eyes, she asked forgiveness for everything that had happened over the past few weeks. As I listened, she started describing things that had been going through her mind: irrational thoughts, hallucinations, disordered moods, anger, suicidal thoughts, self-neglect. None of what she was describing was a surprise to me. I said to her, "Now that you have done what you wanted—had an abortion—you should be feeling well and better now. Shouldn't you?"

She remained silent for a few seconds and didn't say a word. Visibly, she appeared fine, but I could also tell from her countenance and body language that something was amiss. A strange moment of silence clouded the atmosphere in the room. Then, she proceeded to tell me that we should get back together again as a couple, as if nothing had happened. I thanked her for the offer, but I declined, and at the same time took a step backward. She informed me that she had recently found out about a medical treatment that could have helped her if she had known. She "reassured" me that what had happened before would not occur again if I would agree that we become a couple once more.

I was in disbelief. I shook my head, hugged her, and wished her well. I told her that I was very glad to see her feeling better after everything we had been through, but I suggested we amicably part ways and find our happiness differently. Upon those words, there was nothing else to say. I thanked her for the visit.

It was at that moment that she confessed to me the reason why she had gone to court and made up a story to get a restraining order. It was not that her motivation mattered to me, but I let her talk. She explained that after she'd had the abortion, the strange voices buzzing inside her head had asked her to do so, otherwise I might come to hurt her, given that I had never given her my consent to go through with the procedure. As I heard this revelation, I was stunned, but not surprised.

"Good-bye, Lisa," I said.

With those words, I knew I had made my peace with her. I reiterated to her that I no longer bore any grudge against her. Truth be told, I informed her that I had been praying for her to regain good health as well. She thanked me for those words, too, but she did not want to leave. Her last request to me that evening was for us to have sex one last time before bidding adieu to each other.

"God, help me!" I murmured. I pushed back on that. I thanked her for the offer but let her know that I was not interested. Not only were my feelings for her not quite what they had been, but she could also have used any brief sexual encounter to claim rape or something of that nature. I had witnessed the abyss into which her mental illness took her. I was more uncomfortable in her presence at that moment than at any other time before. It felt very strange and eerie. There was no way I would have let myself succumb to the temptation at that moment. I was in control of my feelings and emotions. However, I didn't lose my humanity. I gave her a very light and measured embrace and wished her well. I started to glance repeatedly at the door. She took it as her cue. She acquiesced and agreed to leave.

Over the next few days after Lisa's unannounced visit to my house, she sent me a flurry of e-mails. I was not too eager to reply to them, but occasionally I did out of courtesy, without a modicum of enthusiasm. It wouldn't have been appropriate for me to give her any hint of a possibility of the revival of what we'd had before.

Days went by. All of a sudden, her e-mails stopped. For about two weeks, I didn't hear anything from her, and that was not a matter of concern for me, given that we had already agreed to part ways. I was more focused on my job and working on projects. For me, it was good riddance.

One day, I was at home when my doorbell rang again. I was not expecting anyone, but as usual, I went to see who it might be. I saw a bald, burly gentleman standing at my front door. The gentleman introduced himself to me and said that he was looking for Herve. He was a hired private detective. I said that indeed, I was the person he was looking for, and I asked him what the matter could be. He asked me whether I knew Lisa O'Donnell. I said yes. My heart sank. I feared that something bad had happened to her. The private detective informed me that a friend of Lisa's had hired him to find me.

For a moment, I felt confused. The gentleman informed me that it had been several days since Lisa had checked into rehab and behavioral health treatment center in Nevada specializing in drug and alcohol addiction and other health problems, such as mood and anxiety disorders, PTSD, chronic pain, and trauma. It turned out that Lisa's health had deteriorated gravely since the feticide. She had not been able to go to work. She'd been referred to the specialized treatment center for adequate care, because supposedly she couldn't find any in Iowa.

But why had someone hired a private detective to find me? It turned out that Lisa had tried to reach me a few times from the treatment center but hadn't been able to. Thus, she had reached out to a close friend of hers and convinced the latter to find me at all cost. It was a strange thing, because not only had I not changed my phone number, but I was still living at the same address.

In fact, once Lisa checked into the treatment center, she completely lost her grip on reality. The symptoms of mental illness, the depression, the postpartum psychosis had come charging at her in a way that was multiple times more severe than before she'd had the abortion. Once again, I became worried about her. At the treatment center, she wanted someone to lean on. I gave the detective all the information that he requested. After he left, I sat on my couch and started processing what might be going on with her. I became even more concerned for her. The whole situation was something that prompted me to read and educate myself more about mental illness.

The day after the private detective's visit, I received a call from the treatment center. The caller wanted to see if I could schedule a visit there, because Lisa had asked to see me. Although I was angry about everything she had done, I did not hate her. I never wished ill toward her. Two days after that phone call, she herself called me and invited me to come immediately to be with her at the treatment center for the duration of the treatment if necessary.

It was something that would have required me to leave my job for days, even weeks at a time. I did not know—nor did she—how long the treatment would take. It was an inconceivable request for me. I proposed that I could possibly fly from Iowa to Nevada to see her for two to three days, but not more than that. That was not enough for her. She demanded I go to Nevada to be there with her as long as the treatment would take. Per her words, I was the reason she was there, and for that, I should come and be by her side while she was undergoing treatment. For me to go there, the center would have to send me an invitation on behalf of their patient. Given that Lisa and I never agreed on the amount of time I would spend there with her, I never received the invitation. Without it, I couldn't go there of my own volition to see her even for a few hours, as I might have considered doing. Once again, I assured her that she was in good care, and I wished her a prompt recovery.

Days later, Lisa returned home to Iowa. I sent her flowers and a handwritten note expressing how happy I was that she had sought treatment, and how glad I was for her to be back home with her family and friends. I wished her well. Not long after that, I received an e-mail from her in which she attached a letter and asked me to give it to my parents to read. Below is the letter exactly as she wrote it.

Dear Agnes and Alfred,

I am writing this letter because I have never gotten the chance to meet you, and for that, I am truly regretful. I am writing this letter in an effort to explain to you what happened, from my point of view, from my eyes, and from my heart. Please give me a chance to try to explain what happened. I met your son, Herve, at a time in my life after my dad had died, and I was so happy to have met him. Herve is funny, intelligent, sweet, kind and caring. I fell in love with him the instant I met him, and I knew then and there he was the one I wanted to marry. Sometimes there were small arguments and there were times when I was somewhat out of sorts. I know now this is due to a very, very low amount of progesterone in my system where there should have been more. For women who have progesterone deficits, they can have horrible mood swings, feel depressed, gain weight, be agitated, and just feel awful, particularly around the time of their periods. This had been happening to me, and I didn't realize that's what it was—a lack of progesterone. Herve and I had so much love for one another that we wanted to get married and we talked about having a child. We tried, and it happened very quickly. There was very little time to realize that things would soon get dark very quickly. I wanted to have this child with Herve. I wanted him to be the father. However, I began to get very, very depressed. I would stay in bed, and not feel as if I could do anything. I cried every night, and I didn't understand what was happening to me. Until later, when I visited a naturopathic doctor who tested my hormones and said they were not of a healthy level. I began to have obsessive compulsive thoughts about many things that became very big, larger than life, and I was trapped by them. My anxiety was so bad, my stomach and nervous system were in a state of terror and panic. I stayed in this state of mind for months, trying desperately to think of a way it would go away. I was no longer living in the same reality that you, Herve and others were living in. Mine consisted of a deep dark abyss that I couldn't escape. I basically became insane, and I knew I was losing myself. I wasn't able to work my job, and I wasn't able to make clear judgments. The only thing I thought, in my insanity, was if I had a termination, I would get better. I knew the hormones were causing problems, and doctors had offered no support or help to me. They told me I couldn't take them, and I couldn't take much more depression medicine than I had been on. I was trying to take care of things the best way I could. But between the antenatal depression which caused me to push Herve away, and the hormones, I was completely dysfunctional. I couldn't function at work. The pregnancy was a scary nightmare for me, not the joyous, happy, wonderful occasion I was expecting. It caused me to become suicidal—I almost had committed suicide, and it was getting to be unmanageable.

Did I ask for any of this? Absolutely not. I kept wondering what I had done to deserve this. My father had just passed away from devastating cancer. I diligently took care of him while starting a new English program at the school I had just started at. Why would this happen? Why would God allow this to happen? Why wouldn't he make me cognizant enough to know that what I did wouldn't solve the problems? Why didn't I deserve a chance to be happy like everyone else? I would've been a good mother, who loved her child so much. Why did this have to happen??? I didn't do this to hurt Herve. I just got so depressed, anxious and out of my mind that I couldn't recognize the choice I made for what it was. I was too far gone.

Please, please, please know that I didn't do any of this to hurt you or any of your family.

The worst part is how much I loved Herve, and now I have lost him. I know you don't approve of me, but I wish you could have had the chance to meet me. To see firsthand how I like to cook, clean and take care of Herve. Maybe he never told you those things. I still care so much for your son, it doesn't just shut off. I went through an amazing hell, that I know you understand some about. But please, understand, what happened was because my hormones were EXTREMELY unbalanced. The doctor I told you about earlier has put me on hormone replacement with bio identicals. I realize what happened makes me sound like a crazy witch. But I am such a loving, kind person. I love children, and I love Africa, and I love everything about Herve. I just wonder if you knew me, or knew what I was like, whether you could ever find it in your heart to forgive me and to allow me to love your son. I want to give him the family he would love and deserves. I play the piano, and I am very creative—the child would be musical, smart and intelligent.

Could you please, please, please, find it in your heart to try to get to know me, and to allow me another chance? I can't make up for what was lost, and believe me I cry every day of sadness for what was lost. But things are getting better, and there was an answer for why things happened the way they were. It was scientific, and I didn't know. I believe I could make your son very happy if you give me a chance. I know there are very hurt feelings and distrust. But you don't know me. I could give you names of friends and family who would tell you what a good person I am, but that I was very, very sick. And that the person who did what I did wasn't who I normally am. Even Herve knows this.

I just wanted a chance to tell you from my side of the situation. My heart is broken, in so many ways. I know I've gotten better, and I know I could make your son happy. If there is something I could do, talk to you on the phone or Skype, I would like to personally tell you I'm sorry.

Sincerely,
Lisa

CHAPTER 23

A More Promising Horizon Lies Ahead . . .

It was time I refocused on my assignment at work on one hand, and on some of my personal projects on the other hand. In mid-2015, I was all in. At work, I was juggling design peer reviews, design improvement meetings, project delivery deadlines, and troubleshooting of electronic hardware. I really enjoyed going to work.

My dedication to my job and the progress that I had shown had earned me some respect. Soon, I found myself entrusted with more work and advanced electronic circuit design challenges. Having a career there would have been easy for me. However, there was too much politics with regard to advancement and a host of other things that I didn't find appealing. Overall, my working relationships with most of my colleagues were good. But there was at least one with whom things were not going as well as they should: Clarence. I had done my best to maintain a professional relationship with the gentleman. It was not an easy thing to do, because he was someone who clearly had an anger issue and who could go off at any time. For some reason, the senior management had not kept him in check. I didn't like it at all. Perhaps it was a factor that Clarence was going through a bitter divorce at the time.

Another company employee who had worked with him a few years prior reached out to me in person when he first learned that I was assigned to work with Clarence. That employee, Kevin,* had had such a bad working relationship with Clarence that he thought he should warn me about him. Kevin plainly advised me to find a way to move to another department or program inside the company. The candidness in Kevin's words was unmistakable. He said he didn't want me to go through the same ordeal he had endured while working with Clarence a few years before. I thanked him for his advice. It was a tip that I welcomed, but I had to go through my own experience.

Because it was a small company, there was not much flexibility to move around easily between departments. One single employee could have too much clout over another person's career there. You had to make sure that every person you interacted with would put in a good word for you, with zero unflattering comments, if you were going to see success. I was there to work and perform, give due respect accordingly to all my colleagues and others with more seniority, but not to fawn over anyone. It was not something I wanted to do. Therefore, I started planning to leave the company altogether. It had gotten to the point where I had resolved myself to leave that work environment as soon as I could.

I had thought about that a long time ago. The thing was, I was already deep inside my project assignment, and it would have been very awkward, rude, inconsiderate, and even unprofessional to try to give everything up just to take a position in another department within the company or even to abruptly resign. My design project was scheduled to be delivered in a few months, so I elected to endure, to stay until it was completed and reached the point where someone else could take it over and continue easily without me if need be.

In a span of just a year, I had had a lot of friends who'd left Alburnett. Other than my job, there was nothing else keeping me from leaving. Firstly, things hadn't turned out the way I'd wanted with Lisa. Secondly, I liked the job I was doing, but my level of happiness at work was not where I wanted it to be. I wanted a breath of fresh air. I wanted something new and different. Thus, I started seriously considering leaving

---

*   Some names have been changed.

the city and the company and maybe heading back to St. Louis, where the majority of my friends and relatives still resided. As a professional, I also knew that it wouldn't be appropriate at my age to just go back to Missouri because my friends and relatives lived there. But not only was I a skilled engineer, I also had acquired a lot of experience. Therefore, I was convinced that I would do well anywhere else that I wanted to go.

By the end of that year, once the project was completed, I gave two weeks' notice at my job. Even without another job offer lined up, I was relieved with the decision to leave the company.

With no job offer on the horizon, I decided to take leisure trips around the country and later go and see my parents. Before I went on my first trip, one of the companies with which I'd applied for a job contacted me through a professional networking site. They sent me a personal note in my inbox inviting me to attend a recruiting event in St. Louis. Since the drive from Alburnett to St. Louis is about 5 hours, I was not too eager to drive 10 hours round trip. So I elected to fly to St. Louis instead. It would be a perfect opportunity to see friends and relatives I hadn't seen in years. I thought it would be ideal to get another job offer before I went on my leisure trip. I couldn't ask for anything better.

The welcome that I got when I returned to St. Louis was very warming. Alicia and her family could barely contain their joy at seeing me again. They gave me the royal treatment. Alicia, who is an expert in African cuisine, went to great lengths to cook my favorite dishes for me. My friends with whom I used to play soccer, my friends at the Fee Fee Baptist Church, and the church pastor were also delighted to see me again after all those years. For a moment, I felt like just returning and staying in St. Louis for good, but I knew that my plans far exceeded the mere convenience of living close to friends and family.

While in St. Louis, I attended the recruiting event, which took place at the Renaissance Hotel. The event went so well for me that the engineering company invited me for a face-to-face interview at its headquarters in Arizona. After returning home to Alburnett, I embarked on the well-deserved vacation I'd planned, traveling around the country and going to see my parents as well. It was cathartic. Upon returning from vacation, I honored my appointment with the Arizona company. The interview went very well, and in the end, everything turned out the way I wanted. I had a lot to be thankful for.

In Southern Arizona, I have started a new life. Ever since, happiness has come to me in a way I hadn't anticipated. My career has shifted into high gear. The weather is good most of the year, but it is very hot during the summer. It's a climate that sometimes reminds me of my native land.

When I arrived in early 2016, the fervor surrounding the upcoming general election scheduled for that November was palpable. Unlike in Missouri and Iowa where I had lived before, in Arizona, it felt like each house and business was very proud to show their support for the candidate of their choice.

As someone who followed politics, I witnessed in the 2016 presidential election one of the rudest, distasteful, bizarre, and uncivil elections in recent memory. The incumbent President Obama, due to the presidential term limit, was not running for reelection. The presidential seat was up for grabs between Republicans and Democrats, who had fought a yearlong battle during the caucuses and primaries to select their new party nominees. In the end, the Democrats ended up selecting former US senator from New York and US secretary of state Hillary Clinton as their party nominee. The Republicans on their side gave the party nomination to real estate investor and businessman Donald Trump. Historians suggested that it was the first time in the history of American politics that the two candidates going head-to-head against each other were this unpopular with the American people. One had been dogged by an investigation surrounding the handling of her e-mails while she was secretary of state. The other infamously rose to national prominence for leading "birtherism" and was notorious for denying facts and evidence.

The stubborn refusal by someone to believe in facts and evidence is clearly something that normally will not make that person popular. Here is the reason: The president of the United States is someone who will always be confronted with making informed decisions. If the president is someone known not to believe in what is true, that person might make decisions that will put the country at risk.

Since my naturalization ceremony years ago, I had started paying more attention to the current state of affairs in a way that I hadn't before. Though not perfect, the United States is a very good place to be, depending upon one's goals, offering a promise of peace and stability that has drawn folks from all around the world. In 2016, for the first time in a long time, I questioned whether that peace and stability were in jeopardy. I had just moved to a new state and into a new house, and I became worried while pondering everything that was going on politically in the country. Where was the country headed? Would civility prevail?

There was a presidential candidate inciting violence—in the United States—and promising to assist and to pay the legal fees of his supporters who might become offenders. I was baffled. I had seen the country ideologically divided in a way that conjured up bad memories.

Any hint or semblance of incitement of violence in a political climate brings bad memories to my mind: the genocide of Rwanda and the possibility of a civil war. As I was following the presidential campaign that year and seeing that there were indeed a candidate's supporters going out of their way to inflict harm on his behalf, it didn't take me long to liken that to the seeds of carnage and massacre that triggered the Rwandan genocide in 1994. Despite being young at that time, I was old enough to remember how it started. The people who went on a killing spree by butchering and slaughtering their neighbors and others were following orders from elected officials and media. The killers did so believing that there was a system in place that would protect them because those who had encouraged them to commit violence against their fellow countrymen would later protect them from possible prosecution.

I was still living on the African continent when all that happened. For a moment, I sensed the United States heading down that path, but I was hopeful that civility would eventually prevail. Thoughts of neighbors of opposite political persuasions shooting at each other were flashing in my head. It is a possible scenario, and it could easily spread across the continental United States. The prospect of things deteriorating and getting out of hand was constantly on my mind.

Whether it is a Rwandan-style atrocity or a civil war, there are not many nations on this planet that can claim that something like that will never occur in their country. The United States, for instance, has proven to be a politically stable country and also a model of democracy around the world. But it is not completely insulated from an inner crisis that may develop and could potentially result in an upheaval within its borders. Incitement to violence—from people seeking power, and people in power—relayed by sympathetic media is usually what brings disruption and chaos to a country. That was how the genocide in Rwanda started, and that is how civil wars usually start. The last time a civil war was fought in the United States was from 1861 to 1865. Yes, it's been a long time, but was it really the only one that would ever occur in our history? It all depends upon the civility of the people toward each other. Unfortunately, civility has not always existed among folks in the United States.

First of all, according to a survey conducted by the *Washington Post* in 2017, it was estimated that there were more than 393 million guns in the United States. In other words, there are enough firearms for every man, woman, and child to own one. That being said, I do not believe that the country would ever recover from a modern-day civil war—even one lasting just one week—in this nation where almost everyone is armed to the teeth and the fear of "the other" is still not tamed.

Secondly, as much as there is unity among the states, the same cannot always be said about the people. The "us against them" mentality, the fear of the "other," the tribalism, the clannishness, the nativism and questionable policies have allowed a climate of distrust, scapegoating, and hostility.

Thirdly, the fight for control and supremacy between the Republican and Democratic parties is very polarizing.

Working on issues in a bipartisan way is even viewed as a weakness leading to political peril for candidates of both parties. I am a very big fan of debates about policy, because they give me the opportunity to do a mental exercise about the intended results of those policies and the possible ramifications for the society as a whole.

In politics, one side vilifies the other. One side calls the other's members' actions "un-American." Based on the three points that I've just mentioned, there is indeed enough going on to precipitate the country—God forbid—into unimaginable chaos. This is something I do not wish for, of course, but the political climate can be volatile at times. Liberty and political stability should not be taken for granted in the United States.

Words may not hurt, but they do matter in a political and social ecosystem where people look for inspiration to take action or behave in a certain way. The most extreme ideology of white supremacy is now finding galvanized "soldiers" who are willing to commit acts of terrorism against their sworn enemies as suggested by their credo: nonwhites. There isn't currently a statute to address this kind of domestic terrorism to put it on par with the other known forms of criminal enterprises that have drained much of the budget earmarked accordingly by the US government.

To the best of my belief, the most efficient way to seriously address this type of ideology, especially its radical and violent fringe, is to treat it the same way that we do the religious extremists that have been ideologically hell-bent on undermining our way of life and calling us "infidels." Crafting laws to hamper the most radical fringe of white supremacy will undoubtedly result in the challenge of civil liberty and racial profiling of the demographic that makes up the majority of Americans. To this effect, there would be some pushback. The lawmakers would have to trudge a fine line so as not to infringe on the constitutional rights of those people. Most of them are fine, caring, and law-abiding citizens. One way or the other, draconian deterrent measures will have to be taken so that every citizen in this country can live without fear of their compatriots.

I believe that sooner or later, Congress will have no other choice but to tackle it perforce and head-on.

Citizens should find their voices to call out anyone saying or trying to do things that could lead to their fellow countrymen turning against each other. Most of the time, the upheaval I have just mentioned starts with a single incident, escalates and quickly becomes unmanageable. We pray that something like that never happens, but those who believe that it will never happen may be in for a rude awakening.

Does the two-party political system contribute to the stability of the country, or does it do more to undermine it? I wish there were some plurality in our choice of political parties other than the big two that we have. The antagonism between the Republicans and Democrats in Congress has often made me wonder who those public elected officials think they are, and for whom on Earth they think they are working.

For example, every year, there is a threat of government shutdown because of disputes over the content of a proposed or upcoming budget and government spending. A government shutdown affects federal workers because they don't get paid. I have in the past lived many months without pay, and I understand the pain that it can cause for families. When I lost my job several years ago to a wave of layoffs that swept the home improvement store, it was painful for me, and I hate it a lot when the executive and legislative branches fail to quickly agree over government spending, to the detriment of the employees. Most of the time, it is one party disagreeing and whining over the contents of the budget.

The complete breakdown of civility and decorum during and after the presidential election of 2016 was shocking but not surprising. I saw politicians of the country that I call home wallowing in boorishness, bellicosity and tacit xenophobia. As I read the newspapers and saw images on TV about emboldened fanatics spreading hate, homophobic and anti-Semitic messages, I had flashbacks to the pre-World War II Nazi Germany in Europe, as well as a not-so-distant past in America. The preamble of the United States Constitution laid out a vision to form a more perfect union and to ensure domestic tranquility. I saw the latter put to the test.

In the summer of 1858, when the nation was doing some soul-searching about the issue of slavery which was back then the bone of contention, Abraham Lincoln who later became President of the United States gave a consequential speech in that regard in which he said:

A house divided against itself cannot stand.

The issues facing the nation today are not precisely the same ones from that era, but President Lincoln's wisdom during that oration is still relevant in our current political and social environment. Concord is what I want to see more often, inside our Republic.

I was glad that things went well during the election itself that year. I was happy that the transition of power happened peacefully, ushering us into a new era. I hope that stability, justice for all and the promotion of general welfare as clearly stated in the Constitution will endure long enough in the United States for the nation to remain the beacon of a promise of opportunity and a better life that has drawn thousands of people—including me—from every corner of the world. Some people refer to America as a place where everything is possible. The opportunities are indeed inexhaustible, and I hope that the inspiring dynamism of its technological advancement continues. I hope that the American people will always come together as one to be good stewards of the ideologies enshrined in the founding documents such as equal treatment of all people . . . life, liberty, and the pursuit of happiness.

Lightning Source UK Ltd.
Milton Keynes UK
UKHW022148291119
354427UK00006B/171/P